**Christoph Delius and Matthias Gatzemeier,
Deniz Sertcan, Kathleen Wünscher**

The Story
of Philosophy

FROM ANTIQUITY TO THE PRESENT

KÖNEMANN

Contents

GREEK PHILOSOPHY

From Myth to *Logos*

"From the beginning, wonder has made men philosophize, and it still does." This saying of Aristotle's, which goes back to Plato, is still valid today. Aristotle takes "philosophical wonder" to mean our amazement at inexplicable phenomena. This amazement gives rise to asking questions about causes, but it also addresses the problem of the origin and beginning of philosophy itself. It is not only academic, professional philosophy that contains philosophical knowledge, but also myth, because myth too is motivated by wondering, by questions searching for explanations. Indeed the boundaries between myth, pre-philosophical thinking and philosophy are less clear-cut than one might assume from the chapter headings of histories of philosophy. The material with which each is concerned, in other words the question of the origin of the universe, and the explanation of natural phenomena and social norms and institutions, is common to both philosophy and myth. However they do differ in the way in which they deal with these matters, or to be more precise, in the particular way each verbalizes these things. The much-quoted transition from myth to *logos* is marked by the difference between the narrative language of stories of gods and heroes on the one hand, and strict argument on the other. Instead of using gods to explain the world, men increasingly sought a rational form of coming to terms with it. Aristotle clarifies this distinction as follows: "Mythologists only thought in the way they could understand, and paid little attention to us. For when they raise gods to the status of principles, have gods create everything, and assert that everything that does not feed on nectar and ambrosia is mortal, it is clear that they are stating something comprehensible to them, while saying something totally incomprehensible for us when it comes to the effects of these causes. But we do not need to give any serious thought to mythical insights. On the contrary, we must seek information from those who argue with proofs." The origin of philosophy in the narrower sense is the discovery of argument.

Greek philosophy did not arise on the Greek mainland (it only arrived in Athens in the second half of the 5th century B.C., and never really settled in Sparta at all), but in the Greek colonies of Asia Minor (Miletus) and southern Italy (e.g. Croton and Elea). This is because in these places the confrontation with new questions and problems and with other ways of thinking was more conducive to theoretical discussion than in

CLASSICAL ANTIQUITY

The **origins of Western philosophy** are to be found in Ancient Greece. The Greeks began to express thought in philosophical terms in c. 600 B.C. This period was characterized by far-reaching economic and social change, which led to a crisis of the aristocratic state and finally to new forms of rule (tyranny, democracy).

These changes were accompanied by what is known as the **transition from myth to *logos***. In other words, mythological or religious interpretations of the world (e.g. stories of the gods which told of the origin and course of the world and its contents) were increasingly replaced by a philosophical, scientific, and rational explanation of the world. This transition was only very gradual, however, so that mythical influences are still apparent in many ancient thinkers.

Ancient philosophy begins with the **Presocratics (c. 650– 500 B.C.)**, including the Milesians (Thales, Anaximander), the Pythagoreans, the Eleatics (Xenophanes, Parmenides) and the Atomists (Leucippus, Democritus).

Pythagoras, Engraving,
16th century,
Bibliothèque Nationale, Paris

Presocratic philosophy centers on the question of the basic principle permeating the world and the primal substance from which the world and the things in it arose.

The succeeding **classical period (c. 480–c. 320 B.C.)** was the **heyday** of Greek civilization, in which the Greeks produced their highest achievements in the visual arts (enlargement of the Acropolis under Pericles; important sculptors: Myron, Phidias, Polycletus); literature (period of the greatest representatives of Attic tragedy: Aeschylus, Sophocles, Euripides); and philosophy (Socrates, Plato, Aristotle). Athens became the center of philosophy at this time, and it was here that the new form of state, the *polis* or city-state, attained its highest expression.

The **Hellenistic period (323– c. 1st century B.C.)** was the age in which a mixed culture arose as the result of the absorption of oriental elements. The Greek influence, however, remained paramount. During this period, the Greeks ruled over large areas of the Middle East as far as northern India. Science, scholarship and trade flourished. The centers of culture were Alexandria and Pergamon. Characteristic of Hellenistic art and architecture was the juxtaposition of different styles. Literature and philosophy were marked by a cosmopolitan attitude. New philosophical schools arose (Stoics, Epicureans).

the motherland. The needs of transport and particularly trade far beyond the confines of the city-state did indeed demand new, reliable, and transparent linguistic forms of argumentation and communication.

The central themes of Greek philosophy encompass the three areas of Physics (the theory of nature), Ethics, and Logic. Physics included not only the stars and the earth, natural phenomena, time, space, and movement, but also theology, understood as the study of the gods based on the observation of nature. Ancient historians of philosophy assign these three areas to historical periods, so that the Presocratics are seen as the creators of Physics, Socrates and Plato as the founders of Ethics, and Aristotle as the inventor of the study of Logic.

The Presocratics

The transition from myth to *logos* was a gradual process. One group of thinkers, for example, the Orphics – named after the mythical singer Orpheus – employed the language of myth to ask philosophical questions about the origin of things and about a uniform world principle, while using the names of gods in a recognizably metaphorical way, re-interpreting the myths allegorically.

These questions also form the core of Ionian natural philosophy, based in Miletus, which now turned its back uncompromisingly on the language of myth to seek a strictly rational explanation of the world. For Thales, the basis of creation – the origin *(archë)* of the world – resided in water, for Anaximander in the quality-free and eternal infinite, and for Anaximenes in the air, which he saw as divine, dynamic and life-giving. Common to all these thinkers, whom Aristotle regarded as the founders of Greek philosophy in the narrower sense, is a concern to find a single explanation for the origin of the world. The Pythagoreans saw number as the principle both of the material world and of society. The nature of things seemed to them to be based on numbers. It was number which gave order to the cosmos, by demarcating and thus defining the undefined. The Pythagoreans established the canon of the four Pythagorean sciences of arithmetic, geometry, astronomy, and acoustics (the rational study of harmony), which later, as the quadrivium, was to form

the basis of the Seven Liberal Arts. Both theoretically and practically, they concerned themselves intensively with ethical and political problems, and thus created a philosophical focus which was taken up again explicitly only later, by the Sophists, and then by Socrates and Plato.

The basis of every insight for Heraclitus, a lone figure among the Presocratics, was the empirical observation of the multiplicity of things, which led him to the conviction that the whole world consisted of opposites. The father of all things was war, in other words the battle of opposites. These, however, would eventually be subsumed in an all-embracing unity in the eternal reason of the world *(logos)*. "All shall become the One, and the One shall become All."

One radical critic of custom and tradition, especially of anthropomorphic notions of the gods, was Xenophanes, the founder of epistemological skepticism. With his thesis of the unity, motionlessness and eternity of the universe, he can be seen as the pioneer of Eleatism, whose founder, Parmenides of Elea (critically turning his back on Heraclitus) developed a static, Monistic ontology (theory of existence) on the basis of the following

Group of Philosophers,
Roman mosaic from Pompeii,
1st century A.D.,
Museo Nazionale Archeologico, Naples

The "Seven Wise Men," in fact comprising far more than seven statesmen in changing configurations in the 6th and 7th centuries B.C., were regarded in Greek tradition as the founders of a rule-based, and altogether practical, form of thinking and acting that was only later systematized in philosohpical terms. Handed down from them we have such proverbial expressions as: "Know thyself," "Nothing in excess," "Master thy desires," "Everything in its proper time," "Most people are bad."
Whether the Pompeian mosaic, which is probably based on a Hellenistic model, really does depict the "Seven Wise Men" is questionable, but not completely impossible, for representations of this motif are known from classical Antiquity (e.g. in Cologne). The mosaic has also been seen as a depiction of the Platonic Academy. In that case, Plato would be the seated figure beneath the tree, drawing in the sand with a stick or pointing to a ball which might be construed as an armillary sphere (a heavenly sphere with the orbits of the planets). Whatever the case, the lively picture, of a group of sages in conversation demonstrates the ongoing interest among educated Romans in the philosophy which they had originally inherited from Greece.

Socrates, 470 – 399 B.C.,
Portrait bust, Marble,
So-called Farnese herm,
Museo Archeologico, Naples

The name "Socrates" and a
quotation from his last dialogues
as handed down by Plato are
chiseled into the lower part of
this herm. Thus the sculptor has
enabled us to identify numerous
other examples of the portrait,
whose original was probably
commissioned by Socrates' pupils.
The quotation refers to the power
of rational arguments and the
moral responsibility to follow
them. With his patient and
thorough discussion of this
attitude, Socrates created a new
emphasis in contrast to the
predominantly natural
philosophical approach of
earlier philosophers.

The Discus Thrower by Myron,
c. 450 B.C., Roman copy,
Museo delle Terme, Rome

In the famous thought-experiment in
which he had Achilles race a tortoise,
Zeno of Elea pointed to the difficulties
in the conceptual understanding of time
and movement. Achilles gives the
tortoise a head start: it starts at point A.
When Achilles reaches point A, the
tortoise is at point B. When Achilles
reaches B, the tortoise is at C, and so
on. Hence, even though the distance
between them gets ever shorter,
Achilles can never catch up. Zeno
wanted to show that our experience of
variety and movement is based on
appearance and therefore contradicts
logic. Reason should lead to the
realization that the True is only the
One Immutable. The discus thrower
is shown at a precise moment of
motionlessness, a transition from the
preparatory movement to the final
fling. But for every beholder, this
moment contains within it the
preceding and succeeding movements.
This dynamic conception of time and
movement, in which a point of time
is only a transition and not a real,
isolated moment, leads beyond
Zeno's paradoxes.

strictly logical and linguistic argumentation. His basic epistemological principle, that thinking and being are the same, implies that if something is impossible to imagine, then it cannot exist. As statements about change always imply the non-existence of the preceding or subsequent situation, therefore there can be no change, because non-existence cannot be imagined, nor even meaningfully uttered. So being can only be imagined as an unchanging unity which has not begun and will not cease (Monism). This gives rise to a paradox, because our everyday experience is that things do change, all the time. Parmenides resolves this paradox by viewing perception as appearance, deception and mere opinion (doxa) in contrast to thought. Thus thought and empirical experience are kept strictly apart.

Empedocles' theory of the elements represents a compromise between Heraclitus and Parmenides. Being is not unitary, but consists in the end of the qualitatively different elements of earth, fire, air and water. The multiplicity of empirical objects results from these elements being mixed in different proportions. Empedocles explains and rescues the phenomenon of obviously observable change by interpreting it as the separation, or union as the case may be, of elements.

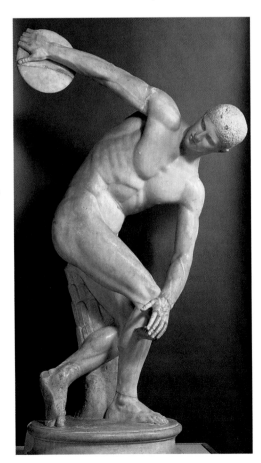

This separation or union does not come about mechanistically or by chance, but through love and strife, the two forces ruling the cosmos. Anaxagoras posits not four, but infinitely many, unchanging and invisible basic substances, whose mixing and interaction is guided by the mind-spirit (nous) which controls the whole universe.

The Atomists Leucippus and Democritus also attempted to overcome the contradiction in the positions taken by Heraclitus and Parmenides, albeit without invoking a mental or metaphysical principle which guides the universe. They postulated minute indivisible basic particles, atoms, which differ in their form and arrangement. It is the changes in these configurations, which come about purely mechanically and by chance, which cause the changes we see in the world.

The Sophists ushered in a new era in Greek philosophy. The focus of interest shifted from natural philosophical, cosmological, and ontological issues to ethical and social questions. It was they who brought philosophy to Athens, provoking, not least by their very extensive influence, the counter-movement we know as Socratic-Platonic and Aristotelian philosophy, which was motivated primarily by the epistemological and ethical skepticism of the Sophists. From the pragmatic experience that perceptions and judgments are relative and subjective, the Sophists arrived at the general position that no secure foundation for knowledge was achievable. As a logical consequence, they abandoned philosophy's claim to truth, seeking no longer to convince by argument, but rather to persuade by rhetorical skill.

The development and expansion of the philosophy of communication is due to this priority given to rhetoric. The Sophists were teachers who traveled the cities of Greece teaching the politically ambitious younger generation, especially the art of public speaking, with the promise that in litigation or political dispute they could thereby turn the weaker position into the stronger. (For these services they charged fees which in some cases were enormous, a practice vehemently criticized by Plato and Socrates.) Among the best-known Sophists is Protagoras, who gave particular emphasis to the relativity of things. In his opinion, a statement could be true in one situation and false in another. This gave

Socrates and his Pupils,
Engraving after a painting by Pinelli

In 399 B.C. Socrates was condemned to death after being accused of atheism and corrupting the young. He turned down an opportunity to flee, arranged by his friends, because he regarded this as an admission of guilt. The last hours of Socrates are reported by Plato in his dialogue *Phaedo*. As this is an idealized picture, it is difficult to test the historical truth of the account. There is little doubt, however, that Socrates met his death calmly, and that he spent his final hours in prison in the company of his friends and pupils. It was in line with Greek custom that friends took priority over family responsibilities. Socrates was executed by being made to drink hemlock. It is reported that he took the cup of poison without fear and with a cheerful countenance. He did not even lose his sense of irony, because before downing the draft, he asked whether he should not sacrifice a few drops to the gods.

rise to his famous dictum asserting human subjectivity as the basis of all knowledge: "man is the measure of all things, of things that are that they are, and of things that are not that they are not." Sophistry exerted a great influence on the succeeding period of classical Greek philosophy (Socrates, Plato, Aristotle).

Socrates

Socrates was condemned to death in 399 B.C. and executed by being made to drink hemlock; his principal alleged crime was to have corrupted the youth of Athens with his sophistic philosophy. His response to the Sophists' art of disputation, the aim of which was solely to win the argument, but not to discover the truth, was his concept of true debate, of philosophical dialogue.

The foundation of his dialectic is the Socratic Question, by which the interlocutor is induced, through having contradictions pointed out to him, to reflect upon and revise the theoretical and practical convictions which he had hitherto taken for granted; and thence to work out a properly founded knowledge of himself and about moral and political life. In these dialogues, Socrates starts out by presenting himself as the ignorant seeker after knowledge, in order that his interlocutor might have no shyness about entering into conversation with him. By dint of targeted questioning, Socrates succeeds in persuading his interlocutor to adopt a critical view of the topic under discussion. Socrates sees this dialogue as useful even if it does not produce any unambiguous result, but merely clarifies the problem and brings a solution nearer. This form of dialogue frightened off many discussion partners, but some recognized its educational value.

Socrates understood himself not as a teacher, but as a midwife easing the birth of critical self-reflection. He said ironically of himself that the only thing he knew was that he knew nothing. Although he was the author of no philosophical writings (his philosophy is known to us primarily through the works of Plato and other contemporaries), his influence was extraordinarily great. Numerous pupils of his founded their own schools of philosophy: Plato the Academy, Antisthenes the Cynics, and Aristippus the hedonistic version, the Cyrenaican school.

Plato

Main Features of his Philosophy

Plato often used a critical disputation with his predecessors – in particular Pythagoras, Heraclitus, Parmenides, and the Sophists –

The Platonic solids assigned to the ancient elements from:
Johannes Kepler, *Harmonices Mundi*, libri V, Linz, 1619, Bayerische Akademie der Wissenschaften, Kepler-Kommission

In his dialogue *Timaeus*, Plato sets out his picture of the origin and properties of the cosmos. Even before the physical existence of the five elements fire, air, water, earth, and ether, matter structured itself while taking on form, as Plato claims, according to ideal geometric solids, whose faces are identical regular polygons and whose vertices lie on the surface of a circumscribing sphere. There are precisely five polyhedra which fulfill these conditions. The mathematical relationships of these solids and the relationships of the elements to one another allowed numerous speculative attempts at analogy.

to help him arrive at his own philosophical position. His dialectic approach to philosophy meant that he largely avoided representing material statements as assured knowledge. Methodological insights, by contrast, whether epistemological, logical or linguistic, he did as a rule present as permanent.

Among the knowledge presented as assured, we find general assertions of the kind that there must be ideas, in particular the idea of the Good, that doing wrong is worse than suffering wrong, that the possibility of learning and of knowledge must be recognized, and that a life of reason is to be preferred to its opposite. A conspicuous feature of Platonic philosophy is the way it freely uses myths and parables; these do not however represent a relapse into mythical thinking – they serve to illustrate, explain and supplement the argumentation, not to replace it, and do not contradict it. His philosophy centers on ethics. His main concern is to prove the possibility of assured knowledge. While Socrates' ethical disputes were predominantly related to problems of individual ethics, Plato emphasized the comprehensive aspect of social ethics, in which context the question of proper upbringing and education played an important role.

Plato's Theory of Ideas

The purpose of Plato's theory of "ideas" (sometimes known in English as "forms") was to establish a philosophical platform from which to oppose the subjectivism and relativism of the Sophists by showing that objective knowledge of truth was possible. The starting point for his considerations was the epistemological axiom that like is only recognized by like, that is to say, that the objects of knowledge correspond to the capacity for knowledge (and vice versa), which means in particular that the assurance of knowledge depends on the objects concerned, for which reason the changing objects of the empirical world can never lead to permanently assured knowledge. In order to show that permanently assured knowledge is possible nonetheless, Plato postulates the existence of "ideas" as objects of knowledge of a particular kind, which – by analogy with

Parmenides' concept of being – are seen as immutable, eternal and (in contrast to the changing empirical world) as inaccessible to perception by the senses and only knowable through intellect. Anyone who has recognized these ideas (which, incidentally, Plato never claimed to have done himself) has immutable, permanently assured knowledge, in contrast to mere opinion *(doxa)*, with which the broad masses are content and which represents the most that can be achieved in the whole sphere of perception.

There are ideas for the whole range of knowable things: for the things of nature (e.g. animals or trees), for artifacts (e.g. tables), for ethical or political concepts (e.g. virtues or forms of government), and not least for the objects of geometry (e.g. circles or triangles). Above all in respect of the last-named, on the pattern of which Plato obviously conceived his theory, but also in respect of social structures, it is immediately plausible that empirical reality never corresponds to the ideal, for which reason they almost cry out for an *a priori* ideal construction. In this way, Plato's theory of ideas creates a critical apparatus with which to consider the prevailing conditions relating to morals, tradition and the state.

In order to make plausible the possibility of knowing these ideas, Plato relates a myth, according to which souls, assumed to be immortal, have, in their pre-natal state, seen all ideas; birth dissipates this knowledge, but it can be re-activated by recollection *(anamnesis)*. For him, learning is not the filling of a blank sheet, but progress into recollection. Psychologically, the road to the knowledge of ideas begins with different perceptual impressions of the same kind (e.g. of beautiful objects or people), until finally the all-embracing and unitary idea of beauty itself appears. Plato describes the epistemological road as a succession of five steps: 1) naming; 2) definition; 3) image; 4) insight and science; 5) spontaneous, sudden illumination of the idea. The final step, the vision of ideas, is only attainable after one has progressed through all the others, and it is only manifested to those who have practiced a philosophical life over a long period in association with others.

Ontology, the theory of different kinds and spheres of existence, derives immediately from the theory of ideas. At the pinnacle of the hierarchy of existence are the ideas. Only they are, in the true sense of the word, existing. They serve as original patterns for the world of the senses. By contrast, the empirical world, the physical, perceptible, transitory things of the senses, Plato regards as having no independent existence, but only existing by virtue of their "participation" in the ideas, of which they are mere copies or images. This division of the spheres of existence is reflected in the division of capacity for knowledge into intellect and perception. However, in his late work, *Timaeus*, Plato blurs this strict separation of the different spheres of existence and knowledge, in part at least, by introducing undefined space or featureless material, or (derived from Pythagorean tradition) the ideal numbers, as mediating instances between the ideas and the world of the senses, and introducing the notion of correct or true opinion, which lies between truth on the one hand, assigned to intellect and ideas, and mere opinion on the other, which relates to the empirical world.

Plato's Ethics and Political Philosophy
The guiding light of all individual and social action, and also of every theoretical effort, is the idea of the Good, which stands at the pinnacle of the cosmos of ideas, or, put another way, stands out above all other ideas. It should be noted in passing that Plato nowhere provides a closer definition of this concept of the Good. As the overarching idea, it is responsible for securing the existence of the other ideas and thus of the whole world, to guarantee the usefulness of the ideas in science and action, to prevent the misuse of knowledge and skills, and to determine the proper relationship between ends and means in concrete instances. The analyses developed in the early dialogues of various social virtues (bravery, justice, etc.) hold up a model idealized picture in opposition to actual social practice, which in Plato's eyes was totally corrupt. This picture was at the same time to serve as criticism of prejudices and widespread values, in particular the opinions of Sophists and politicians. The thesis of the teachability of virtue, put forward in the dialogue *Meno*, is based on the presupposition that virtue is a

The School of Athens,
Fresco by Raphael, 1508–1511, Vatican Museums, Rome

In its symphonic variety, Raphael's fresco appears to depict not just many philosophers, but philosophy itself, and to illustrate the abstract halls of thought through an architectural analogy. Knowledge of Antiquity at the time of the Renaissance was in fact fragmentary, but few beholders would suspect this in view of the artist's casual and virtuoso assemblage of characters and movements into a panorama of visualized topics, investigations and positions. Raphael was aware of course that not all the philosophers shown were alive at the same time; he was not depicting a historical scene. Relatively few of the figures can be unambiguously identified. In the middle, Plato, with the *Timaeus* under his arm, points casually to the "heaven of ideas" above, while his pupil Aristotle holds his arm stretched out horizontally before him. He did not believe, and this is the symbolism here, in the Platonic ideas; for him, the Universal and the Particular were both conveyed through earthly things. Socrates, with his back turned to both, is counting arguments on his fingers. In the left foreground, Pythagoras sits and writes, a tablet in front of him showing the harmonic numerical ratios. Diogenes lies half-dressed but unembarrassed on the staircase, while on the far right, Ptolemy, as a crowned king, holds a globe.

Plato, 427 – 347 B.C.,
Portrait bust, Roman copy
of Greek original, Marble,
Louvre, Paris

Like his teacher Socrates, Plato
thought that truth could not be
reduced to formulas and then
trotted out at any time regardless
of context. Rather, it had to be
discovered by each person for
himself, but not in isolation –
partners in discussion were
indispensable. For this reason all
his writings are in the form of
dialogues, in which two or more
persons converse.
For Plato, however, true insights
are not concerned with the
sphere of the contingent. Things
that come into being and pass
away are separated by a basic
gulf from the timeless sphere of
ideas, which, independently of
whether they are in anyone's
mind or not, exist as real entities
and as originals for empirical
objects.

form of knowledge and that no one can
act against his better knowledge. A similar
argumentation underlies Plato's ethical and
political theory as a whole. Given one's
human self-awareness as a reasonable
being, no one of sufficient insight, faced
with the choice of leading a reasonable or
unreasonable life, can possibly decide on
the latter. The most important goal of
upbringing and education is thus to
enlighten people about themselves.

In his wide-ranging work, *The Republic,*
Plato worked out a comprehensive educational, social and constitutional theory. He
breaks down the state into three classes or
estates. 1) The ruling class of Guardians,
charged with administering the state. They
are required to have a high standard of
education in every area of knowledge.
Plato discusses in detail the training of
the Guardians in gymnastics and music
(in the wider sense including poetry
and rhythm), as well as in the four
Pythagorean sciences, to which he adds
stereometry. This comprehensive education
in preparation for government is not concluded until the age of 49. 2) The Soldiers,
a combination of police and army. Their
responsibility is internal and external security. 3) The General Population. They are
responsible for providing food, for trade
and for crafts. For each of these estates,
the appropriate virtues are understanding,
bravery, and moderation respectively. The
fourth cardinal virtue, justice, comprehends
all the others and thus extends to all the

estates, by regulating solidarity and the
mutual relationship of the virtues and the
social classes. For the first two estates,
Plato postulates that goods, women and
children be regarded as common property.
Only in this way, in other words by total
renunciation of private property and other
private claims, can the worst evils for the
state – namely acquisitiveness and its resulting disputes – be avoided. By virtue of their
all-round education, which serves not only
to impart knowledge but should also lead
them to the Platonic ideas, the Guardians
acquire the right and the duty to serve the
state as philosopher-kings, an office that
Plato expressly holds open for women
too. In the context of the discussion on
educational theory, Plato draws up a harsh
critique of poets. He would ban poets from
his republic, because they 1) lie, in other
words neither know the truth nor dissemi-
nate it; 2) lead children and young people
astray with false notions and keep them
away from the knowledge of the ideas; and
3) present and copy not the ideas, nor even
the images of the ideas, but images of the
images (i.e. artifacts).

Plato's Natural Philosophy
The theory of causes and the explanation
of the origin of the world are the main
themes of Plato's natural philosophy.
He lists the causes necessary for a complete explanation of the events in the world
as: 1) the material of which something
consists; 2) the physical cause, which brings

Plato's simile of the cave, Engraving
by Jan Saenredam, after Cornelis van
Haarlem, 1604, Albertina, Vienna

Plato's "simile of the cave" is to be
found in his dialogue *The Republic.*
People chained up for life in a cave
constantly see in the firelight the
shadows of things which they cannot
see, and they regard the shadows as
the things themselves. However the
things themselves are mere images of
an ideal existence, represented by the
sun shining outside the cave. Plato uses
this simile to describe the path to
recognition of the ideas, which, as real
originals, are superordinate to the world
of concrete, visible things which are
mere copies of them.
The engraving reproduced here was
commissioned by a scholarly humanist
in Amsterdam, who also prescribed the
outlines of the content. It thus demonstrates the way in which memorable
classical images can be adapted to the
changing spirit of the age.

ANTRVM PLATONICVM.

about an effect; 3) the purpose an event or process is supposed to serve; 4) the ideas, according to which – in the end – every event in the world unfolds. This is the basis of the classical four-cause doctrine (material, formal, efficient and final, discussed in more detail by Aristotle). Cause in the true sense is for Plato the idea of the best, or in other words the form of the Good.

He portrays the origin of the world in a mythical manner. An architect of the world (demiurge) arranges the primal chaos into a cosmos, in other words an ordered unitary whole, and in such a way as to assemble the best of all possible worlds from the pre-existing material, while keeping the ideas constantly in view. This notion was later to be seized upon by Leibniz. We are not talking here of creation from nothing (creatio ex nihilo); such a notion is alien to all Greek philosophy, because the demiurge has to work with existing forms and material.

To explain the structure of the world, Plato has recourse to Empedocles' four-element theory. As a preliminary stage he postulates immaterial geometrical forms, to be precise the five regular polyhedra (tetrahedron, octahedron, icosahedron, cube and dodecahedron, later known as the Platonic solids), which he reduces to two primal triangles. Prior to these it is numbers, and prior to them it is the ideas which determine the world, so that we have the following ontological hierarchy of the cosmos: ideas, numbers, geometrical solids, elements, concrete objects.

Aristotle

Main Features of his Philosophy

Aristotle's philosophy covers an extraordinarily broad and encyclopedic range of themes. For the first time in the history of philosophy, some internal differentiation can be discerned, which later led to the establishment of the various branches of learning (e.g. psychology, logic, zoology). A careful, strictly thought-out methodology can be discerned in every area, using the consistent terminology and definitions which Aristotle introduced. He can be seen as the founder of the historiography of philosophy, because on almost every theme he quotes, criticizes and reconstructs in

detail the theories of other philosophers. His work is thus a treasure trove of the otherwise largely lost works of the Presocratics. Aristotle has adopted only the linguistic and logical theoretical approaches from Plato, along with a thoroughgoing teleology not only of actions but also of natural phenomena. He uncompromisingly rejects the theory of ideas, dismissing it as empty words and poetic metaphors. In the place of the transcendental ideas as the basic principles of the world, he postulates ideas immanently acting in things.

A further important difference from Plato is Aristotle's decided interest in individual research into nature, in particular in the analysis and explanation of the problem of change and becoming, in the context of which he developed the famous and historically important distinctions between matter and form and between actuality and potentiality.

Logic and Linguistic Philosophy

Aristotle's writings on logic are usually brought together under the term Organon ("instrument"). His greatest achievement in the area of logic is the discovery of the syllogism, and with it the insight that particular conclusions can be regarded as valid solely on the basis of their form. A syllogism consists of two premises and a conclusion. For example: major premise, "All men are mortal"; minor premise, "All kings are men"; conclusion, "Therefore all kings are mortal." "Men" in this example is the middle term, which disappears in the conclusion. The

Symposium, Greek vase-painting, c. 460–450 B.C., Outer surface of a dish, Louvre, Paris

The "symposium" in ancient Greece was an all-male dinner and drinking party. Each symposium was presided over by a symposiarch, who dictated the subjects of conversation (often a matter of controversy) and decided at what moment how much of the customary mixture of wine and water should be drunk, and in what proportions. Doubtless love (including the love of boys) was often a topic, and eros was also one of the subjects of the most famous work of the literary symposium genre, namely Plato's description of such an event. He, however, treats eros as a demonic power, mediating between the human and the divine. Following an impressive raising and deepening of the persuasiveness of successive arguments, eros here appears as a ribbon holding the cosmos together, and as a condition for recognizing the idea of the Beautiful, which merges with the supreme idea of the Good. For philosophical reasons, Plato disliked interpreting the world through myths, but in his Symposium he expounds views which would be difficult to represent otherwise in the form of mythical tales related by Socrates. Thus, perfectly in keeping with the theme of the dialogue, poetry is also given a place.

conclusion is necessarily true if the premises
are true. Syllogisms of this kind Aristotle calls
apodeictic, or proofs. If the truth of the
premises is not provable, as is usually the
case in ethical or rhetorical argumentation,
he calls them dialectic, or probable conclusions. With regard to the basic problem of
the syllogism, namely establishing the non-
derivable true premises, Aristotle refers to
our ability, in simple and direct perception,
to recognize something as something, for
example to recognize an object as the man
Callias, and to formulate this recognition as
a perceptual judgment.

In his linguistic philosophy, Aristotle takes
over the definition of a sentence with a
definite truth-value as consisting of subject
and predicate from Plato. In addition, in his
work, *The Categories,* he develops a theory
according to which all expressions possible
in statements of assertion can be sub-
divided into the following predicate types
(categories): substance, quantity, quality,
relation, place, time, position, situation,
action and affection. In the case of substance, he distinguishes between primary
substance, which relates to concrete individual things, and secondary substance, which
expresses the essence (or the definition) of a
thing. In contrast to Plato's ontology, priority
is given to primary substance, because
without its presence, nothing else could
either exist or be expressed.

Aristotle's Theory of Nature

Aristotle defines nature as the sphere of
those things which contain in themselves

the principle (the origin) of movement
and rest, and includes not only physical
bodies but also the four elements. His primary problem therefore is to analyze and
explain the phenomenon of movement.
(This includes not just locomotion, but every
form of change.) Parmenides had asserted
that "movement" was not conceivable.
Aristotle refutes this opinion by introducing
the distinction between the negation of
existence and negation of predication,
which opens up the possibility that in
statements about motion, it is not existence,
but merely the attribution of a predicate
that is negated.

In this way, he obtains the following analysis of movement. 1) There is something
constant, which outlasts the whole movement process: matter (*hylë*; 2) in addition,
there are two definitions of form, one for the
beginning of the process and one for the
end. As Aristotle believed that all natural
changes were teleological (i.e. had a purpose), the initial state is a not-yet, a lack,
a deprivation of the final definition; the final
stage by contrast marks the attainment of
a goal (or intermediate goal as the case
may be). Put another way, the beginning
is the state of the possible (*dynamis,*
potentiality); the end is the state of reality
(*energeia,* actuality), or of fulfillment (*entelecheia*). Aristotle explains this by refering
to the sentence "A man is being educated,"
whose complete formulation reveals all
the elements mentioned. An uneducated
(definition of form as deprivation; potentiality) man (matter) becomes an educated
(definition of form as goal; reality) man
(matter).

Aristotle's Metaphysics

Aristotle recognized no transcendental
entities such as Plato's ideas. The Platonic
dualism between idea and real object is
something he wants to overcome. For him,
the essence of things lies in themselves,
whereby this essence is only potentially
within them. The essence achieves actuality
through a definite form, in other words
matter and form combine to create a unity
in the object. He distinguishes between
animate and inanimate as different forms of
being, and further differentiates the animate,
according to different capacities of the

soul, into plants (capacity for feeding and growth), animals (in addition, capacity for locomotion and perception), and people (in addition, capacity for thought).

Metaphysics, the general theory of wisdom, or the "original philosophy," is the basic theory of the first causes and principles of being and of thinking. In respect of being, Aristotle discusses the four-cause theory (known to us from Plato) and the most general characteristics of existent things, such as unity, identity, substantiality, potentiality, reality, materiality and formal purpose; these basic definitions are, at the same time, characteristics of things and principles of thought.

Pursuing the chain of causes of events in the world further and further would lead to the risk of falling into the methodologically unacceptable situation of infinite regress. In order to avoid this, Aristotle postulates the existence of a being, the cause of all other things, but not itself caused: the unmoved mover. This being is eternal, immutable, unmoved, the object of striving (and thus causing movement), pure actuality (without potentiality), immaterial, reason. It is a philosophical basic principle to explain the world; but while Aristotle calls this entity "God," it did not create the world, nor does it guide the world now or take any part in it.

Ethics and Political Philosophy

Aristotle's ethics is an ethics of happiness and virtue. Starting from the fact that all action (whether theoretical, practical or political) has a goal which determines the respective activity as a guiding principle, he defines the Good as the goal of action (and not, like Plato, as a transcendental concept). The question of a general good embracing all goals of action leads him to divide actions into those we undertake in the pursuit of further goals, and those we perform for their own sake. Only the latter can serve as general purposes of action, and only happiness, or bliss, fulfills the conditions of a supreme goal pursued for no other purpose.

Aristotle arrives at a material definition of happiness by inquiring after the activities and capabilities specific to human beings as human beings. They reside in the conditions of the soul which raise human beings above animals. Hence we have the following definition of happiness: it is an activity of the (human) soul by reason of its specific capacity, namely reason. In the process, Aristotle does not forget to point out that a minimum of outward features of happiness (such as property and health) is indispensable for the attainment of perfect happiness.

The activity of reason can be related to the sphere of practical action or to that of theory, giving rise to a division of the virtues into ethical and dianoetic. The ethical virtues (alongside the four cardinal virtues, Aristotle analyzes a whole series of further practically related forms of behavior) consist in the pursuit of the golden mean between two extremes: bravery, for example, is the mean between cowardice and recklessness. By

Aristotle, 384–322 B.C., Marble, Kunsthistorisches Museum, Vienna

Aristotle was a member of Plato's Academy for twenty years before becoming tutor to Alexander the Great, and subsequently founding a school of philosophy of his own in Athens. What he criticized in Plato's philosophy was the unbridgeable gap between the ideas and the world of experience, between the essence and the actual object. For him, the essence of things lay in themselves, and not in some transcendental idea of them. The Platonic theory of the vision of ideas was, for him, knowledge of the universal, which formed a supplement to experience, or knowledge of the individual. Aristotle is regarded as a great systematizer of philosophy. A major concern of his school was to classify the multiplicity of phenomena.

The School of Aristotle, Fresco by Gustav Adolph Spangenberg, 1883–1888, University of Halle

Attalos Stoa, Built 159–132 BC., Reconstructed 1952–1956, Athens

The *stoa* was a covered public promenade found in classical sacred buildings and large public spaces. The best-known example in Athens was the *stoa poikile* ("painted hall"), which was decorated with pictures by famous painters and used as a meeting place for the Stoic school of philosophers named after it. As the founders of the Stoics did not have enough money to buy land, they used this public building for teaching purposes.

According to the Stoics, all of nature is imbued with the principle of divine reason. Only those who live in harmony with this principle can achieve bliss. A life in harmony with oneself and nature can be achieved by liberating oneself from feelings of fear and desire, which disturb the desired impassivity. Freedom from these emotions *(apathia)* was one of the Stoics' highest ideals.

the dianoetic, or intellectual, virtues he is referring to the five kinds of scientific activity, which is why he also discusses these in his *Nichomachean Ethics.* They are not defined in terms of a mean, but of the attainable optimum.

Aristotle's political theory, in contrast to Plato's utopia, whose community of goods and women he emphatically rejects, is pragmatic in conception. He too discusses problems of upbringing in detail, in particular musical education, but devotes a major part of his *Politics* to questions of economics, civic rights, and the division of offices. Anticipating the modern notion of the separation of powers, he distinguishes between the legislative, the executive and the judiciary as elements of state power. He defines the state in terms of its ethical goal as a self-sufficient autonomous community of equals with the purpose of achieving the best possible life, in other words to make possible the happiness of the citizens. The best form of state or constitution, in other words the one most beneficial to the majority of people with the least danger of misuse for selfish ends, he sees – pragmatically and applying his principle of the golden mean – in a mixture of democracy and oligarchy, in which extreme poverty and excessive wealth are both avoided, and the most rights assigned to the middle class of citizens.

The Philosophy of the Hellenistic Age

Alongside the Academy founded by Plato, and the Peripatetic School founded by Aristotle, the Garden of Epicurus, and the Porch or Stoa, were the main schools of classical philosophy.

In addition there were a few other schools, e.g. the Cynics, who looked back to Socrates' pupil Antisthenes or to the Pythagorean, Diodoros of Aspendos. But it was only with Diogenes of Sinope (nicknamed *kynikos,* doglike, because of his outrageous behavior, hence the name "Cynic") that the school itself was established; it survived into the 5th century A.D.

Characteristic of philosophical Cynicism was a mordant, cynical criticism of customs, institutions and religious opinions, coupled with a withdrawal into a private sphere, free of social constraints, where one could live in accordance with one's convictions. The supreme goal in life was happiness, which could be obtained by avoiding misfortune and by leading a life of self-realization, understood as a life led according to "back to nature" principles, and thus as self-sufficient in contrast to the prevailing outward measures of happiness such as honor, wealth and health. This attitude was made possible by training the faculty of reason, by reducing needs (asceticism) and avoiding the main causes of misfortune, namely ignorance, pursuit of luxury, and unthinking pursuit of desires.

Epicurus founded his school in Athens in about 307 B.C. as a rival to the Academy and the Peripatos, as Aristotle's school was known. Epicureanism is also a philosophy of individual happiness, which consists of a life of joy and pleasure from which pain and worry are absent. The basic condition is *ataraxia,* unwavering intellectual detachment, which can be attained above all by philosophical insight and a life of withdrawal. The widespread charge that the Epicureans were devoted to unrestrained pleasure is without foundation. Understanding the processes of nature imparts not just theoretical knowledge, but also, and especially, practical enlightenment, which liberates man from the fear of the gods and the fear of death.

According to Epicurus' epistemology, which goes back to the Atomists and Democritus' theory of perception, sensory impressions are due to emanations from objects, which are composed of atoms. The human soul, which disappears at death, also consists of atoms. Gods are understood as immortal configurations of atoms.

The Stoic school was founded by Zeno of Citium in the Stoa Poikile, a brightly painted roofed promenade in Athens, in about 300 B.C. It remained in existence until the middle of the 3rd century A.D. Early Stoicism showed some affinity with Cynicism, and likewise saw itself as a successor to Socrates, and in critical, at times polemical, opposition to the Academy and to the Peripatetics.

Like Socrates, Zeno sought, in a world of political and social instability and of epistemological uncertainty above all due to the skepticism of the Sophists, to construct an intellectual edifice which would ensure theoretical certainty and practical reliability. His main concern was to establish a philosophy which would help individuals to run their own lives, and unlike that of the Epicureans and Cynics, one that tended to political stability. Happiness, the goal of humanity, consisted in living a life of harmony with oneself and with nature, and this could be achieved by investigating the laws of nature and orienting oneself consistently to reason, by overcoming false prejudices and inclinations, and the striving for purely outward qualities; virtue alone should be the guide of action. The basis of knowledge is perception, which provides infallibly true mental images, from which, with the help of logic, further firm conclusions can be drawn. He interprets the world, the cosmos, as a unitary living organism, which is totally

Epicurus, c. 342–271 B.C., Hellenistic bust, Louvre, Paris

The philosophy of Epicurus centered on the doctrine of blissful life. The principle of pleasure, which forms the basis of happiness, was defined by Epicurus as the absence of physical and emotional pain. The ideal of Epicurean philosophy consisted in a simple life, which would allow people to satisfy basic needs and face crises with equanimity. The pleasure praised by Epicurus has nothing to do with sensual pleasure and indulgence: a man should also avoid experiences which guaranteed momentary pleasure but could have painful and unfortunate consequences.

Diogenes in his tub, receiving a visit from Alexander the Great, Outline engraving after a Roman relief

Diogenes of Sinope, here depicted in his shelter (a tub or maybe a large clay pitcher), must not be confused with Diogenes Laertios, the author of the only extant classical history of philosophy, who lived five hundred years later. The "message" of the man from Sinope, who spent many years in Athens, consisted in his lifestyle and in the witty answers and aphorisms which he uttered and demonstrated in real life. He confronted the Athenian establishment with an existence which, free of possessions, strove for equanimity and contentment. It was provocatively designed to reveal human vanity and demonstrate natural humanity. He went around the marketplace in daylight with a burning lantern, saying he was looking for an honest man (i.e. not grubs absorbed in the constraints of social convention). Legend has it that Alexander the Great offered to fulfill a wish. "Move a little out of my sunlight," he replied. Disparagingly, but altogether to his approval, he was nicknamed *kynikos* ("doglike"); accordingly, he and those contemporaries who shared his attitude became known as "cynics."

Chrysippus,
Marble statue, 3rd century B.C., Louvre, Paris

Chrysippus was the third head of the Stoic school in Athens. Like the other Stoics, he divided science into physics, ethics and logic, and believed that the whole of nature emanated from one rational principle. He systematized the theses of his predecessors in numerous writings. The statue shows in highly impressive manner the individualizing realism of Hellenistic art. It represents a moment of concentration, suggested especially in the eyes and the "speaking" hand. At the same time the generalized, typical aspect of his posture, the general formula of a thinking man, is not neglected. This formula, which also relates to the situation of the teacher in front of listeners, became standard for the representation of philosophers. When certain Roman emperors later had themselves portrayed thus, they underlined their claim to be philosopher-rulers.

imbued with fire as its general principle, and by the divine breath *(pneuma)* of the *logos*, and also is totally determined by divine providence. As the universal world-*logos* also determines political life, the application of the system to political theory necessarily demands a turning away from the Greek *polis* ("city-state") in favor of a broader cosmopolitanism.

As he re-formulated and systematized its philosophical position, Chrysippus is regarded as the second founder of Stoicism. The focus of his interest is dialectics, understood as a basic science of logic and argumentation, which, alongside formal logic, encompassed linguistics, semantics, epistemology and rhetoric. The famous Stoic logic is due largely to him.

In epistemology, he combined Empiricism and Rationalism. The (potentially fallible) impression of the senses, from which that part of the soul endowed with reason develops an idea *(phantasia)*, gives rise to truth and knowledge, but not before this idea itself has been examined by reason. With the help of memory, and the capacity to compare and abstract, we form the tested ideas into experiences, which lead to definitions and concepts. Chrysippus relates the basic Stoic maxim of living in harmony with nature directly to the rational nature of man. Although human beings are in principle subject to the all-determining world-*logos,* they nonetheless have the possibility to maintain self-sufficient self-determination through the exercise of free will.

With Panaetius, the founder of the middle Stoic period, Greek philosophy began to orient itself to imperial Roman thought. He is less concerned with dialectics and physics, the centers of his predecessors' interest, than with problems of ethics, and especially its pragmatic and political aspects. He rejected earlier Stoicism's rigorously ascetic ethics, with its suppression of natural urges, and put a positive judgment on pleasure and the possession of outward goods. In contrast to the ideal of the unworldly Stoic sage prevalent hitherto, he developed a practical doctrine of political duty, which went down extremely well with Rome's political and intellectual elite (Cicero, Scipio).

ROMAN PHILOSOPHY

Preservation of the Greek Heritage
The philosophy of Ancient Rome leant heavily on that of Greece, without any originality worthy of the name, and was not characterized by any ongoing formation of schools. As far as the historical legacy is concerned, the major service performed by Rome to philosophy was to transmit philosophical thought to the Roman Empire and to develop a Latin terminology which formed the basis for the dissemination of philosophy in the Middle Ages.

Lucretius wrote a didactic poem, *De rerum natura* ("On the Nature of Things"), in which he combined the teaching of Epicurus with the Atomism of Democritus. The whole work is imbued by a concern to provide a consistently rational explanation of natural processes, and thus to liberate people from the fear of death, priests and the gods.

In his work, Cicero combined the various philosophical trends of Antiquity. In epistemology, he adhered to the skeptical variant of the Academy; in ethics, anthropology and theology, he adhered to Stoicism. It is to him that Greek philosophy owes its acknowledgment by the Romans, whose attitude to philosophizing was one of less than wholehearted approval. He deserves respect above all as a translator and conveyor of Greek philosophy, having brought Greek theories of ethics and politics to the Roman world. As a thoughtful and at the same time pragmatic politician, he saw the ideal life in a synthesis of philosophy and rhetoric, and always in the service of the state, which he defined as an association based on legal consensus and community of interest. In order to prevent the misuse of rhetoric, he required that speakers have not just rhetorical skills, but moral dignity too.

In his epistemology, he denied the possibility of absolutely assured knowledge, and, consistent with this view, spoke out against all dogmatism. He did however demand precise examination of one's own judgments by carefully weighing up all possible counter-arguments.

Seneca was also actively involved in Roman politics. Nero's teacher and tutor, he later committed suicide at his pupil's behest. He vehemently rejected the Atomist theory, and oriented himself primarily toward early Stoicism, Cynicism and Epicureanism. His main philosophical concern was a practical, even folksy, ethics, based on the Stoic doctrine of goods. One's role model, he said, should be the imperturbable Stoic sage, characterized in particular by control of the passions and composure in the face of death. Like Lucretius, he placed scientific research at the service of enlightenment and ethics.

Marcus Aurelius, the "philosopher on the Imperial throne," generally adhered to the ethical and political philosophies of the Stoics. His linking of ethics and religion led to the thesis that unreasonable behavior was tantamount to disobedience to God. From the rational identity of all people he derived a cosmopolitan political ideal, which also formed the ideological legitimation of Rome's imperial claim.

Late Antiquity

Classical philosophy experienced a major revival in the form of Neoplatonism (3rd–6th century), which, from its inception until the rediscovery of Aristotle's writings in the Middle Ages, was the dominant intellectual force, almost totally displacing all the other philosophical schools and trends. Its founder, Plotinus, constructed a unitary explanatory model embracing all spheres of existence and thought; based on Plato's ontology, but differing in significant ways, it divided the world into a hierarchy of levels of being (hypostases): the One, Mind *(nous),* and Soul. Each level emanates from the one above, without the latter undergoing any diminution of its being. The ground and origin of all that exists is the One, which he also called the Good or the Divine. It transcends all being and thought. It is incorporeal and without qualities. The second level, *nous* (variously translated as "mind," "spirit" or "intellect"), constitutes the location of plurality and ideas, and thus of what truly exists. The third level, Soul, is thought of in part as the soul of the world, in part as the individual soul of each human being, animal, and plant. By imbuing the whole world, it shapes the cosmos into a single organism. Below these three come the imperfect hypostases of the world of material things, which Plotinus disparaged, equating material with evil. In so doing, he laid the foundation for a long tradition of hostility to the body. The highest ethical and spiritual goal of man consisted, he said, in transcendental union with the One; this presupposed a detachment from everything to do with the body, a state which in its turn could only be achieved by strict asceticism.

Like many Neoplatonists, Boethius regarded the philosophy of Plato and Aristotle as a unity; he saw it as his main task to translate their works into Latin and provide them with a commentary. With his writings on Aristotle's *Organon* he became the channel by which the logic of the Ancient World was transmitted to the Middle Ages. After being condemned by Theoderic for high treason, he composed the *Consolation of Philosophy* in his cell; in it, he described all earthly goods as worthless, and praised God as the highest good.

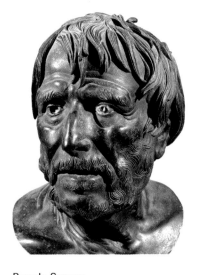

Pseudo-Seneca,
Roman copy of Greek original, Bronze, Museo Nazionale Archeologico, Naples

The beginning of the 19th century saw the discovery of the only known portrait of Seneca to bear an inscription with his name. It has very little similarity to the bronze head depicted here, which also exists in numerous marble versions, and had been regarded as a portrait of Seneca since the end of the 16th century. As there was a sort of Seneca renaissance in the 17th and 18th centuries, numerous art collections acquired plaster casts or paintings of this head.
The Roman philosopher and poet was admired not only as a paragon of virtue on account of his ethical attitude, but also as an important dramatist, whose tragedies exercised a certain influence on the French and German literature of the Baroque.

The Middle Ages

FAITH AND KNOWLEDGE

From Late Antiquity to the Middle Ages

In the 4th century, the civilization of classical Antiquity was subjected to far-reaching changes. Increasing pressure from Germanic tribes to the north, together with internal symptoms of dissolution, finally led, in the late 4th century, to the division of the Roman Empire into the Eastern and Western Empires. Some time after, Rome, the capital of the Western Empire, was sacked by barbarian tribes, and in A.D. 476, the Western Empire collapsed. The Eastern Empire, by contrast, with its capital at Constantinople, survived until 1453, when the city fell to the Turks. This period of almost a thousand years between the collapse of the two empires, Western and Eastern, is roughly what we generally know today as the Middle Ages, or medieval period.

A symbolic date for the transition from classical to medieval, that is to say Christian, philosophy is the year A.D. 529, when in the East, Plato's Academy in Athens was closed by Emperor Justinian. That very same year saw the foundation of the first great monastic order in the West, that of St. Benedict. From then on, the monasteries became the centers of scholarship and teaching in western Europe.

The beginning of the Middle Ages also marks the beginning of the spread of Christianity in Europe. There had long been Christian congregations in the major cities of the Empire, but they played no very significant role. Things now changed. In the early 4th century, Emperor Constantine decreed that Christianity should enjoy equal status alongside the pagan religions. About a hundred years later, Christianity was made the sole religion of the state. Within another four centuries, the whole of Europe had been Christianized.

The spread of Christianity in Europe was accompanied by a change in philosophy. Medieval philosophy consists above all in an intermeshing of philosophy and theology. Its basic concern was the question of the relationship between faith and knowledge. Its foundation was Christian doctrine, which had to be defended, a position known as Christian apologetics. However, it will become clear that medieval philosophy did not represent a complete break with that of classical Antiquity. Many scholars sought to understand the philosophical theories of the Ancient World and to reconcile them with Christian teaching.

One of these scholars was Aurelius Augustinus, who as St. Augustine has become known as the most important philosopher of the transitional period between late Antiquity and the Middle Ages. His thinking was influenced above all by Plato and the

THE MIDDLE AGES

Medieval philosophy consists primarily of the **union of philosophy and theology,** because it was based on Christian doctrine, which it was required to defend and put on a rational foundation.

One of the main themes of medieval philosophy was therefore the question of the **relationship between faith and knowledge** and the related attempt to overcome the apparently irreconcilable difference between revealed truth and philosophical insight.

The **first period (c. 200–700)** overlaps with that of late Antiquity. Its most important representative is **St. Augustine,** who laid the foundations for the whole of medieval philosophy.

The theological and philosophical doctrine of medieval western Europe is known as **Scholasticism** (from the Latin *schola,* "school"). This term also refers to the manner in which the verities of faith were explained (the "scholastic method" practiced in the monastic schools).

The development of Scholasticism proceeded in three stages. The first stage, that of **Early Scholasticism (c. 800–1200),** saw the emergence of the scholastic method and the first confrontation with the writings of Aristotle, which were becoming known in this period.

The earth as a disk surrounded by the ocean, French manuscript illumination, 15th century, Bibliothèque Nationale, Paris

The succeeding period of **High Scholasticism (c. 1150–1300)** is seen as the heyday of the movement. It is characterized by the discovery of Aristotle's remaining works, and by the attempt **to unite Aristotelian**

philosophy with Christian teaching (St. Thomas Aquinas). In addition, there was a confrontation with Arab philosophy. The last period, that of **Late Scholasticism (c. 1300–1400),** was already marked by decline.

Among the core issues of medieval philosophy was the **problem of universals.** This was concerned with whether general terms had any reality, or whether they were simply constructs of thought and language.

Important for the development of Scholasticism was the **foundation of universities** (from the 12th century), which quickly evolved into centers of intellectual life.

Neoplatonists. From the latter, Augustine adopted the view that the whole of existence has a divine origin. He shared the Platonic theory of ideas, but viewed them in relation to God's creation. God created things, he said, on the basis of the ideas already present in His mind. For Augustine as for Plato, the ideas are primal patterns, but they are patterns "thought" by God, according to which He created things. In this way Augustine succeeded in reconciling the Platonic concept of ideas with holy scripture. Augustine's view of evil also generally accords with that of Neoplatonism. As evil is merely the negation of good, it has no independent existence.

Augustine's entire thought is directed towards God. For him, Christianity is the fount of all truth. What needed to be clarified was whether this truth could only be revealed by faith, or whether it could also be discovered by reason. Reason and faith were, for Augustine, inseparable. Reason lay in faith, and in faith lay reason. Thus knowledge and faith follow the same road, the road to God. According to Augustine, this road led via the innermost workings of the soul. The foundation of knowledge and truth lay in certain knowledge of the self. One can reasonably doubt the existence of all external things which are only perceptible to the senses. But by doubting, people become aware of themselves as doubters. The importance of this self-certainty lies in its transcendence of sensory perception and the knowledge that the latter provides. The more people penetrate into their innermost being, the nearer they approach truth, which in Augustine's view "dwells in the inner person." Self-certainty, for Augustine, stands in relationship to God from the beginning. Certainty of self implies certainty of God, for God created Man in His image.

THE EMERGENCE OF SCHOLASTICISM

The Scholastic Method

By the 9th century, the problem was no longer either to demarcate or unite Christian and classical teachings, but rather to develop a systematic total picture and

a rational explanation of the verities of faith. The venues for this wide-ranging enterprise were the schools where Latin was taught, hence the term Scholasticism, from the Latin *schola,* "school." Philosophy, which was either subordinated to theology or subsumed under it, was given the task of reconciling the – in some cases apparently irreconcilable – contradictions between revealed truth and philosophical insight. The intention was to remove all the objections to revealed faith and to provide a rational basis for Christian doctrine, rather than merely defend it as hitherto.

For this purpose a particular procedure was used, known as the scholastic method. Developed by a number of scholars, it was practiced in the monastic schools. Examination of a text meant first of all preparing a commentary on the basis of the authorities (i.e. the Bible and the Church Fathers), and then to use the methods of logic to pursue a "disputation" for the purposes of clarifying any unsolved questions. Differing views were opposed in order to seek a solution to the problem. This procedure thus kept very largely within the existing interpretations as enunciated by the Fathers (e.g. St. Augustine), who had already laid down the dogmatic foundations of the faith. The important

Albertus Magnus at his Desk,
Fresco by Tommaso da Modena, 1352,
Capitolo dei Dominicani, Treviso

Aristotle's writings became known in Europe during the 12th century via the medium of Arab philosophers. The world of Christian scholarship was thus confronted with new insights in the fields of logic, metaphysics and natural philosophy. Many however saw a contradiction between Aristotelian teaching and the Christian faith, for which reason some universities banned the use of his works. It was to Albertus Magnus that Aristotelian philosophy owed its breakthrough. He was of the opinion that the application of Aristotelian thought to the investigation of nature would necessarily lead to true philosophy. It was however his pupil, St. Thomas Aquinas, who succeeded in the attempt to combine the systematic scientific philosophy of Aristotle with theological tradition.

The Seven Liberal Arts, from Herrad von Landsperg, *Hortus deliciarum,* Outline drawing after a manuscript destroyed by fire in the Strasbourg library, c. 1170, later colored

Education in the Middle Ages was based on the system, deriving from the Ancient World, of the Seven Liberal Arts. In classical Antiquity, they were seen as a form of introduction to philosophy, while in the Middle Ages they took on the character of a general curriculum embracing the whole of non-theological studies. Two stages were distinguished: the lower, or *trivium,* comprising what were known as the "speaking" arts (grammar, rhetoric, logic), and the upper, or *quadrivium,* comprising the "calculating" arts of music, arithmetic, geometry and astronomy. The Seven Liberal Arts formed the basic curriculum at every medieval university.

role of logic within this method need not surprise us: after all, it was one of the Seven Liberal Arts which constituted the entire non-theological element of the medieval curriculum and thus characterized the whole of higher education. The first, lower, stage in the study of the Seven Liberal Arts comprised rhetoric, grammar, and dialectics (or logic); this was known as the *trivium.* The second stage comprised arithmetic, geometry, astronomy and music; this was the *quadrivium.*

Scholasticism developed in three main stages. The first stage, that of Early Scholasticism (c. 800–1200) saw the emergence of the scholastic method, and the first confrontation with the writings of Aristotle, which became known during this period. The period of High Scholasticism (c. 1150–1300) is regarded as the heyday of scholasticism; its main features were the discovery of the remaining works of Aristotle, and the attempt to combine his philosophy with Christianity (St. Thomas Aquinas). In addition, there was a confrontation with Arab philosophy. Late Scholasticism (c. 1300–1400) was a period of decline.

The Problem of Universals

The scholastic method was developed primarily by Peter Abelard, whose importance rests on his solution to the problem of universals, one of the core issues in medieval philosophy. Simply stated, the problem is this: do general terms (universals)

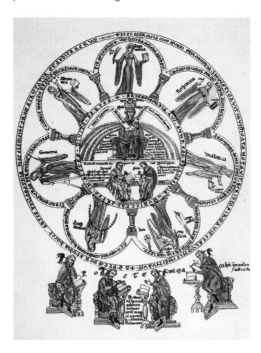

have any reality of their own? When using the term "man," say, or "animal," in a general sense (as for example in the sentence "All men are mortal"), this does not refer to any real individual, because otherwise the talk would be of this or that particular man or animal. And yet these terms refer to something and have a particular meaning. The question is: does this universal have any existence in reality? Or put another way: is there such a thing in reality as "manhood" or "animalhood" in the way that there are individual men and individual animals? Or again: are there universal entities to which a reality can be attributed, independent of the existence of the individual things?

In the history of philosophical problems, the question of universals goes back to Aristotle's criticism and re-interpretation of Plato's theory of ideas. For Plato, the ideas had a real existence, while Aristotle regarded this kind of transcendentalism as a superfluous construct.

There are two approaches to solving the problem of universals, quite apart from numerous variants, some of which cannot unambiguously be assigned to either of the two basic solutions. The first approach assumes that the universal exists only as a name (i.e. word or sign) and only after the individual thing *(universalia sunt nomina post rem).* This view is known as nominalism (from Latin *nomen* [plural *nomina*] "name"). By contrast, those who assume that universals are real things, or original patterns, are representatives of the "realist" school of thought. For realists (in this sense), the universal is a reality which existed before the individual thing *(universalia sunt realia ante rem).*

The main representative of nominalism is Roscelin of Compiègne. He said that universals were articulated sounds, with no correspondence in reality. This makes them mere products of language – an untenable position for adherents of realism. William of Champeaux, one of the latter, starts from an entity common to things which exists independently of the things themselves. The general term thus corresponds to a real substance identical with this entity. The differences between individual specimens lie, for him, in the different proportions in which properties and conditions are mixed.

Alongside the realist and nominalist solutions, there are other ways of answering the question of universals. An interesting example is the proposal by Peter Abelard. He knew the divergent views of Roscelin and William, and subjected both to critical examination. He believed that Roscelin underestimated the meaningful nature of universals, because there is no doubt that these general terms refer to something, so that they cannot just be arbitrary bundles of sounds. But Abelard also criticized William's position. What universals refer to cannot be real substance, because a universal with a real existence would have to have different, mutually contradictory, properties. If there was such a thing as a universal "living organism," for example, it would have to be sentient and non-sentient at the same time. A universal for Peter Abelard was not something with a real existence, but an abstraction created by men. Universals are only general in subjective thought. But the abstract terms are not arbitrary. They are abstractions derived by the intellect from individual things by determining and summarizing the similarities of the latter. This view of Abelard's points to the creative, active role of human beings in their experience of the world, which, in view of the widespread medieval concept of man as a merely passive receptor, represents an extremely modern aspect of his philosophy.

The Influence of Aristotle on High Scholasticism

During the 8th century, the Arabs occupied large areas of Spain, which not only contributed to the spread of oriental science and culture, but also led to the most important writings of Aristotle becoming known in western Europe. The arrival of Aristotle's writings brought about major changes within scholasticism toward the middle of the 12th century. Via Syria, the Arab world had assimilated elements of Greek culture. The works of Greek scholars were translated into Arabic, and on the basis of this, an Islamic philosophy was constructed. Above all, it was the writings of Aristotle that were studied and provided with commentaries. A philosopher

named Al-Farabi, for example, was the first to apply Aristotle's logic to revealed religion. An important contribution to this commentary was made by Ibn Rushd (known in the West by the Latinized form of his name, Averroes), who worked on the systemization of Islamic teaching. It is through him that Aristotle's *Metaphysics,* especially, became known. Like the Scholastics, Averroes assumed that the eternal truths contained in religion could be given a rational foundation through the use of reason.

Aristotle's writings, together with the commentaries on them by Arab (and also Jewish) scholars, were finally translated from Greek or Arabic into Latin. The dissemination of these writings led to new philosophical approaches within Christian philosophy, as well as to new philosophical methods.

Christian scholars were confronted with new insights in the areas of logic, metaphysics and natural philosophy, whose connection with revealed religion was not

The Ebstorf World Map,
c. 1283, formerly in Ebstorf Monastery near Uelzen

While the Greeks were familiar with the idea that the earth was spherical, the Middle Ages regarded this view as incompatible with Christian scripture, and countered with the proposal that the earth was a disk. As in this famous 13th-century map, the earth was mostly seen as a circular area surrounded by the ocean; this area is divided into the continents of Europe, Africa, and Asia, the largest. In the center is Jerusalem, which was indeed regarded as the center of the world. The disk is borne by the figure of Christ, whose head, hands and feet point east, south, north, and west respectively.

It is immediately obvious that this representation of the world is highly simplified and not to scale. This is partly due to the fact that the location of a place was not determined by modern methods of calculation. On the other hand, geographical accuracy was not a primary concern. Medieval maps are more narrative in character. They tell the story of the world, starting from the creation, and report miracles in the spirit of the tradition of the age. Thus they resemble chronicles rather than scale maps of the earth's surface.

immediately obvious. In addition, the arrival of Aristotle led to an increase in respect for such sciences as astronomy, physics, mathematics and medicine. These areas had hitherto been without exception subordinated to theology. It now became increasingly clear that each discipline (including theology itself) had its own material and methods. This was also true of philosophy, which likewise was in the service of theology. It could now be seen how Islamic philosophers dealt with philosophical topics without constant recourse to authority. There was thus renewed attention given to the question of the relationship between theology and philosophy.

It was St. Thomas Aquinas who, like no other thinker of his age, sought a synthesis between theology and philosophy, while at the same time acknowledging the autonomy of each in respect of their methods. Theology rested on faith, philosophy on reason. Thomas was of the opinion that some truths could be explained both by Christian revelation and by reason. Thus theology and philosophy represented two different ways of pursuing a common aim, namely the search for truth. These two paths to knowledge did not, however, merely exist in parallel; rather, they impinged on each other, and thus contributed to a better understanding to the approach of the other. One of Thomas' main concerns was the defense of theological statements by means of philosophical arguments. However he believed that there were certain limits to reason, as reason was not capable of answering every question. There were some truths open only to revelation, such as, for example, the Trinity and the Incarnation. Thomas succeeded in creating a synthesis of philosophy and theology on the basis of his familiarity with Aristotle. It is in the works of St. Thomas Aquinas that the influence of Aristotle on the Middle Ages reached its high point. The doctrine of the creation is an example of how he sought to unite Christian teaching with Aristotelian science.

Thomas agreed with the Neoplatonic thesis, according to which all existence was created by God from the void. This assumption forms the foundation of his understanding of Aristotelian science. According to Aristotle, one must start from the particular in order to express the essence of things. The essence of things lies in themselves. From his distinction between material and form, Aristotle derived his doctrine of becoming. According to Aristotle, essence is present in material only potentially. Only through form does potentiality become reality. Movement and becoming are constant changes in relation to material and form. As a result, all that exists is structured level by level, from the first material as mere potentiality, to God as pure reality.

Unlike Aristotle, Thomas identified this principle with God the Creator. God as the Prime Mover had placed the relationship between potentiality and reality in the world, and thus triggered the process of coming into being and dying. The principle is thus the expression of divine reason. Why and how God created the world are not accessible to human reason, however, as creation was an act of freedom.

Late Scholasticism

The late Middle Ages (from approximately the 14th century) were a period of crisis, not only in respect of economic and social developments, but also with regard to the relationship between theology and philosophy. The contrast between the two was becoming increasingly clearer, and a synthesis in the manner of St. Thomas Aquinas increasingly impossible. Characteristic of the philosophical projects of this period was the determined search for certainty, with the question of the foundations of human knowledge being given more and more emphasis.

The philosophy of William of Occam (or Ockham) is an example of this new emphasis and of late medieval attempts at finding a solution. His thought basically rested on two principles: that of omnipotence and that of economy. The first stated that God created things by His own free will, in other words that He could have created them differently. The consequence of this is that the world can no longer be seen as a necessary world, but only as one of any number of possible worlds. Apart from God (to whom alone a necessary existence can be attributed), everything is contingent (i.e. existing by chance) rather than necessary. Accordingly reason can comprehend the world as rational, but not as necessary, and can therefore not gain any complete insight into the essence and creative freedom of God. While St. Augustine had still assumed that access to the ideas of God was possible through the enlightenment *(illuminatio)* of human understanding, Occam sees human capacity for knowledge as finite. The separation between philosophy and theology was becoming clearer.

The principle of economy is encapsulated in the maxim known as "Occam's Razor," which states that "entities are not to be multiplied beyond necessity." In other words, all superfluous explanations of anything are pointless and should be avoided. The point of this thesis consists in the avoidance of one-to-one correspondences of terms and objects, because terms are deceptive and not every description corresponds to an object with real existence. There are for example things to which different terms are assigned. What Occam was trying to point out with his "razor" was that superfluous explanations or terms

possibly lead to false assumptions (of the actual existence of the thing described). Thus he was setting up a kind of scientific maxim.

With regard to the problem of universals, Occam was a nominalist. In his opinion, general terms are names in the sense of signs, or meaning-bearers, which act as place-holders for concrete objects when one is thinking, and which human thought uses to describe things. For Occam, only individual things had any existence, for which reason knowledge must be directed toward them.

Occam distinguishes intuitive from abstract knowledge. The former relates to immediately present and directly perceivable objects and facts, and to inward self-experience; the latter leads to statements on the basis of concepts without the immediate presence of an object. In the former case, therefore, one turns immediately to realities, while in the latter the results are derivative. Intuitive knowledge for Occam is the precondition for abstract knowledge. Knowledge of individual things and empirical experience thus become the basic principle of science. For this reason it is impossible to prove the existence of God, because the term "God" is only derivative and has no foundation in experience. This is why, according to Occam, there can only be faith in, but not knowledge of, God. An important feature of Occam's explanation is the fact that the difference between intuitive and abstract knowledge is not based in the different objects with which one happens to be concerned, but in the kind of knowledge itself; in other words, it is the process of knowing rather than the object of knowledge that is central.

Occam's late medieval nominalism prepared the way for the skeptical and critical approaches characteristic of the philosophy of the modern period. Occam and some of his contemporaries were representatives of the "new way" *(via moderna)* which was gradually replacing the "old way" *(via antiqua)* of such schools as those of St. Thomas Aquinas and Albertus Magnus. These two factions were to disagree for a long time, but at the universities it was the *via moderna* which increasingly set the tone.

Duns Scotus in a painting by Pedro Berruguete, Palazzo Ducale, Urbino

At the end of the 13th century, philosophical theology in the sense of the synthesis achieved by St. Thomas Aquinas was increasingly regarded as a threat to revealed theology. In connection with a reconsideration of St. Augustine, Duns Scotus strictly separated theology and philosophy once again.

The Schoolmaster Teaching, Manuscript illumination, Zurich, c. 1310–40, from the Heidelberger Liederhandschrift (Codex Manesse)

The goal of medieval education was to raise people as members of the Christian community and instruct them in faith. Teachers were in holy orders until the late Middle Ages. Schools started with the monastic schools, which enjoyed their heyday in the time of Charlemagne. Alongside these, cathedral and other collegiate schools developed in the 8th century. These then evolved into universities during the renaissance of scholarship in the 12th and 13th centuries.

A Time of Transition

The Renaissance

THE DAWN OF MODERNITY

Renaissance and Humanism

The Renaissance, the Middle Ages, the Modern era – the continuum of European history is divided up into these familiar epochs, demarcating one type of civilization from another. The possibility of such a demarcation was realized as long ago as the 15th century, at the dawn of the Modern era; the Middle Ages by contrast had recognized a quite different division, based on biblical and theological statements and thought to be anchored in a completed plan of creation. During the 18th century, people finally became convinced that for about three centuries they had been living in a new era, and in fact the modern concept of a succession of eras emerged at about this time.

And indeed, it was the 18th century which saw the culmination of many of the developments which started in what is now often called the early modern period, namely the age of the Renaissance. The post-medieval system of states was by now established, Christian and feudal political values were thoroughly relativized by the thinkers of the Enlightenment, cultural institutions and the whole image of the world were secularized (in other words freed from ecclesiastical ties and dogmas).

The sciences played a decisive and autonomous role, the remnants of Scholasticism were eliminated. Natural phenomena and peoples from all over the world were compared and classified, a cosmopolitan middle class developed an awareness of themselves as a broadly based and indispensable stratum of society with revolutionary potential, and the individual discovered novel forms of self-expression.

This 18th-century state of affairs had its early modern roots not least in the decisive practical innovations (or improved applications, as the case may be) of the 14th century, as listed by Francis Bacon in a book published in 1620: "printing, gunpowder and the compass. These three changed the shape and face of things in the world; they were followed by numerous other changes, and it seems that no empire, no sect, no constellation, has exercised a greater influence on human affairs than these mechanical things."

These "three things" really can be linked with the historical facts which characterized the beginning of the modern era: printing with the humanist scholarship of the Renaissance and with the pamphlets and writings of the Reformation; the introduction of firearms with the ending of chivalry and thus with the development of new forms of state; and the invention of the compass

The Three Philosophers,
Painting by Giorgione, c. 1508, Kunsthistorisches Museum, Vienna

The title by which this painting is known today was not given to it by the artist himself. However, it is appropriate enough, even though the three men are by no means unambiguously identifiable as philosophers in the modern sense of the word. During the Renaissance, "philosopher" was the name given not only to theoretical metaphysicians, moralists and theologians, but also to naturalists. Astronomical research, suggested by the figures on the parchment held by the old man on the right of the picture, also fell under the heading of philosophy. Giorgione depicts three ages of Man, three relationships with the world. Impartial contemplation, decisiveness in action, skeptical wisdom coupled with possible magical abilities – these are the stereotyped attitudes distinguished in traditional philosophical definitions of human existence. Giorgione combines the general theme with lively individuality. The integration of the three men in the landscape is uncontrived, and gives the intellectual and general significance an intimate touch of reality.

with the epoch-making geographical discoveries of such explorers as Columbus and Vasco da Gama.

In the mid 16th century, the painter and architect Giorgio Vasari published biographies of famous artists; the series begins with the first "vanquishers" of the Gothic style, which Vasari dismissed as "barbaric." Here the Middle Ages are disparaged compared to classical Antiquity and its rebirth (or "renaissance") in the Italian art of the 14th century (Giotto) and then, above all, of the 15th and early 16th centuries (e.g. Leonardo, Michelangelo, Raphael). During the 19th century the term "Renaissance" came to be used for a whole cultural epoch, lasting from about 1400 to about 1530 or even as late as 1600, but largely restricted to Italy, or at least seen as originating there.

In view of its origin, the term "Renaissance" is clearest when applied to the history of art;

in other fields, it is far more difficult to establish a demarcation between it and the Middle Ages at one end and the Baroque at the other. Today, the Renaissance is no longer seen as a unitary phenomenon covering the whole of culture, but rather as a "threshold period," in which outstandingly new things are interwoven with medieval tradition.

Many of the epoch-making innovations of this age can be found in the sphere of the visual arts. In the early 15th century, architects and painters discovered the technique of central perspective, which created a visual illusion of depth and made possible the representation of people and things in space in such a way that proportions were correctly reproduced. In contrast to the image-creation procedures of medieval painting structured by symbols and pictorial formulae, perspective imaging rests on the

Idealized Townscape, 15th century, Palazzo Ducale, Urbino

The art and architecture of the Renaissance is characterized by a striving for perfect harmony and beauty. In Antiquity, it was thought, these esthetic ideals had already been realized. The rediscovery of classical knowledge can be seen, for example, in painting and architecture. Particular importance was attached to balanced relationships and harmonized proportions, and research was conducted into the rules by which these symmetries were created. Central perspective in the shaping of space in the ideal town accorded with this striving for harmony.

THE RENAISSANCE

In his *History of France*, the French historian Jules Michelet summed up the innovations of the 15th and 16th centuries as the "discovery of the world and the discovery of man", when for the first time, in 1854, he used the word "Renaissance" or **"rebirth"** to describe a historical period.

A restoration of classical republican constitutions had already been attempted in a Roman insurrection led by Cola di Rienzi (1347). With reference to this, the political theoretician Machiavelli spoke in the early 16th century of a re-birth.

Likewise in the 16th century, the idea of a re-birth of classical Antiquity in contemporary art became general.

In geography, astronomy and natural history, horizons broadened by leaps and bounds.

1543 saw the publication of Copernicus' astronomical theses, which put the **sun in the center of the planetary system.** The philosopher Giordano Bruno supported the thesis and extended it by asserting that the universe was infinite.

In combination with a rise in city-states and their middle classes, **printing,** developed by Johannes Gutenberg in about 1440, revolutionized the education and information system.

By nailing his theses to the church door in Wittenberg (1517), Martin Luther unleashed the **Reformation,** which sought a re-birth of the pristine convictions and religious practices of revealed Christian faith.

The Catholic **Counter-Reformation,** associated among other things with a

re-organization of the Inquisition, started with the Council of Trent (1545–63).

Humanism, which like the Renaissance generally was above all an Italian phenomenon, had since Francesco Petrarch (1304–74) been concerned with how to lead a life in the spirit of cultivated language combined with moral philosophy, based on the knowledge of classical literature.

The **philosophy** of this transitional period between the Middle Ages and the Modern era was increasingly **concerned with Man, history, and nature.**

Petrarch (Francesco Petrarca), Painting by Justus of Ghent, after 1476, Palazzo Ducale, Urbino

Francesco Petrarch understood history as memory, an inner understanding of the factual world which conveys the subjective and objective.

Nicolas of Cusa (1401–64), Detail of a Crucifixion painting in the chapel of St. Nikolaus Hospital in his home town of Bernkastel-Kues, c. 1463–80

Entirely in the spirit of the Renaissance image of humanity, Cusa emphasized the creative aspect of human capacity for knowledge, which for him had parallels with God's creation of the world. Just as God had created natural forms, Man creates what exists in thought (artificial forms).

Group of Reformers, (Among those depicted are Martin Luther, Johannes Bugenhagen, Erasmus of Rotterdam, Philipp Melanchthon and Johannes Forster), Copy after the Meienburg Epitaph for Lucas Cranach the Younger, Wittenberg, Lutherhalle

When Luther nailed his theses to the church door in Wittenberg (1517), the Reformation thus unleashed was aimed at a late scholastic theology which had moved away from biblical teaching, and also against the financial practices of the Church. The reformers' goal was a renewal of the Church in the spirit of the gospels. For Luther, the individual had a direct relationship with God, thus making redundant the intermediary function claimed by the Catholic Church. Luther adopted the doctrine of predestination formulated by St. Augustine, according to which salvation and damnation are pre-ordained by God. This restriction on Man's freedom of will brought him into conflict with some of the humanists, e.g. Erasmus of Rotterdam, for whom human self-determination formed the basis of a humane culture. Philipp Melanchthon too, a close collaborator of Luther's, stressed Man's free will, and attempted to unite Christian and humanistic approaches.

respective relationship, in each case, of the subject, the field and the viewpoint of the beholder, making the picture the "function" of these elements. Scientifically and rationally, the picture is defined as an exact image of reality as it appears to the vision of the beholder. This was the harbinger both of modern rationality with its mathematical view of space and nature, and of an understanding of the world, whereby the subject (and beholder) put his mental construction on what he saw.

Just as the viewpoint was an integral part of the perspective picture, aimed at the individual beholder, the new genre of portrait painting made its topic the individuality of the sitter. In fact, the dignity and uniqueness of individual human beings were emphasized quite generally during the Renaissance. Here too we see an incipient break with the Middle Ages, which was characterized more by the idea of a collective community of faith, in the spirit of the monastic orders. What was new above all was that not only princes were praised and crowned, but also writers and "craftsmen" like Giotto and Michelangelo.

The first poet of the Modern era to be crowned with the laurel wreath on the Capitol in Rome, following classical tradition, was Petrarch, the first great humanist. Humanism as a literary-philosophical movement and attitude within the Renaissance refers to the learning and scholarship in the arts and sciences, which was what characterized the "human" in human beings. *Humanistae* in the 15th century was the name given to professors who drew on classical sources to teach grammar, history, literature and moral philosophy.

The humanists were scholars of Latin, and gradually also of Greek literature. But at the same time most of them were excellent stylists and rhetoricians in their own right. Petrarch, like his successors, demanded a rebirth of humanity out of the spirit of Antiquity, and asserted the indivisibility of rational thought and cultivated language. His political exemplar was the Roman republic; the same was true for, among others, the Florentine humanist Leonardo Bruni, who gave expression to his republican convictions both in his writings and in an important government office. The union of theory and practice was quite generally one of the demands of humanism, and led to the Renaissance ideal of the *uomo universale,* the man of all-round education, a sound moral foundation, and perfectly cultivated manners.

Humanism was not limited to Italy. The greatest contemporary connoisseur of classical and Christian literature was Erasmus of Rotterdam, who conducted an extensive

correspondence with people across the whole of Europe. His tolerant thought sought compromise in questions of human passion, religious conflict and the contradiction between Antiquity and Christianity. Humanists were active in England and France, too, and in Germany Ulrich von Hutten could proclaim, in the midst of all the confusion of the age: "O century, o science, it is a pleasure to be alive! The sciences are blossoming, and spirits are moving."

THE PHILOSOPHY OF THE RENAISSANCE

Nicholas of Cusa
Conscious Ignorance of Infinity

The modern concern with the linguistic and historical reality of the human world, which has its parallel in the realism of Renaissance artists, led the humanists time and again to criticize Scholasticism with its unnatural, logically over-sophisticated, epistemological metaphysics and its endless commentaries on Aristotle. Petrarch brought in the ethical teachings of Plato, against Aristotle, through whom, he said, one became cleverer but not better, and thus ushered in a development which led to the Platonic Academy in Florence.

In Plato's philosophy, and in particular in his idea of the Good, Petrarch saw an approach to divine truth, as adumbrated in his work *De sui ipsius et multorum ignorantia* ("On One's Own and the Multitude's Ignorance"). The "ignorance" referred to is that of the Christian, to whom the ultimate truths are only accessible through faith. This point became programmatic for the ecclesiastical diplomat, humanist, cardinal, and philosopher Nicholas of Cusa (otherwise known as Nikolaus von Kues or Nikolaus Cusanus). In his book *De docta ignorantia* ("On Learned Ignorance" or "On Conscious Ignorance," 1440), he accepts the incomprehensibility of the infinity of God and takes this negative insight as the starting point for a positive definition of precisely this incomprehensibility.

If infinity is the totally "alien" aspect of the created world and of individual things, the "absolute" in contrast to the relative, then it cannot be approached with the logical apparatus of the Scholastics, which is based on opposition/exclusion or agreement/inclusion.

In the absolute, these relative relationships cannot occur. The absolute, according to Cusa, must be thought of as that in which opposites come together. Cusa illustrated this with a geometric example: the tangent of a circle of a particular size touches the circumference at just one point; if the circle becomes infinitely large, it becomes one with the tangent. This is apparent, but really not imaginable. Cusa was trying to grasp this limit to comprehensibility, in order to thus look at his own ignorance and to understand it in its essence. To this end, he investigated how we know anything, and thus came to define the relationship between human and divine mental activity.

The mind compares and distinguishes things, creates numerical relationships, measures and calculates. The knowledge thus gained about things is, however, always relative and incomplete, because there are always more things to be discovered about the relationships between the infinite things of the world.

Melancholy, Engraving by Albrecht Dürer, 1514

The doctrine of the four humors, their combinations and their cosmic relationships which linked human characteristics with the world order, was a recurrent theme of Renaissance philosophy. The melancholy humor, dominated by the planet Saturn, was associated on the one hand with the vice of dark indolence or even with mental disorder, but on the other hand was the precondition of creative genius. Dürer's allegory certainly shows not just a psychological type according to the imagination of the time, but is also a self-depiction of art, united with philosophy and science, as a medium for the creation of inexhaustible meanings. "A good painter," said Dürer, "is inwardly full of figures, and even if he lived for ever, he would be able to draw from within on the ideas, of which Plato writes, in order to pour out something new through his work."

Symbolic representation of the break-out from the medieval world-image,
Colored woodcut in 16th-century style, from: Camille Flammarion, *L'atmosphère. Météorologie populaire*, Paris, 1888

Reproductions of this illustration from a successful 19th-century work of popular science were for a long time wrongly thought to be copies of an authentic Renaissance woodcut. The medieval cosmos in stylized form is represented as one no longer to be taken seriously, neither in respect of the flat earth, nor of the clearly delimited celestial sphere, nor of what lies beyond.
A curious researcher breaks through the old doctrinal structure of Scholasticism and discovers, beyond the horizon hitherto regarded as the limit of the universe, a new, strange world. In the philosophy of Giordano Bruno, the disappearance of this boundary became explicit in the 16th century. Unlike Copernicus, whose – in itself revolutionary – heliocentric system continued to presuppose an outer sphere for the fixed stars, Bruno regarded the stars as suns with their own planetary systems, extending without end into an infinite universe.

Only with an absolute standard could an individual thing be definitively measured, and only through the absolute union of opposites could the never-ending differentiation of the world be perfected and abolished. According to Cusa, reason embraces understanding and, while not comprehending the absolute, at least "touches" it. Thanks to this contact, reason can imagine measurability as such and unity as such, and this imaginability is the basis of mental activity, which, without it, would only differentiate in an aimless manner. This connection between reason and understanding shows the human mind how it can enable the creation of its own knowledge, instead of totally adapting to the pre-ordained reality of things. The mind autonomously "supposes" unity as the foundation of counting and mathematics, just as it supposes all the units of measurement, for example, which Cusa calls *hypotheses* ("suppositions"). With the help of hypotheses, man deduces the relationship between things, which, however, remains always opaque to a certain degree. This is a creative activity analogous to the creativity of God: "For as God is the Creator of what really exists and of natural forms, so Man is the creator of what exists in thought and of artificial forms; these are nothing other than similarities of his mind, just as creatures are similarities of the divine mind."

Renaissance Platonism

With his assumption of an absolute principle (God), from whom ultimately – thanks to the contact of reason with this absolute – all things knowable arise, Cusa was adopting a (Neo-) Platonic concept. He was not the only one: the 15th century witnessed a veritable renaissance of Platonism. Since the time of Petrarch, the humanistic source-text hunters had tracked down all of Plato's writings in the original Greek. Marsilio Ficino translated all of them into Latin for the first time, and thus made them accessible to all the scholars of Europe. Ficino and like-minded humanists had an important sponsor in the person of Cosimo de' Medici, banker, patron of the arts and unofficial ruler of the official Republic of Florence. From time to time since the late 1450s, they had gathered at one of Cosimo's country residences: this circle has been known ever since as the Platonic Academy of Florence.
Ficino saw in Plato's philosophy a very topical teaching, which he thought allowed a synthesis of all the opposing tendencies of the age. It could, he said, reconcile religion and philosophy, as well as metaphysics and science, which were everywhere going their separate ways. Plato's thought not only contained within it Christian doctrine, in advance so to speak, but also transmitted ancient wisdoms in which the one fundamental divine revelation

found its purest expression. Ficino's "Platonic Theology" (1474) sought to demonstrate this integrating power of a "philosophical religion" by presenting mind and nature and all levels of existence as a single continuum. In a re-interpretation of the Plotinian Neoplatonic tradition, Ficino named these levels as: divine being; the sphere of pure intelligences (the world of angels); soul; physical qualities (color, warmth etc.); body (formless matter, purely material quantity). The center of being is the world-soul. It has its correspondence and representation in the soul (or spirit) of man, who now moves to the center of the universe. Human capacity for knowledge can unite the extremes of God and body, and reflects (indeed in a certain sense first creates) the permanent unity of being.

Perception and knowledge are for Ficino not passive acts of registering and processing, but a turning of the soul towards the thing known, which is only possible because the soul is involved in all levels of existence. Goethe expressed this Plotinian concept of the correspondence between knower and known in a verse (here given in prose translation): "If the eye did not partake of the sun, it could never see the sun; if God's own strength were not within us, how could the divine delight us?" The thought that the soul had the chance to rise to sublime union with God, and an esthetic view of the world whose luminous harmony we experience in the harmony of our soul, have often made Ficino's teaching look like the philosophical reflection of Renaissance art.

Self-portrait in Convex Mirror,
Painting by Parmigianino, c. 1523–24, Kunsthistorisches Museum, Vienna

There had as yet been no very long tradition of the portrait as a genre in itself when Parmigianino painted this self-portrait, which comes across as remarkably modern even today. The development of portrait painting reflected the increasing value placed on the individual by the Renaissance. In self-portraits, the genre was additionally characterized by a publicly expressed confidence in the artist's own creative productivity. Medieval thought attributed creativity only to God; the artist could only produce what had been, either in a real or ideal sense, pre-formed. Now, though, the artist began to take on God-like features. Parmigianino has brilliantly demonstrated his ability to reproduce the materiality of a soap-bubble, an appearance in a mirror, a virtual image. In virtuoso fashion, he has painted the phenomenon he sees, liberating himself from the rectangular objectivity, so to speak, of the "real" world. He shows how the artist, as the subjective center, is actually the precondition for phenomena, how he orients the phenomena toward himself, and how he can experience and preserve them in their appearance as such.

The free and central position of Man, as in Ficino, was also emphasized by his pupil Pico della Mirandola. In a now famous speech "On Human Dignity," he had God the Father say to Adam: "The nature of other beings is determined by the laws we have laid down, and is thus kept within bounds; you are not bound by any insuperable limits. I have made you the center of the world, in order that you may from there comfortably look around to see all the things that there are in the world. We have created you neither as a heavenly nor as an earthly creature, neither as mortal nor immortal, in order that you may determine, being your own free and creative sculptor and poet, the form you wish to live in."

Man as the center of the world – this is clearly not to be understood that Man, as the image of God, is from the outset the measure of all things. Rather, the center, here, is an indefinite place in contrast to the definite place occupied by the rest of creation. The center implies a non-orientation, which, as positive openness, is the potential for freedom.

The Platonic philosophy of the mind was by no means unopposed during the Renaissance. Thus Christofero Landino saw Man as a unity of body and soul, and as a social being. He gave the *vita activa* or "active life" a higher status than the *vita contemplativa* or "contemplative life" praised by the Platonists. "Nature as a most excellent mother has produced us for active participation in social life and to maintain the human community." The indissoluble factuality of the union of body and soul was emphasized by Petro Pomponazzi, who was trained in the Aristotelian school. He even denied the possibility that the soul might be immortal – at that date, a bold assertion indeed.

Plato in a painting by Pedro Berruguete, c. 1477, Louvre, Paris

The rediscovery of Plato is the distinctive feature of the philosophy of the Renaissance, in particular in Italy. The main representative of this trend was Marsilio Ficino, who translated all of Plato's writings into Latin, and thus made them accessible to all the scholars of Europe. It was Plato's idea of the good that particularly appealed to the humanistic tendencies of the age. For Ficino, mind and nature and all the levels of existence represent one single continuum. In line with Neoplatonic tradition, he regarded the level of Divine Being (the sphere of ideas) as the highest.

In Cosimo de' Medici the Italian Renaissance philosophers found an important patron. In 1459, he founded the Platonic Academy of Florence, a conversation circle on the pattern of Plato's own philosophical school in classical Athens.

A NEW UNDERSTANDING OF SCIENCE

Philosophical Consciousness

The study of nature, looking beyond the closed cosmos, the idea of consciousness, and the appreciation of human individuality – all these began to emerge in the Renaissance; in the Baroque period which followed, they were enlarged upon and fleshed out, and above all, placed on new foundations. Nature now came to be studied very successfully by quantitative methods in experiments based on mathematically oriented hypotheses. The old model of the cosmos with its stationary earth at the center was now definitely obsolete, and the new model of the solar system gradually came to be taken for granted by all those who enjoyed the privilege of education.

Sober, rational thinkers no longer saw Man as occupying a special position in the history of creation, but rather as a particular species with certain affective reactions and with an innate tendency to construct social forms of living. And consciousness became a philosophical concept, a place of pure thought opposed to the world of things, seeking principles of knowledge in itself, in order to bring systematic unity into the mass of what was there to be explored.

The question concerning rationally responsible principles of knowledge was becoming more and more urgent with the rise of natural science. For on the one hand, philosophical theses ought, it was thought, to be testable in the same way as physical hypotheses and explanations, and, taken together, shown to be compatible with reality as it was experienced. Finding and consistently applying a particular method ensured the constructive transparency of the theses. It became normal to speak of philosophical "systems," namely those tasks whose formulations and solutions were methodologically closed, and whose meaning could be measured against their preconditions and the success of their explanations (of the world, for example).

On the other hand, while "philosophy" remained the superordinate term for science generally (Newton's chief work on mechanics and the cosmic system, published in 1687, was entitled *Philosophiae naturalis principia mathematica* ["Mathematical Principles of Natural Philosophy"] for example), in actual fact physics had already declared its independence. For this reason, philosophy now concentrated particularly on fundamental assumptions, which in the individual sciences were consciously or unconsciously acknowledged as preconditions, without their forming part of the respective subject matter.

What actually "is," what is the "substance" which underlies appearance and

THE 17TH CENTURY

After the end of the wars of religion which occupied the first half of the 17th century, the second half witnessed a consolidation of a **Europe of modern territorial states.** The Papacy lost its international political importance. 1625 saw the appearance of a tract entitled *On the Law of War and Peace* by Hugo Grotius, a notable foundation of modern international law.

In France, which became a leading power, Louis XIV and Cardinal Richelieu were establishing the system of **centralized absolutism,** which became the pattern for many other states, and for which Thomas Hobbes, among others, sought a philosophical justification.

The **bourgeoisie gained increasing influence** in Holland and England, but also in France.

Not least for this reason, general human reason was raised to a central principle of philosophy.

Also important were **considerations of natural law,** usually linked with theses on anthropology and the original formation of state "commonwealths" (the social contract). The foundations of natural law were often sought in the rational order of things; and there were demands that, independent of the form of government, the laws of a country should not contradict this natural law.

The **new methods of mathematical natural research** and their integration into metaphysics set the course for the development of the Western world.

Louis XIV in a painting by Hyacinthe Rigaud, 1701, Louvre, Paris

René Descartes made a major contribution to the development of modern science with his discovery of analytical geometry, and he also provided its philosophical foundation.

Following from Descartes, a **dualistic and mechanistic image of the world** became widespread, in which the world of physical extension, which functioned like a machine, was imagined as separated in substance from the world of the mind or of reason. In his "Monadology" Leibniz set up an opposing view.

Philosophical **Rationalists** (including Descartes, Spinoza, Leibniz) saw thought as the basis of our knowledge of reality. Systematic thought embraced not only the causes of the data of experience, but also the ultimate reasons for the structure of the world.

The **Empiricists** (including Locke, Berkeley, Hume) were decidedly skeptical toward such claims. They sought to return reason to within the boundaries of experience.

is preserved when chance phenomena come and go? Or might it be that nothing can be said about any such thing as substance? Are only individual perceptions real? What do the answers to these questions imply for our understanding of "truth" and for statements which claim general validity? These problems do of course constitute a primal domain of philosophy. They are problems of metaphysics, which now took on a distinctly modern epistemological coloration. One can explain it like this: the thinking and the existence of the thing thought are distinguished in the thinking process itself. Philosophy had recognized this opposition since ancient times; rules for particular mental operations (logic) were just as old, as were theories on the relationship between thought and existence, and on how true statements might be made about God and the world. But in the modern era, thinking came to be directed towards itself, and insulated itself against the "outside world." Taken to philosophical extremes, this outside world need not even exist except as generated by some abstract "I." It must be said, however, that this extreme view only arose later, and not during the 17th century.

The philosopher John Locke wrote a comprehensive work on human understanding which was anticipated by nothing in classical or medieval thought. The way thinking "functions" was investigated in great detail. A little later, David Hume allowed consciousness and knowledge to consist of nothing but sensory perceptions, their reproductions and associations, and he rejected all statements about substance and any reality independent of perception.

In this context, Descartes' statement "I think, therefore I am" was intended as the starting point for the objective discovery of reality. But it is also the motto of the new position of thought and existence: reality exists for us only in the framework of mental constructs. Mathematics became the methodological ideal of philosophy. "Those who seek the correct path to truth must not concern themselves with any object of which they cannot obtain the same certainty as they would with arithmetic and geometric proofs."

Nature is such an object if it is seen as material determined purely causally by

natural laws. The immediate unity of Man and nature, or the cosmos, as experienced by the Renaissance, was thus abolished. Philosophers now distinguished between what could be stated with certainty in accordance with the conditions of knowledge and things in themselves, beyond any reference to knowledge. To discover harmony and beauty in geometric proportions and their counterparts in nature was still, for the Renaissance, to discover true and necessary characteristics in the blueprint of the world. Modern rationalism, by contrast, in many places cut the mystic ribbon linking the meanings of things, human understanding, and the divine order.

Thus one can see how Hegel, for example, lecturing on the history of philosophy in about 1820, while discerning the beginnings of a new age in the general culture of the Renaissance and Reformation, postponed the corresponding rebirth of philosophy to the 17th century and Descartes. While this attitude underestimated the thinkers of the Renaissance, it should nevertheless be

Las Meninas, Painting by Diego Velásquez, 1656, Prado, Madrid

In his book *The Order of Things* (1966), the French philosopher Michel Foucault sought a reconstruction of the modern "systems of thought," i.e. the basic convictions which organize and structure the knowledge and science of an epoch. Above all, he sought to demarcate the 17th and 18th centuries from the Renaissance and the incipient modernity of the 19th century. In his introduction, Foucault characterizes the thought of the 17th and 18th centuries by analyzing the famous painting by Velásquez as a model of the age. "Representation," according to Foucault, was a decisive basic concept of the period. Ideas represent things, and order them into a comprehensive "tableau" of signs, and, in accordance with contemporary subjectivity, can also represent themselves as such, just as the painter can show himself in the act of painting. In contrast to the modern period, however, there were still limits to self-referential subjectivity. The determining factor of the game of courtly representation, the Spanish royal couple, is not represented in the body, but appears only schematically in the mirror on the back wall of the room in the painting.

Perspective Illustration,

From: Abraham Bosse *Manière uni-
verselle de M. Desargues*, Paris, 1648

In the 17th century, even more than in
the Renaissance, perspective, as the
expression of subject-related rationality
and the mathematization of space,
agreed with the basic scientific and
philosophical attitudes of the time. This
illustration is taken from a teaching
manual of perspective. Bosse was an
engraver who later taught perspective at
the Paris Academy of Art, founded in
1648. Here he explains a construction
procedure discovered and published by
the mathematician Girard Desargues.
The procedure was practical without
being mathematically innovative.
However Desargues did add a
description of the perspective vanishing
point as the point of intersection of
planes, which demonstrates a new
understanding. In the Renaissance, the
main concern had been the correct
perspective foreshortening of objects; by
the 17th century, the rules of
perspective were no more than a
special case of general laws of
projection.

Francis Bacon,1561–1626,
Copperplate engraving by
William Marshall, 1640,
Bibliothèque Nationale, Paris

The goal of Bacon's philosophy
was the scientific control of nature,
for "knowledge is power." The task
of philosophy was thus the
systematization of the sciences. To
gain a true knowledge of things,
one first had to liberate oneself
from prejudice and misjudgment.
In his major work, *Novum
Organon,* Bacon explained how
to avoid these illusions, or "idols."
For Bacon, the correct procedure
for obtaining true knowledge was
the inductive method, by which the
general forms of nature were
derived by collecting and
comparing observations and
carrying out experiments.

remembered that in the 18th century and up
to Hegel, the most important impulses in the
philosophical tradition – leaving aside the
classical authorities – came from Descartes,
Locke, Leibniz and their contemporaries, and
only rarely from as far back as Ficino or even
Giordano Bruno.

Francis Bacon

The Inductive Method

Entirely in the spirit of the technical objecti-
fication of the world, the Englishman Francis
Bacon set out on a round tour of knowledge. His main concerns were the place
of experience and the practical applications
of philosophy.

Instauratio Magna ("Great Innovation") was
the collective title of a planned six-volume
work of which only fragments were ever
written. First of all, learning is sub-divided
according to the psychological faculties of
memory, imagination and understanding
into history, "poesy" and philosophy, each of
which is further sub-divided. A heading "first
philosophy" covers the foundations valid
for all areas of knowledge. The *Novum
Organon* (or "New Instrument," ambitiously
named after the *Organon* of Aristotle, whom
Bacon criticized) devised a program for an
inductive method, by which generally valid
statements were to be obtained from the
investigation of a large number of specific
cases. It thus differed from the scholastic
deductive method, by which categories for
nature were established by logical reasoning

on the basis of presupposed basic principles,
quite possibly at the expense of actual facts.
In accordance with the title of the book,
Bacon's pithy style was dominated by an
optimistic missionary spirit. Bacon himself,
born a commoner, was created a peer
of the realm as Viscount St. Albans and rose
to become Lord Chancellor, before falling
from grace on account of receiving gifts
while in office, a practice that was perfectly
normal at that time.

He begins his philosophical program in a
critically didactic manner with his particularly famous doctrine of the four classes of
"idol," in other words prejudices or fallacies.
In the interest of objectivity, it was first
necessary to expose these and put them
aside. The first class was the "idols of the
tribe" *(idola tribus)*, namely projection of
our understanding and behavior, which is
characterized by feeling and purpose, on
and toward natural processes or other inap-
propriate objects. The "idols of the cave"
(idola specus) worked at an individual
level: allowing our prior knowledge, circumstances and opinions to cloud our
judgment. The "idols of the marketplace"
(idola fori) involved the common coin of
human communication, namely custom and
agreement and the use of language, which
put their own shape on things themselves.
In order to perceive the truth about these
things, the conceptual networks of the philosophical schools *(idola theatri* or "idols of
the theater") would in particular have to go.
Once all this had been achieved, the
truth still would not simply lie open to
the senses. True, Bacon attributed considerable importance to sensory perception,
but only within the total framework of
experience and knowledge, in other words
a chain of connections whose potential
required not only perception but also
understanding. For knowledge, and hence
orientation in the world, came about, he
said, in a methodical fashion: through
targeted questioning, the gathering of
corresponding observations, and the subsequent drawing of conclusions regarding
the truth or falsehood of assumptions.

The way in which Bacon began to subject
knowledge to the facts is reminiscent
of gathering circumstantial evidence in a
criminal investigation. In order to pin down

a phenomenon scientifically, e.g. heat, as many instances as possible of this phenomenon must be listed in tabular form. The accompanying circumstances are of course in most cases very different: heat appears together with light, living bodies, fermentation, friction etc. The table reveals numerous features, of which a particular bundle, or maybe just a single one, always appear together with the phenomenon in question, and can thus be abstracted as its essence. Also important are cases in which a putative characteristic feature is missing; it can thus be dismissed as non-essential.

The same method also allows the discovery of regularities as rules linking the occurrence of different phenomena. Bacon was particularly interested in processes and their regularities, because he wanted to encompass nature less in static existence than in development. Accordingly, to explain something meant to have it arise from its conditions, almost literally to regenerate it in thought. To a certain extent, Bacon also granted hypotheses containing elements that went beyond experience as explanations, as long as what emerged from the hypotheses could still be tested. Heat he explained convincingly as the movement of tiny particles, although these could not be directly observed.

Knowledge is Power

The goal of research was the application of discoveries to inventions, to the use and exploitation of nature, to everything which could advance the progress of civilization. "Human knowledge and human ability (or human power) come together, because it is ignorance of cause that robs us of success. For we only take power over nature by giving way to it, and what appears as the cause when we observe, should serve us as a rule when we implement." This formulation of technical goals as possibilities of "applied" natural law was at that time certainly not something to be taken for granted. Thus the Italian mathematician G. U. del Monte, in a widely read tract on mechanics, regarded the subject of his book as including everything "that is done by carpenters, builders etc. in the face of resistant natural laws."

The passage just quoted on the identification of knowledge with ability or power is

the clearest possible expression of the practical, world-changing character of this empirical scientific philosophy. Francis Bacon became the father-figure for many empirical researchers. True, his idea of the "beings" or "forms," which as individual, substantial and quasi-organic units constitute the natural laws or the "cohesion" of a thing in accordance with these laws, is still largely Aristotelian and medieval. But both his tabular method and his attempt to explain developments in a thing from its original condition represent a major step toward the modern replacement of substantial essences by functional structural descriptions.

"Knowledge is power" – this statement, which is attributed to Bacon and in spirit imbues his whole teaching, could, in this or similar form, have been made earlier; but now, in the age of the Baroque, it developed its full resonance. Virtually no limits were now set to potential knowledge; great things were expected from technology. Leibniz, for example, who like Pascal before him constructed a calculating machine, considered surprisingly many tasks not only of a practical, but also of a calculatory nature, to be capable of mechanical solution, and in this came close to predicting the industrial and computer age. Such expectations arose not least from the increasing transparency of that greatest of all machines, the universe.

Representation of the Relative Distances of the Planets from the Sun by Johannes Kepler

While he was Professor of Mathematics at Graz, Johannes Kepler became intensely interested in astronomy, giving thought to the size, distance and movement of the planets. One important foundation of his investigations was Plato's dialogue, the *Timaeus*, in which the philosopher expounds his views on physics. According to Plato, the world represents a natural harmony, created by God on the basis of the "ideas." This divine harmony was most perfectly expressed by mathematical forms and numerical relationships, which can be seen, for example, in the regular polyhedra (tetrahedron, cube, octahedron, dodecahedron and icosahedron) which according to Plato were the symbols of the five elements (fire, earth, air, heaven, water). Kepler tried to project this mathematical harmony on to the planetary system, by linking the spheres of the planets with the five Platonic solids.

Dialogue Concerning the Two Major World Systems by Galileo Galilei Copperplate engraving by Joseph Mulder, 1700

A literal translation of the original Italian title of this work, published in 1632, would be "Dialogue. In which in Four Days the Two Major World Systems, the Ptolemaic and the Copernican, are Disputed, whereby the Philosophical and Scientific Grounds for Both Sides are Presented, Without a Decision being Reached." The final qualification was a mere precautionary measure, for Galileo was altogether convinced of the correctness of the heliocentric Copernican model rejected by the Church. Ptolemy, who lived in the 2nd century A.D., is depicted in the center of the title page holding a geocentric model of the cosmos, next to Aristotle (seated), whom he partly followed in his representation of cosmic motion. His system was virtually undisputed for almost 1500 years.

Heaven and Earth

"Before they will change anything in Aristotle's heaven, they brazenly deny what they see in nature's heaven," said Galileo of his hidebound colleagues in natural philosophy at the university. And indeed there were unfamiliar things to see, if you looked through the telescope. This was a Dutch invention, which had probably come about quite by chance in the handling of optical lenses, but as soon as Galileo heard of it, he built the instrument for himself, and made a considerable impression in Italy with it. He described his observations of the Moon and the stars in 1610 in a little book which went round the world. But what did "Aristotle's heaven" look like, which suffered so much as a result?

It consisted of an unimaginably large, but yet finite ball, whose outer layer and boundary, the sphere of the fixed stars, surrounded a series of other concentric spheres of crystalline, liquid or airy substance, whose sole visible elements were the planets. In their circular motions, which followed the rotation of the outer sphere but at different speeds, they remained for ever unchanging, in contrast to the stationary world in the center of the ball, namely the "sublunary" earthly region, which was subject to change and death. Sphere and circle were understood as ideal primal forms, the hallmark of perfection at ease with itself. Hence moon and stars must immaculately embody these forms. But now, through his telescope, Galileo saw the craters on the moon, irregularities resembling those on earth. This, together with the much-discussed observation of a "superlunary" comet (a body "above the moon"), belied the doctrine of the untouchability of the heavens and shook the Aristotelian cosmos to its foundations. Galileo went further, by drawing Copernicus' description of a heliocentric universe to the attention of a public hitherto not reached, and provided arguments in its support.

What Copernicus had produced in 1543 were also arguments, not proofs. His starting point was belief in a creation comprehensible to Man, whose principles were meaningful to him, and to that extent tailored to him, irrespective of his physical location in the cosmos. Now the geocentric world system caused more problems in respect of its comprehensibility than the Aristotelian model suggested. Even in classical Antiquity, precise measurements had shown that while the fixed stars circle the earth – provided the latter stood still – in exemplary fashion, the planets moved irregularly, changing not only their distance from the earth, but also their velocity and even their direction of motion. How these complicated movements result from the "simple" motions of the solar system has been clear ever since Copernicus. Let us start from his hypothetical basic model, in which the earth and the planets move in "circles" at whose center is the sun. Then, seen from the earth, the planets first of all circle the sun, and secondly (appear to) circle with the sun around the earth, in other words they follow epicyclical paths.

An epicycle is a circle around a point on the circumference of another circle. When both circles turn, a point on the epicycle describes not a circle but, for example, a ring of loops. Depending on the relative directions and rotational velocities of the circle and the epicycle, the point can move along an elliptical, "dented" or even rectangular path. Thus in the 2nd century, Ptolemy construed the planetary orbits as epicyclical figures. He assumed the earth to be at rest, worked out each orbit individually, and gave no thought whatever to the physical explanation for the dance of the planets. He was expressly interested exclusively in mathematical reconstruction, and thus also with the prediction of

Milton Visiting Galileo, Painting by Tito Lessi, 1880

In 1632 Galileo published his *Dialogue Concerning the Two Major World Systems, the Ptolemaic and the Copernican,* which soon led to his trial. A year later he was forced by the Inquisition to recant his statements that the Earth was a planet of the Sun. From this time on, he lived in total isolation in his house in Arcetri under the strict surveillance of the local clergy, and was banned from taking part in meetings with friends. But from his base in Arcetri Galileo did succeed in communicating with foreign scientists and scholars. In Protestant countries there was great interest in his work and fate. From time to time a visitor managed to gain access to his "dungeon," as he called his house. One such was the philosopher Thomas Hobbes, who told him of the translation of the *Dialogue* into English. The young poet John Milton also paid a short visit at this time. There has been much speculation as to the subject of their conversation. Milton was doubtless shocked by the suffering inflicted on the famous Galileo. In his best-known work, *Paradise Lost,* Tuscany is the sphere of influence of Satan.

the movements. The fact that his orbits were incompatible with the rotating spheres of Aristotle, who certainly had concerned himself with a physical explanation of the cosmos, was played down then and later, partly for religious reasons.

Even in Galileo's day it was still possible for the symmetric Aristotelian heaven and the strongly eccentric epicycle stricture to exist side by side, and to be used without any sense of incongruity to answer specific questions one way or the other. Neither did Ptolemy have any problems covering various irregularities in the planetary movements with more and more new, disparate and overlapping constructions. The one uniform condition he did retain was the conviction that all cosmic movement must be circular and regular, which admittedly applied only to the individual components of his compound orbits, in other words to the basic circles and the epicycles. And even this regularity could only be maintained with the help of artificial constructs; in practice, it had been lost. It was precisely this that Copernicus could not accept. He still full-heartedly maintained the conviction of regularity, and he wanted to return to Aristotelian clarity and physical probability,

or at least clear imaginability. He thus sought to transform the Ptolemaic structure into uniform and simple structures. In the course of this laborious undertaking, he realized that the sun could be at the center of all the epicycles, and that in this case, because the earth, seen from the sun, orbited like all the other planets, all the epicycles were redundant.

The heliocentric system was intended to make do with one orbital shape, the circle, and this undreamed-of simplicity was Copernicus' great selling-point. If there were two possible descriptions which both produced the right answers, one ugly and complicated, and the other clear and simple, the second must reflect reality. God could not have created the ugly complicated version. In its practical implementation, however, the new theory lost its simplicity. In order to harmonize observational evidence with the presumed circular orbits, new and different epicycles had to be introduced.

It was Johannes Kepler who, as one of the few convinced adherents of Copernicus, finally managed to explain the observations completely by assuming elliptical planetary orbits and irregular movements (*Astronomia Nova* ["New Astronomy"], 1609). Even for

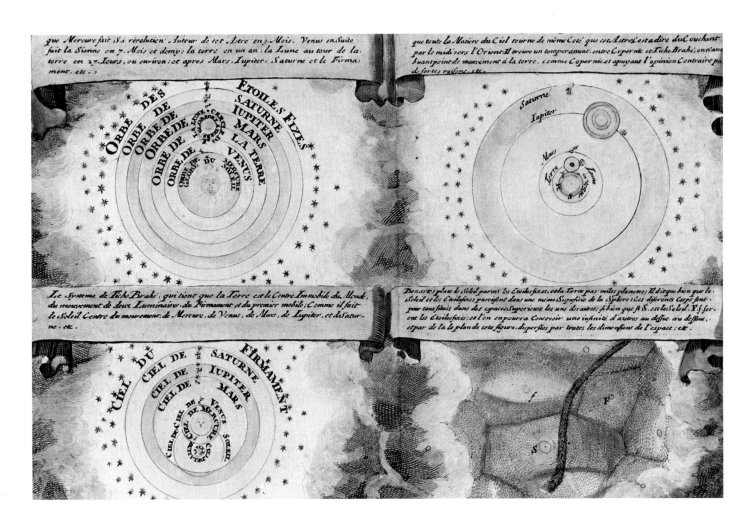

The handwritten French text within the engraving reads:

que Mercure fait sa revolution Autour de cet Astre en 3 Mois. Venus en suite fait la Sienne en 7 Mois et demy; la terre en un an. la Lune au tour de la terre en 27 Iours, ou environ; et apres Mars, Iupiter, Saturne et le Firmament. etc.

que toute la Matiere du Ciel tourne de même Coté que cet Astre, et à dire du Couchant par le midi vers l'Orient il trouve un temperament, entre Copernic et Tiche Brahe, en n'attribuant point de mouvement à la terre, comme Copernic et apuyant l'opinion Contraire par de fortes raisons. etc.

ORBE DES ÉTOILES FIXES
ORBE DE SATURNE
ORBE DE IUPITER
ORBE DE MARS
ORBE DE LA TERRE
ORBE DE VENUS
ORBE DE MERCURE
ORBE DU SOLEIL

Le Systeme de Ticho Brahé, qui tient que la Terre est le Centre Immobile du Monde, du mouvement de deux Luminaires du Firmament et du premier mobile; Comme il fait le Soleil Centre du mouvement de Mercure, de Venus, de Mars, de Iupiter, et de Saturne. etc.

Descartes place le Soleil parmi les Etoiles fixes, et la Terre par miles planetes; Il dit qu bien que le Soleil et les Étoilesfixes paroissent dans une même Superficie de la Sphere; Ces diferentes Corps sont pour tant situés dans des espaces Superieurs les uns des autres; si bien que le S. est le Soleil. Y.f. seront les Étoilesfixes; et l'on en pourra Concevoir une infinité d'autres au dessus au dessous et par de la le plan de cete figure, dispersées par toutes les dimensions de l'espace; etc.

CIEL DU FIRMAMENT
CIEL DE SATURNE
CIEL DE IUPITER
CIEL DE MARS
CIEL DE VENUS
CIEL DE MERCURE
CIEL DU SOLEIL

Comparative Representation of the Three World Systems According to Nicholas Copernicus, Tycho Brahe, and René Descartes, Copperplate engraving, color added, 17th century, private collection, Paris

Above left is a sketch of the solar system according to Copernicus, below it is the model proposed by Tycho Brahe, which has the Earth at its center, but follows Copernicus in having the planets orbit the sun. The depiction on the right does not really belong. It does not show a complete system, but reproduces an illustration from Descartes' *Principles of Philosophy* (1644). In this important work, metaphysical and epistemological foundations are first developed before Descartes goes on to demonstrate their methodological consequences in the later parts of the book, in which comprehensive theses on physics and cosmology are proposed. The illustration shows the Sun and some of the fixed stars, surrounded by a celestial material (shown as dots), which Descartes imagined as a fine liquid. Thus he was able not only to describe the cosmic movements, but to provide a causal explanation for them, as vortices, on the analogy of his hydrodynamic observations. In this model, everything is due to the direct mutual pressure and impact of tiny particles.

Kepler, it was a major step to abandon the ideal, philosophically sacrosanct circle, which Copernicus had kept alive by retaining the old spherical model and changing its center. He took this step during his long and thrilling evaluation of the very precise measurements made by the Danish astronomer Tycho Brahe, whose assistant he was for a time. Brahe himself had worked out a system of the universe which had the earth at its center, but where the planets circled a moving sun. This was less thoroughgoing than the Copernican model, but at the time had just as much going for it, and it was certainly an advance on Ptolemy. Kepler, though, described it as a "warmed-up bread roll."

Tycho's model went down well with the more conservative natural philosophers of the 17th century, and it was also theologically acceptable. Galileo by contrast was forced by the Roman Inquisition in 1633 to recant his statements that the earth was one of the sun's planets. He spent the rest of his life under surveillance and house-arrest. It was an astonishing measure – after all, Copernicus' book had not been banned or opposed in its time. But Galileo's appearance

changed the situation. He had his admirers and patrons, not least in high ecclesiastical circles in Rome, and thus a doctrine was on the verge of spreading which contradicted the scholastic Christian tradition and could only be supressed by force.

In 1616, Copernicus' book was placed on the *Index librorum prohibitorum,* the Roman Catholic Church's list of banned books. Established in 1559, it lived on until 1948. This index was a product of the Counter-Reformation, following the re-introduction into Italy of the Inquisition, which had first been set up in the 13th century, and in 16th-century Spain had become institutionalized and very powerful. In Galileo's day, a period of ongoing religious war, Counter-Reformation activity was at its height. It was led in many areas – including science – by the Jesuits, among whom Galileo had particular enemies. In connection with the Copernicus ban he received a caution, and for years said nothing more on any sensitive issues. But then, strengthened in his resolve by many to whom he had spoken, in 1632 he published his *Dialogue Concerning the Two Chief World Systems – Ptolemaic and Copernican,* which soon led to his trial and conviction.

Mathematical Science

The "celestial machine," wrote Kepler, should be seen not as a kind of living organism, but rather as a kind of clockwork, thereby coming up with a central example of the mechanistic tendencies of his age. In the modern senses of the words, "machine" and "living organism," with reference to the same entity, are mutually exclusive from the outset. But in classical Antiquity, the division between animate and inanimate was less clear-cut, and although this changed with the coming of Christianity, animistic ideas never disappeared completely. In explanations of the cause of movement, for example – including the mechanical movement of machines – there were, in the Middle Ages and the Renaissance, as well as with Aristotle, more or less concealed analogies with conscious human movement.

Even Kepler still understood the minimum velocity of a planet when furthest from the sun as a weakening of the strength of the "soul" of the planet. He retained the notion of planetary souls, even though at the same time, as a modern scientist, he had changed his mind on the causes of motion after finding a correspondence between two different phenomena which pointed to a regularity which could be stated in quantitative terms. "When I considered that the cause of the motion of the planets declines in proportion to their distance from the sun, just as light grows weaker the further one goes from the sun, I concluded that this cause must be something physical." This is the origin of the mathematical physical explanation of the solar system, which Newton went on to perfect. Kepler stated three laws of planetary motion. The first two concern the shape of the orbits (ellipses, as we said, with the sun at one focus) and changes in velocity, while the third derives a numerical relationship between the orbital period of a planet and its mean distance from the sun.

Galileo too, who, seven years Kepler's senior, was still unable to appreciate his insights, was looking for physical regularities. True, his main area of research was not astronomy, but he never lost sight of the goal of supporting the Copernican thesis and unifying the physics of heaven and earth. With respect to quantitative laws of nature, he was concerned not merely with specific formulations, but with the – still new – "idea" of such laws. In his much-read, relatively easy to understand texts, he fought vehemently against the old natural philosophy. So where were the differences?

Quantity – size, number, the divisible, the measurable, the countable – was linked by Aristotle to geometric structures, number, time and space. Mathematics operated at a quantitative level, it measured like against like, identified numerical values with numerical values. Astronomy could use such methods; it was involved with objects that behaved like ideal geometric structures. But that was already the limit of the applicability of mathematics to nature. Terrestrial physics was concerned with changing, transitory things determined by inward qualities and purposes. Qualities are characteristics with irreducible essences of their own. Qualities like colors, smells, and feelings could have different degrees of intensity, and thus also be examined under a quantitative aspect, but they were not mutually comparable or measurable on any common scale. In principle, no natural process could be subject to mathematical analysis any more than could a human life. In total contrast to this view is Galileo's famous statement: "Philosophy is written in the great book that lies open before the eyes of all of us, the universe. But we can only read it if we know its letters and have learnt its language. It is written in the language of

Astrolabe owned by Galileo,
Museo delle Scienze, Florence

In the 14th century European astronomers and seafarers came to know the astrolabe, which – used in principle since Antiquity – had been continuously improved by Islamic astronomers.
The astrolabe can be seen as the precursor of modern charts for astro-navigation. It allows visible sections of the sky to be set against the date and time of day.

Blaise Pascal's Measurement of Atmospheric Pressure by Means of a Barometer, After a drawing by August Dressel, c. 1890, later colored.

Blaise Pascal is famous as the author of the philosophical ruminations contained in his *Pensées*, but he also made a name for himself as a mathematician and physicist. In clever and on occasions spectacular public experiments, he was able to extend and confirm the theses on atmospheric pressure which Torricelli had established by means of experiments using an early form of barometer. The fact that a column of mercury or water in a tube (closed at the top, but with its open bottom end standing in a reservoir of the liquid) falls to a particular height depending on air pressure, leaving a vacuum above it, so that in a sense a "void" is produced, led to highly animated disputes among natural philosophers. If, like Descartes, one was unwilling to allow the possibility of empty space, one had to hypothesize the existence of a fine material which permeated all other substances.

Thomas Hobbes: *Leviathan*, Title-page of the first edition, London, 1651

Homo homini lupus ("Man is a wolf to man") is one of Thomas Hobbes' best-known sayings. In *Leviathan*, his major work of constitutional theory, he explains that each man's pursuit of his own interest will inevitably lead to a war of each against all. But as no one wants to see his existence subjected to constant threat, individual power is surrendered and put in the hands of the law and a ruler (the state). The title page is an apt image of this concept. The body of the state-monster, the Leviathan, is composed of the totality of citizens. These constituent individuals are seen from behind, they are all looking toward the head of the ruler, which owes its existence to them. They have set up this head, but in consequence they must, as one body, obey its will. The highest power in the state is untrammeled and indivisible. The sovereign ruler of a peaceful commonwealth is a spiritual and temporal lord – hence the crosier and sword in his hands.

mathematics, and its letters are triangles, circles and other geometric figures. Without these means, it is impossible for Man to understand a single word."

Galileo, Descartes and their contemporaries sought to reduce the degrees of qualities like heat or atmospheric pressure to linear, measurable spatial quantities. What was non-quantifiable and non-mathematizable was largely jettisoned from their physics, as was the concept of purpose. It was against the latter in particular that they directed their energies. Like Francis Bacon, they saw in it an animistic "idol," a confusing prejudice that had to be replaced by an approach that sought causes, not goals.

Portrait of an Italian Condottiere (once thought to depict Cesare Borgia), Painting by Altobello Meloni, c. 1520, Accademia Carrara, Bergamo

"A man who only ever desired the Good would be ruined in the midst of so many men who are not good": the words of Machiavelli in his book *The Prince* (1513), which set a new course for the political philosophy of the time. The basis of an orderly state consisted for him in the ruler's will to power. In order to preserve his power, the ruler must not do only good, even though he makes himself appear just and is respected by his people. For Machiavelli, the model of this ruler-figure was Cesare Borgia, whom some considered a frivolous amoral adventurer, but others a calculating politician.

Constitutional and Social Theories

In 1576 Jean Bodin published a book in which he provided useful arguments for absolutist opinions and coined the term "sovereignty," defined as supreme power over citizens and subjects, untrammeled by the law. This did not describe any existing government, but was a blueprint for an ideal one. So why is the sovereign "untrammeled by the law?" This seems not to be a desirable state of affairs, and yet on this point Bodin was in agreement with most of his contemporaries.

In his work *The Prince*, written in 1513, probably the best-known political handbook of the Renaissance, Niccolò Machiavelli had already demanded unlimited freedom of action for the prince; he should take account only of implementing the purposes of the state and the government. This was written against the background of a strife-torn Italy engaged in continual war. Machiavelli abandoned moral legitimization for political action in favor of the goal of a united state, in which there would certainly be scope for justice to prevail.

Unlike Machiavelli, other authors did not abandon the traditional moral foundation of political theory. Thus we find constant legal norms said to be based on "natural law." All we can say of this concept, which was construed in various ways, is that it was a counterweight to the divine right of the ruler and to that extent revealed a certain tendency towards enlightenment. Another element of political theory which constantly recurred until well into the 18th century was the "social contract," which provided a foundation for the commonwealth or state. Thomas Hobbes integrated this contractual theory into a comprehensive philosophical system. Oriented toward Francis Bacon and above all toward Galileo, Hobbes worked out a scientific philosophy whose method was "the rational discovery of effects or phenomena from their known causes, and conversely of the possible causative grounds from their known effects." Going further than Bacon, he developed the "genetic definition" which represented a conceptually constructive generation of what was to be defined. Accordingly, in his *Leviathan* (1651), his chief work of constitutional theory, Hobbes had his social contract arise physically, so to speak, from two forces: ruthless self-interest, entirely justified by nature, which leads to the struggle of each against all, and the will to end this state of war. In this view, there is no social instinct binding men together; in an imaginary lawless and stateless situation, every individual seeks to obtain whatever he can at the expense of the interests and lives of others. All men have power, and yet they cannot desire this insecurity nor the constant threat to this power and to their existence. All individual power is thus surrendered, and by virtue of a covenant, where each concludes with each, transferred to a person or an assembly. This is then the sovereign, or the commonwealth, or the Leviathan – for reasons which are not quite clear, Hobbes chose the name of the biblical sea-monster as a synonym for the state. Its founding, once established, could not be undone; all were thenceforth unconditionally subject to it. The sole remaining inalienable right was that of self-defense in the face of a direct attack. Naturally there were other laws; these however were not immutable, but rather dependent upon the will of the sovereign.

In Hobbes' model, there are only metaphorical atoms or points in geometric space, which form a Leviathan molecule or state figure. The commonwealth is rooted in the will of free individuals, who have to assert themselves in the "market."

RATIONALISM

Skepticism and Certainty

The *Essais* of Michel de Montaigne, published in 1580, inaugurated a new literary genre. The word in French means "attempt," and an essay was an attempt at exploring a theme through the witty presentation of thoughts and ideas. Montaigne's outlook was characterized not least by the sectarian confusion of his time. In view of the violent consequences of rigid religious attitudes, he sought out for himself a subjective standpoint which produced emotional tranquillity from a self-irony conscious of the transitory nature of things, and a reticence with regard to allegedly objective rational structures. His choice of the essay form was appropriate to this attitude.

"We are all put together from patches and in such a motley fashion that every piece plays its own part at every moment."

Here Montaigne was looking back to the Skeptics of the ancient world, for example Pyrrho; during the period of the Counter-Reformation, this viewpoint was not without consequences. Skeptical reticence was seen not least as a chance to keep oneself free, in spiritual humility, for the revealed faith of Christianity. Religiously motivated skepticism was thus opposed to constructive reason, or *ratio*. This reason was dangerously threatened, because the Skeptics understood how to undermine its foundations. In Descartes, we can see how he tried to use his own self to overcome Skepticism. Secure truths, in which reality can be "correctly" described, had to be found by assuring oneself that knowledge was possible.

The term "Rationalism" had already been applied to this attitude in the 16th and 17th centuries. The opposite term, however, is usually not "Skepticism" but "Empiricism," which refers to a philosophy that built on sensory experience (from the Greek *empeiria*, "experience"). Skepticism and Empiricism are, however, often found allied against Rationalism, for example when they only admit "phenomena" – what appears to us – without drawing any conclusion concerning objective existence. Incidentally, while the adjective "empirical" is old, it is only since the end of the 18th century that "Empiricism" has been used to denote a particular philosophy.

Vanity Still Life, Painting by Pieter Claesz, 1630, Mauritshuis, The Hague

In his *Essais*, Montaigne continually returns to the theme of the vanity and transitoriness of all earthly things. The heading for one of this wide-ranging work's 107 chapters, based on a classical proverb, is "To philosophize means to learn how to die." This is reflected in the form of the *Essais*. Sudden changes of subject, ironic autobiographical insertions, and a seemingly random juxtaposition of chapters of barely related subject-matter – this all conjures up associations of vanity, of the dissolution of things and thoughts. A similar quality of self-reference, not to say a virtual annulment of what has been created, can be found in the literature and visual arts of the Baroque. It cannot always be demonstrated in allegorical still-lifes on the theme of transitoriness, as illustrated here, but in the brilliance and sensuous splendor with which the materiality of things condemned in the end to rot away is painted, there certainly lies an irony which is reminiscent not least of Montaigne.

With the goal of creating a secure foundation for philosophy, Descartes developed a method of radical doubt which formed the basis of his philosophy. The basic principle of his argument was that it is necessary to examine everything which has been assumed hitherto. In the process of doing so it will turn out that the existence of things, of one's own physical presence, and even of mathematical principles (such as $2 + 3 = 5$) may be an illusion, which means that nothing can be regarded as certain. Descartes did however discover one fact which must be considered true, namely the fact that he was doubting. But if he doubted, then he must also think, in other words, he must be a thinking being. "I think, therefore I am" (*cogito, ergo sum*): this conclusion was the way out of total doubt, and has become one of the most famous statements in philosophy. By defining the "knowing" subject as the original location of certainty, Descartes became the pioneer of all modern philosophy.

The philosophical tendencies of the Baroque and the Enlightenment are often represented in adversarial terms as "rationalist" and "empirical," but this only applied to a certain aspect of the period. "Rationalism" can, then, be a term limited to this epoch of the Modern era. But it should be noted that there is a far broader definition of Rationalism, which would for example also embrace Plato. We shall therefore in the next section describe certain features of Rationalism which also apply to philosophers of Antiquity and the Middle Ages.

In 1607, Francis Bacon came up with the following image: "The men of experiment [Empirical philosophers] are like the ants; they only collect and use; the reasoners [Rationalists] resemble spiders, who make cobwebs out of their own substance. But the bee takes a middle course; it gathers its material from the flowers of the garden and of the field, but transforms and digests by a power of its own. Not unlike this is the true business of philosophy."

Actually all philosophers worthy of the name (including all those discussed in this book) are "bees" in Bacon's sense. The opposition of ants and spiders (and doubtless Bacon had certain contemporaries in mind) does not entirely accord with the terms Empiricist and Rationalist in the history of philosophy as understood today. Descartes and Leibniz do not "make cobwebs," Locke and Hume do not "collect" (or at least not "only"); rather, they discover theories about these activities which also take account of opposing positions and do not always exclude each other in all points.

The Whole Truth

As the Empiricists certainly did not argue irrationally, the use of reason is not a feature distinguishing them from the Rationalists. What is a distinguishing feature, however, is the way reason was regarded as anchored in the whole system of the world. Thus, for example, Spinoza's philosophy can be called "absolute" rationalism, because it proceeds on the basis of the total comprehensibility, the rational structure of the world as a whole. This conviction determines not only the content of Spinoza's philosophy, but also the form in which it is presented. He delivers it *more geometrico,* "in the geometrical manner." Like Euclid in his *Elements,* the basic geometry book of the ancient world, Spinoza starts by listing definitions and establishing axioms (i.e. non-derivable principles). From these, the whole succession of theorems, each based on the preceding one, is derived and proved.

Descartes also gives definitions of those basic terms of his metaphysics which allow such a structure. Something basically inherent to pure reason, the Euclidean logic of proof, thus appears appropriate not only to the ideal (i.e. mentally self-generated) structures of geometry, but also to reality. Put somewhat pointedly: the world can be deduced from first principles. Admittedly, this does not go so far that one could for example proceed from the definition of God to individual objects and thus explain absolutely everything. But a complete explanation of this kind could be seen as the Baroque Rationalist ideal.

According to the view that reveals itself in the aforementioned geometrical presentation, there must be original, simple, basic concepts, which do not just arise from subjective experience, but concern, and as it were depict, true existence. For this reason, knowledge can result in statements that "precede" experience and yet must turn out to be true in experience. Such knowledge is described as *a priori* ("from what went before," i.e. deductive). The Empiricists did not allow this. *A priori* knowledge is usually combined in Rationalism with the conviction that there are "innate ideas." This does not mean ready-made images, present within us from birth, but rather the predisposition, the potential ability, to form particular ideas which cannot be explained by experience alone.

Here we come to another important point: the Rationalists did not in fact view "ideas" as pictures, which arose directly or indirectly from sensory impressions. Ideas were, however this might be understood in individual cases, mental concepts.

According to all this, our knowledge cannot therefore be described as the sum of our experiences. The Rationalists of the Baroque took an ordered whole as the precondition for understanding the individual detail. And correspondingly they tried to develop their theoretical structures as wholes, as comprehensive and ordered systems.

René Descartes

A Tree of Knowledge

Descartes' first book was a slim intellectual autobiography, a succinct and stylized description of the development of a 40-year-old's insights, mental goals and researches. At the same time it is a *Discourse on the Method of Rightly Conducting Reason*. This *Discourse on Method,* as it is generally known, starts off modestly, but unexpectedly develops far-reaching claims. But still in the guise of a personal report, and entirely in this spirit, Descartes speaks not as an academic philosopher, but as a gentleman, who does not lose sight of his orientation in life. His *Discourse,* and his *Meditations,* epoch-making works, are written in a conciliatory tone, full of sovereign concessions to theological authorities, but also to the reader, who is obligingly conducted into the argumentation.

Nowhere does Descartes lose contact with the totality of human goals as regards knowledge. As a talented and innovative mathematician, he saw his discoveries in this field and in science not in isolation, but in connection with a philosophical explanation of the "possibility" of natural science. The latter now already meant the application of mathematics to the world. But in spite of specialization in the sciences, they were, for Descartes above all, not separate from philosophy. "All the sciences are nothing other than human wisdom, which always remains one and the same thing, no matter how many different objects it may be applied to." And yet philosophy was no longer self-evidently an umbrella covering all knowledge of the world; philosophy itself had to become scientific. Descartes summarized his idea of fruitful philosophical and scientific explanation in an image of a tree (as Francis Bacon had already done): the "first philosophy," metaphysics, is the root, physics is the trunk, the branches are medicine, mechanics, and – in the treetop – ethics; and the practical applications of these sciences are the fruit.

It would doubtless be an exaggeration to apply this image to Descartes' work as the root of modern philosophy, but certainly he did usher in a new way of thinking. For this Tree of Knowledge grew out of a methodological ascertainment of what could be stated without unexplored preconditions. And this involved assuring himself: the theory of knowledge and experience proceeded from the "I," from thought and its form; subject and object part company, and the subject is defined as the original location of certainty. This prepared the way for a large proportion of succeeding philosophy, which, a good century and a half later, at the start of a new epoch, was to be even more thorough in making conscious self-reference its absolute foundation.

Methodical Doubt

Like many Renaissance philosophers before him, Descartes was no longer content to regard scholarly familiarity with the written tradition as a basis for secure knowledge. Nor did constant enrichment of this tradition through new experience or even modern

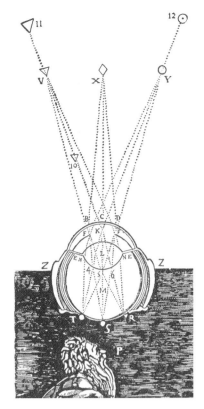

Illustration for the Essay *Dioptrique*
by René Descartes, Amsterdam, 1644

Descartes' work on optics, together with his *Geometry* (which introduced analytical geometry, which among other things was to revolutionize physics) and his *Meteorology,* was published in one volume along with his *Discours de la méthode.* This last sets out the methodological principles which must underlie all research. The three other writings provide examples of the application of these theoretical scientific preconditions. The illustration shows the refraction of light both in the cornea and in the lens of the eye. Descartes stresses that the points from which the light rays reach the eye must be reproduced as points once more on the retina, if sharp vision is to be possible.

Eliezer and Rebecca, Painting by Nicolas Poussin, 1648, Louvre, Paris

Cultural histories of the Baroque era in France often represent Poussin's painting as the artistic counterpart to Descartes' philosophy. In both cases, the dominant features are clarity, distinctness and rationality. As in a geometric plan, one detail is linked to the next in order to illustrate the action. The subjective input of the beholder is also reflected. In the painting illustrated here, for example, the pillar on the right with the sphere on top of and the high building to the left are matched through symmetry and similarity in size and shape. This lessens the perspective effect of the vanishing point in this illusory space. Depth arises in the perception of the beholder – it can be emphasized, but it can also be "overlooked" in favor of a flatter effect.

experimentation open up a way for him out of the labyrinth of scholastic dispute and uncertainty. He wanted a new beginning, he wanted to "build on land that belongs entirely to me."

This was asking for more than just the removal of sources of error, which would only achieve a "relative" improvement in knowledge. It was also asking for more than just the discovery of the respective (and thus relative) first principles of the individual sciences. What he wanted was an "unconditional" new start, an Archimedean firm spot, in a sense the philosophers' dream: "Give me a firm and immovable spot on which to stand, said Archimedes, and I shall move the earth. And I too hope for great things if I find even the smallest thing whose certainty is unshakable." In order to obtain this certain starting-point, everything that was not certain was jettisoned. Systematically, this philosophical new broom "makes use of his intrinsic freedom and assumes that nothing exists if there is the slightest doubt about its existence." His single-mindedness makes clear that this was no existential doubt of desperation. Nor was it the radical skepticism that had entertained the Sophists of Antiquity, whether from conviction or inclination. Radical skepticism states boldly (and maybe in desperation): nothing exists, and if anything did exist, one could not talk about it.

Descartes was quite different. His skepticism presupposed that truth existed and that true statements were in principle possible. His doubt was a methodical experiment to discover the foundation of such statements. So the first step was to abandon for the time being all judgments concerning facts (or alleged facts) perceived by the senses. There are, after all, sensory illusions. And if we have been deceived once, we are programmed to be suspicious. Sometimes we dream in all the colors of reality, although our dream images have no independent existence. In the doubt experiment, we must generalize this experience by assuming that even if we are convinced we are awake and sober, our putative perceptions may have no correspondence in reality.

Secure judgments, then, cannot be made about the outside world, which must be left to the field of doubt. On closer consideration, it will also be apparent that our own body is part of this provisionally non-existent outside world.

There are, however, facts which are judged purely in the mind, and evidently always recognized as they really are. These include mathematical relationships and proofs. The "fact" that a rectangle is bisected by a diagonal into two congruent triangles seems to be inherently true. It is – in this simple case – not only immediately obvious, but also provable, so that any doubt seems senseless. But according to Descartes, in such geometric-logical statements, what is captured is an "ideal" truth. And an imaginary, omnipotent "deceiver-God" or evil demon could turn even this kind of reality into a mere sham, or at the very least trick our memory concerning what has already been proved. Maybe our total memory, and thus our existence to date, is just a figment of the imagination.

"Cogito, ergo sum"

So we finally doubt the objectivity of our judgments and think that all our imagined reality hitherto is non-existent. "But," and here comes the decisive point, "it cannot be that I who thought these things was nothing. For it is a contradiction that the thinker does not exist at the time that he thinks. Accordingly, the statement that 'I think, therefore I am' (cogito, ergo sum) is the first and the most certain of all insights to present itself to any orderly philosopher." One can see that this "I think, therefore I am," one of the most famous statements in philosophy, cannot be taken out of context. In isolation, one would inevitably read the

The Four Philosophers, Painting by Peter Paul Rubens, c. 1611, Palazzo Pitti, Florence

Rubens pictured himself here together with his brother Philipp, the classical scholar Justus Lipsius and Jan van der Wouvere. Lipsius is regarded as the most important theoretician of Absolutism and a major scholar and publisher of the works of Seneca the Stoic. The 16th century saw the rise of neo-Stoicism, which propagated the virtues of courage, duty and composure. The picture is regarded as Rubens' own commitment to neo-Stoicism, and as homage to Lipsius, who had died in 1606, and his pupils. Lipsius is depicted teaching, while his students seem to be occupied with something else. This is to be seen as a sign of their mental independence, for they were trying to put his theories into political practice.

sentence as implying a logical conclusion, in which the "therefore" has a decisive function: I "think," therefore I "am." Without other sentences, whose certainty would have to be demonstrated in their turn, such a conclusion would however be logically meaningless, and would be useless as a philosophical starting point. And while it is sometimes even said, quite generally, that Descartes derives existence from thought, this is actually erroneous.

In fact the sentence should be read as: "I" think, therefore "I am." This corresponds to the Latin version of the passage quoted: *cogito* means "I think." If the personal pronoun *ego* were added, this would imply a particular emphasis. The emphasis suggests itself; after all, the sentence answers the question: What really "is" as I think or perceive it? "That something exists, and something, even an evil spirit, underlies our ideas, was never in doubt." Thus in his *Meditations*, where the whole train of ideas is set out in great detail, Descartes says, instead of *cogito, ergo sum:* "The sentence: 'I think; I am' is, as often as I utter or mentally formulate it, necessarily true." This first certain sentence, we now see, is not some primal formula laden with profound preconditions, but states a simple evident truth, which can be understood at any time. An evident truth, for Descartes, is something that is "clear and distinct," indubitable, and which presents itself to the understanding just as it is.

"I doubt, therefore I am." In another place Descartes uses this formulation to summarize what has been achieved in his thought experiment. Through doubt as an inherent activity of the "I," all existence which is independent of thought is separated off from thought as such. There remains a sphere of pure consciousness – and thereby a new concept is introduced into philosophy. *Conscientia,* previously used in the sense of "conscience," now came to mean "consciousness." It should be added that by "thought" Descartes meant more than the registration of a succession of states of consciousness. "I am a thinking thing *(res cogitans),"* he wrote, and in the form of *res cogitans* something basic, an indivisible "substance," was revealed.

The Reality of God

Did Descartes, with the evident truth of his *cogito,* reach that Archimedean firm spot that he was striving for? A start had certainly been made, but "moving the world" was not yet possible. For the "I" was a captive within itself, and apart from the "thinking thing," the *res cogitans,* nothing was yet known.

True, Descartes also recognized, along with the first certainty, also a criterion of truth: everything must be true which can be known with the same clarity and distinctness as the "I think, therefore I am." This included mathematical proofs or sentences like "Nothing comes of nothing." But the criterion remained, to start with, highly restricted, for it could not dismiss the possibility of the treacherous evil demon. To deal with this, he needed an idea additional to the *cogito*, introducing with indisputable truth something which existed "outside" thought.

According to Descartes, it is the idea of God that fulfills these conditions, for this idea cannot stem from the imagination. Omnipotence and infinity are not something we find already existing in ourselves, or can construct from other ideas. And – here Descartes follows older philosophy – every idea must have a cause, which must have at least as much reality as is imagined in the idea as effect. Therefore there must really be a God to underlie this idea of God. Or put another way: our idea of God attributes to Him every imaginable positive, i.e. non-restrictive, quality. Existence must be seen as one of these qualities. Therefore God exists.

These "proofs of God's existence" sound very strange today, of course. Be that as it may, the argumentation is still based on the thinking "I": "The whole force of the proof lies in the fact that I regard it as impossible that I should exist as I am, namely with the idea of God inside me, if God too did not really exist." God possesses every possible perfection and no faults. "From this it follows obviously enough that this God cannot deceive, for it is clear that lies and deception derive from a fault." Thus the aforementioned criterion of truth is rescued: all things that we perceive clearly and distinctly are true, and God is certainly one of them.

Baruch de Spinoza
All-Oneness and Participation

"When one begins to philosophize, one must first have been a Spinozist. The soul must bathe in this ether of the one substance." Thus declared Hegel in his lectures on the history of philosophy. This is a strange demand, insofar as one can certainly develop philosophical thoughts on every possible question without ever having heard of Spinoza. Hegel would agree, because this statement was not meant literally. To explain it, however, we must first say something about the "one substance." It refers to Spinoza's basic thesis. He formulated it in critical opposition to Descartes, who had distinguished thought and spatial extension as two substances. The third – original and creative – substance was God. For Spinoza, by contrast, thought and extension are not different substances. Not that he had anything whatever against Descartes'

View of Delft, Painting by Jan Vermeer van Delft, Mauritshuis, The Hague

The painter Vermeer and the philosopher Spinoza were both born in Holland in 1632. Vermeer spent his life in Delft, and Spinoza in Amsterdam and The Hague. It is doubtless somewhat bold to assert, alongside this external relationship between the two men, a certain internal relationship in their works. And yet Vermeer's pictures can provide us with a very impressive illustration of the idea of substance in reference to which everything is one: the spaces in his paintings come across as transparent against space as such, and the light does not seem substantially different from what it illuminates. *Determinatio est negatio,* says Spinoza, "definition is negation." Every concept is defined by its being different from other concepts, by what it is "not." It thus takes on a distinct form only by virtue of its place within the totality of things; the whole precedes the individual. And in the same way, the things painted by Vermeer are not put together from ready-made modules, but seem to have emerged into light from the totality of the picture, while the painted points of light derive their material significance only from the picture as a whole.

separation of the world of consciousness from the corporeal world of material nature. But for him thought and extension were nothing other than two attributes of the one and only substance: God, or, as in a famous identification, "God or nature." Spinoza also described it thus: thought and extension are only different "expressions" of the one substance. This makes it clear that this "one" is differentiated within itself and can thus find expression in different ways.

But let us return to Hegel's statement, according to which every entry to philosophy is Spinozist in a certain sense. It is the specific view of the Whole which is addressed here. Everyday planning and action is directed towards individual purposes and things. But we can get away from the direct thing-relatedness of everyday life by taking a step backward, so to speak. Then we become aware of thought-actions as such. "The mind has only a confused power of knowledge whenever it is directed outwardly – in other words when it encounters things by chance – to look at this or that." By contrast the mind knows "clearly and distinctly" (Spinoza takes these words from Descartes) "whenever it is directed inwardly – namely by looking at several things at once – to understand the similarities, differences and contrasts in them."

Without a doubt, philosophy presupposes reflection, but it also presupposes every science, and actually every simple mental problem-solving activity. And yet even this simple consideration of overlapping viewpoints involves a step into the Absolute, into the One, "in which everything we hitherto regarded as true is absorbed" (Hegel). But what is absorbed here is not truth as such, but only the limitation of expedient horizons in which everything usually presents itself to us. For Spinoza, every true thought was a thought in God. And to think God meant for him to think God's necessity and to understand oneself as part of this. Thought and existence at this point are one (and that was later for Hegel and his contemporaries one of the starting points of philosophy). In the understood infinite one substance, there are no purposes, everything flows out from eternal logical necessity.

But to understand this is only the ultimate goal of Spinoza's philosophy. Even individual

Johann Wolfgang von Goethe, Painting by Georg Melchior Kraus, 1775–76, Stiftung Weimarer Klassik

After his death and the publication of the *Ethics*, Spinoza was repeatedly denigrated as an atheist; his God was coarsely misrepresented as a material world-monster. Spinozist Rationalism was subjected to more intelligent criticism in 1785, in a book by the German philosopher Friedrich Heinrich Jacobi, which aroused admiration for the much-criticized thinker. In particular Jacobi's friend Goethe saw himself endorsed in his inclination toward Spinoza. He found in Spinoza the exhilarating calm, so to speak, of an eternal divine order which had nothing to do with purposes and final goals. For Goethe, there was a direct relationship with his own sphere: "Nature and art are too great to be interested in purposes, and they don't need to be either."

insights are, as we said, of importance. By achieving true knowledge, Man obtains a share in the existence which he has always been without being really aware of it.

Precisely this, however, understood somewhat unhistorically as a kind of experience, is perhaps not something totally alien, which can only be understood within Spinoza's system. Do we not sometimes have the feeling, for example when we discover and understand how things hang together, that we are moving in some "truth" that transcends our individuality, a "truth" in which absolutely everything is connected? There are also situations of elation or depression in which "all is one." This is what Hegel meant by his lively image of "the soul bathing in the ether of the one substance." If Spinozism is understood thus, Hegel's assertion is less subjective and one-sided than might at first appear.

Gottfried Wilhelm Leibniz
Structure of the World

A year before his death, Spinoza received a self-confident, well-informed visitor. Leibniz, 30 years old at the time, was stopping over at The Hague on a journey from Paris via London, where he had been in contact with Newton's circle, to Hanover, his future home and workplace. We do not know how far the two philosophers could agree; Leibniz later had only negative comments to make on Spinoza's philosophy, which does, however, have much in common with his own.

Design for a Medallion by Leibniz, 1697–1698, Niedersächsische Landesbibliothek, Hanover

Leibniz developed not only the binary number system, which uses only two signs (e.g. 0 and 1), but also thought of a calculating machine which would use it. The drawing in the illustration demonstrates the system and the way it handles the basic arithmetical operations; it is a design for a medallion for Duke Rudolf August of Wolfenbüttel, who was impressed by the "invention". One cannot help thinking of today's computers, which do indeed use the binary system for their operations, and use binary digits (or bits) to synthesize whole worlds. Leibniz said: "When God calculates, and implements the thought, the world is the result." On the medallion, Leibniz consciously exploits the idea of a complex creation arising from an elementary difference. The heading reads (with reference to 0 and 1 or God): "Nothing but One in All." The thought is illustrated with the elementary contrast between light and dark, which was the first stage of creation and already contained its full abundance.

Calculating Machine by Leibniz, Niedersächsische Landesbibliothek, Hanover

As a universal scholar, Leibniz conducted many and varied researches in the fields of physics, mathematics, linguistics and philosophy. Frederick the Great said of him: "He is a whole academy in himself." One of his most important works in the field of mathematics was the discovery of the differential calculus. In addition, he developed a calculating machine, which, unlike existing adding machines (invented by, among others, Blaise Pascal), could also multiply and divide. This machine for the four basic operations of arithmetic is based on a construction using graduated drums, which is still used today in various fields of engineering. All his life, Leibniz worked to perfect his machine. It is one of his most important technical discoveries and formed the basis of 20th-century mechanical calculating machines.

Leibniz, too, constructed a metaphysical system which combines certain basic personal attitudes with the development of a "mathematically" closed conceptual structure, which was in part still scholastic and in part Cartesian. Like Spinoza, Leibniz attempted to give expression to a universal accommodation of the individual with the whole. Like Spinoza, he rejected the dualism of Descartes' substances – thought and extension. But he dissolved Spinoza's substance into an infinitude of individual substances, which he called monads, and which, like Spinoza's one substance, were eternal, even though (apart from the supreme monad, God) they were not their own cause, but created. From the nature of the substance(s) it necessarily follows that there is an infinite succession or variety of their states in exactly the same way – and here Leibniz and Spinoza use the same metaphor – that the regular properties of a geometrical figure follow from its nature (as for example it follows from the definition of a triangle that the sum of the angles is 180°, that the bisectors of its angles meet at a single point etc.).

Nevertheless Leibniz's metaphysics interacts much more closely with science than does Spinoza's. It can also be said, perhaps, that Leibniz, like Descartes, starts from a logically true and at the same time reality-linked principle. This is how Descartes understood his *cogito*. Leibniz sought his own Archimedean firm spot in the "general nature of truths." Logic and definition of truth play a central role for him.

The Living Force

Since the 17th century, individual sciences have become so specialized that no one can any longer achieve an adequate overview or really be at home, and creatively active, in several different disciplines at the same time. But Leibniz was still able to develop a truly universal learning. He was able to contribute at the highest level to the mathematics, logic, linguistics, technology and, of course, the philosophy of his age.

As an old man, he wrote that when he was young, the whole theoretical world stood open to him. "I remember that as a 15-year-old I was walking alone in a wood near Leipzig, called Rosenthal, to reflect on whether I should retain the substantial forms. Finally the mechanistic theory prevailed, and led me to the study of mathematics." He was one of those rare people in whom mathematical and philosophical interests were to mix and fertilize each other. The epoch-making discovery of a general and relatively easy to apply infinitesimal calculus – it follows numerous approaches dating right back to classical times – led Leibniz immediately to a new view of nature, the "law of continuity," according to which, "nature never takes leaps." Just as an infinitesimal part of a curve can be regarded at the same time as part of a straight line, namely a tangent to the curve, definitive scientific quantities, formerly understood as polar entities, should be seen as limiting values. Rest, for example, was not to be seen laid down in the order of existence as the

opposite of movement, but as the extreme case of minimum of movement. In metaphorical language, this permanence of continuous transitions filled a dynamically permeated space, or indeed a space that only developed through its dynamic effects. This is not the space of pure geometric extension, in which Cartesian physics had unfolded, but which for Leibniz did not allow any explanation of impenetrability or inter-action between bodies. There was for Leibniz something unreal about movement described in purely geometric terms – after all, it is movement that underlies interaction. "For to be precise, movement never has any more actual existence than does time, as it has no parts existing in common, and consequently never exists as a whole. And thus there is nothing real in it except the reality of the momentary state, which is to be defined by its force and by its striving for change. Therefore this covers everything that is present in material nature except the object of geometry or extension."

Descartes' geometric (or "particle") physics had in fact made do without any concept of force, but did use a "movement quantity" with whose help the movement of bodies could be compared, and, above all, the transfer of movement rendered calculable. This movement quantity is the product of a body's mass and velocity (mv); in today's terminology, its momentum. Descartes assumed that the sum of the momenta of all the bodies in the cosmos was constant.

When Cartesians spoke of force, it was to be understood as proportional to momentum. Here, Leibniz discovered a contradiction. He considered that, in analogy with a frictionless pendulum, which after being released would swing up to its starting height, a falling body had, at every point of its descent, obtained as much force (today we would say kinetic [= movement] energy) as it would need to lift it back from this point to its starting height. This means that bodies of different mass, each falling from different heights, can be related in respect of the corresponding forces. It turns out that momentum is redundant as a measure of force. The momentum mv Leibniz called the "dead force," while mv^2 is the true measure of the "living force," whose totality in the universe remains constant. The assumption of the conservation of forces is tantamount to the – not empirical, but "metaphysical" – precondition that the full effect should correspond to the full cause, in other words that nothing gets lost, so to speak.

This living force, according to Leibniz, can be much more unambiguously ascribed to a body, is so to speak more identical with it, than its velocity, which is relative and can be ascribed to all the other bodies relative to

Leibniz Asserting that Two Leaves cannot be Fully Identical, Leibniz at the court of Electress Sophia of Hanover, copperplate engraving by Christian Schule, color added, 1796

As a rationalist, Leibniz held the opinion that the world was ultimately based on rational principles, and was mainly explicable and knowable through reason. Thus he developed his metaphysics from just a few principles. The most important of these were the principle of sufficient reason (everything has sufficient reason for its existence) and the principle of contradiction (nothing can both exist and not exist). The principle of sufficient reason is related to the epistemological view that all truths are expressed in analytical statements. If something is correctly assigned a particular quality, then this quality is already contained in the concept of the thing. Unlike abstract concepts, every thing or every living individual is permanently defined by infinitely many qualities. This results in the "principle of the identity of the non-distinguishable". If two things were totally identical, they would not be two things, but only one identical thing. This is the reference of the illustration: Leibniz demonstrates that leaves of trees, which, for all their similarity, exist each for themselves, cannot ever be fully identical.

which it is measured. The living force indicates a potential for effect, and means that any momentary state of a body "contains" its succeeding states.

Leibniz' Monadology

In his theory of substance, his metaphysical system of the world, Leibniz builds on the central points of his logic on the one hand, and of his physics on the other. His monads (from the Greek *monas,* "unit") are point-like centers of force, whose "definition," i.e. "total concept," contains all the states through which they pass. It is true that only God can have such a total concept, which contains all the definitions of an individual and is thus infinite. He is the original monad, the creator of all the infinitely many monads of which the universe consists. They are all individual substances; like God, they are souls, but unlike God, they have bodies.

The contrast with Descartes' theory is evident. As hinted in the last section, Leibniz could not retain geometric extension as substance. For him, the physical world was permeated by individual energies. However, it is not easy to understand how Leibniz manages to abolish the dualism of body and soul. For the monads are, as we said, souls, spiritual entities, and in no way to be imagined in any spatial sense, not even as located at a particular point on a body. How, then, are we to imagine the connection? Now, in the final analysis, bodies for Leibniz are not real, but phenomena based in the reality of the monads. They have their reality in perceptions and in thoughts, in other words in souls. As we are conscious souls, space and bodies are certainly real "for us." But we cannot say that exist "as such."

It is easier if we start from nature as it exists for us and talk of a universal one-to-one correspondence of bodies and souls, a "total animation." This correspondence does not simply declare that what we register as separate individual things or organisms are embodied monads, but it does apply continuously to the whole material world with no respect to arbitrary boundaries. "The creator of nature could carry out this divine and wonderful artifice, because every piece of material is not only infinitely divisible, but is indeed infinitely divided into parts, each of which has its own movement. From this it

can be seen that in the smallest piece of material there is a world of creatures, of living organisms, of animals, of entelechies, of souls. Every piece of nature can be regarded as a garden full of plants and as a pond full of fishes. But every branch of the plant, every limb of the animal, every drop of its fluids is again such a garden or such a pond." The monads however form a hierarchy. Thus just as God is the "monarch of the divine state of spirits," so there is in organisms, particularly in animals and human beings, a dominant monad, which is what we call the soul in the usual sense. Among the faculties of the human soul is perception, and also the awareness of and reflection on perception ("apperception"). "Lesser" monads do not have the latter, and yet the difference is gradual, because they all have perceptions. These may however be so minimal that one can speak of "unconscious" perception, which in practice amounts to nothing. "Unconscious" perceptions also occur in the human soul, for example when quiet noises are drowned by louder ones. They can then no longer be distinguished, although they continue to exist as part of the total noise. The amount of "drowned noise" in perception is, according to Leibniz, infinitely large. For monads perceive not only what surrounds and touches them, but "any change in any other monad," in other words, everything that happens in the cosmos. Every simple substance is an "ongoing living mirror of the world."

And yet: "The monads have no windows through which anything can go in or go out." Leibniz understands perception not in the usual sense of processing a psychological certainty resulting from an independent reality which impinges on the senses. Nor is there for him any real interaction of body and soul. Perceptions are simply that aspect of monads which changes. Leibniz supposed that the whole of creation was undergoing (constant) change. The manner of this change, the flux of perceptions, is the expression of the striving and the force of the monads; it is a many-ness in the one-ness of substances, and it is what constitutes their respective particularity and uniqueness. Every moment of this flux itself consists in a multitude of perceptions, albeit not all of them conscious. "A soul can only read in itself what is distinctly set before it; it

cannot at a stroke unfold what is folded up within it, for this folding extends to infinity."

In spite of the windowless nature of the monads, their perceptions represent from their own standpoint, as we said, the states of the other monads, of the world. This was possible, according to Leibniz, because God had attuned, in a pre-established harmony, the courses taken by all these perceptions. It was in the relationship of each monad to the universe of monads that the world of phenomena, the world of spatial, perceptible nature came into being. This is why the pre-established harmony also implies the harmonization of perception and physical movement, in other words the mental and physical sides of an individual.

The Best of All Possible Worlds

For Leibniz, we live in "the best of all possible worlds." This thesis is the theme of his *Theodicy* (from the Greek: *theos*, "god," and *dike*, "justice"), in a sense the reasons for acquitting God of the charge of creating positive, autonomous evil and misery in the world. The word "theodicy" has been used since Leibniz in a general sense for arguments for absolving God in this way, but the idea behind it goes back much further. Most

theodicies explain evil in negative terms; in other words, evil is an accidental absence of good and has no autonomous existence. Leibniz's theses, however, were bound to provoke opposition, and indeed outrage, and they still do. Voltaire satirized them in his *Candide*, whose hero – an incurable optimist, blindly trusting the conviction of his tutor Doctor Pangloss (a caricature of Leibniz) – goes out of his way to welcome and praise a whole series of devastating blows. In the *Theodicy*, Leibniz occasionally creates a harmonizing balance between good and evil in worldly affairs, and there is no doubt that Voltaire's attack on this was entirely justified. But this is not the heart of the "principle of the best," according to which a minimum of preconditions (e.g. natural laws) gives rise to a maximum of variety. The whole of existence represents the optimum fulfillment of merely possible existences in real existence. No individual monad as a center of force can unfold its force freely, but only in conjunction with other opposing forces. The Principle of the Best thus means a high degree of "compossibility," i.e. the compatibility of possibilities, or the tendencies of the individual forces. In this interplay, a universal harmony is made known.

Academy of Arts and Sciences, Copperplate engraving by Sebastian Le Clerc, 17th century, British Museum, London

Le Clerc was not only an engraver but also a mathematician and physicist. Here he presents a mighty panorama of an ideal academy, not without some distant reference to Raphael's *School of Athens* (see p.11). Many of the instruments and appliances are reminiscent of the inventories of the chambers of arts and curios in which princes and scholars (and academies too) collected rare antiquities, measuring instruments, scientific demonstration models and other things. The figures are dressed in classical garb, their often fantastical appearance reminiscent of the treasure-hunters depicted in numerous 17th and 18th-century paintings. Here, science is paired with magic, for soothsayers are also depicted. Otherwise, studies are being pursued in perspective, geometry, astronomy, music, anatomy, optics and the various branches of physics. Many important academies were indeed founded in the 17th century, for example the French Academy of Art (1648), the Académie Royale des Sciences (1666), and the Royal Society of London, to which Locke and Newton belonged. These foundations also had an economic purpose: one intention was to improve the quality of important exports, while it was also expected of the scientists that they would come up with industrially usable inventions.

Candide, Novel by Voltaire (1758), Illustration to Chapter 3, Copperplate engraving by Pierre Charles Baquoy, 1787

Leibniz held the view that the actual world was the "best of all possible worlds." This opinion was the expression of his optimistic view of reason. The free man decides in favor of what his reason tells him is good. This was doubted by Voltaire and satirized by him in his novel *Candide, or on Optimism*. Trusting in the goodness of the world, the hero suffers one misfortune after another. He gets caught up in the Lisbon earthquake (illustrated here), falls into the hands of pirates, and comes face to face with lust for power, cruelty, cowardice, theft and murder. The belief in the free, mature individual, which characterized 17th and 18th-century thought, was subjected here to critical examination.

Leibniz's God, unlike Spinoza's, is not the world, nor does he bring it forth out of a necessity generated by his own being. Rather He has created it by His own free will, and so this creation could have been different. That is why it is the best of a conceivable multitude (or perhaps infinitude) of "possible" worlds, in the face of an infinite void of impossible worlds, worlds which in a sense would not work. If the harmonious perfection of creation is thus optimal, this is nevertheless true in a relative and not an absolute sense. The faults in the created finite world are not denied.

EMPIRICISM

John Locke

Human Understanding

Leibniz's theses are mostly preserved in short treatises or only as drafts. However he has left us a lengthy critique, written in dialogue form, of *An Essay Concerning Human Understanding*, the chief work of his contemporary, John Locke. Leibniz's *New Essays Concerning Human Understanding* give the reader a front seat at an encounter between Rationalism and Empiricism (on this contrast, see also the first two sections of the previous chapter, "Rationalism"). It must be said, however, that the two interlocutors have a good foundation of understanding, because Locke was a rationalistic

John Locke, 1632–1704, Detail of a contemporary painting, Bodeian Library, Oxford

Rejecting Rationalist assumptions of pre-experience, "innate" ideas which underlay all knowledge, Locke developed a theory of knowledge which, concentrating totally on the investigation of the origin of our ideas in experience and their processing and combination, had a great influence during the Enlightenment. In his *Two Treatises on Government*, classical tracts on liberalism, Locke (who held political office from time to time) attacked patriarchal views of monarchy and demanded the separation of the legislative and executive powers. Supreme political power, he said, implied a duty to pass laws which protected the life, rights and property of the citizens.

Empiricist. What does this mean? Leibniz quotes the following maxim of the Empiricist position: "Nothing is in the understanding that was not first in the senses." To which Leibniz, along with the other Rationalists, added: "Except understanding itself." And not even Locke could have totally rejected this addition. For he did not attempt to present understanding, memory and all the contents of the mind in a radically empiricist manner as a kind of "self-organization" of sense-impressions, but rather took certain faculties (such as understanding) as given, and above all as active. But he did speak of a *tabula rasa,* an "empty table" (an image which goes back to Aristotle), the original "blank page" of the understanding, which is painted and written on by experience.

Leibniz compared the blank page to a block of marble from which a sculptor can carve any figure he likes. For Leibniz, though, this block has fine veins, whose structure the sculptor respects and which lead to a figure which is in a sense innate in the marble. Without the activity of the sculptor, this figure would remain unformed, virtual, just as permanently valid principles of knowledge cannot become effective without sensory perception. For, in the final analysis, experience and thus all real things and happenings acquire their cohesion, find their true reflection, in pre-constructed ideal orders which lie self-given in the consciousness.

This is how Descartes saw it, too. In one well-known passage in his *Meditations,* he investigated a piece of wax as exemplifying the whole world of things. What, he asked – just as every Empiricist would ask – is the unchanging and permanent part of the perception-object "wax" that makes it into an "object" in itself? Its form is changeable, so is its color, its firmness varies with the temperature, its aroma is volatile and in any case perceived in highly subjective fashion. In fact its spatial extension is the only quality which could not be imagined as different or absent. Neither wax, nor any other thing, is conceivable without pure extension. But it is precisely this which is not a sensory datum. It is a mental construction, and according to Descartes, the possibility of thought preceded all perception. In a similar manner, all the basic concepts of knowledge should be discoverable through quasi-mathematical thinking. For this reason, natural science could, ideally, present itself as a set of absolutely true theorems.

In his own book, Locke confronts this idea on the title page, no less, with the following verse from the Bible (Ecclesiastes 11, 5): "As thou knowest not what is the way of the wind, nor how the bones do grow in the womb of her that is with child, even so thou knowest not the work of God who doeth all." With these words, Locke proclaims a form of agnosticism, i.e. denial of the possibility of knowing something. This something is not what is perceptible to the senses, the substantial aspect of things, let alone "what holds the world together in its innermost parts" (as Goethe put it, speaking through Faust), which Leibniz sought to understand with his "harmony." Locke's attitude was nevertheless not hostile to science. On the contrary. He too was aiming at scientific knowledge. But for him, science consisted in hypothetical statements which described interrelationships and made them predictable, without explaining their ultimate causes. The researcher, so to speak, remained entirely in this world of sensory perception, classifying impressions and drawing up relationships.

In the introduction to his chief work of philosophy, published in 1739, David Hume saw a line of development in thinking which had originated with Francis Bacon. According to Hume, Bacon's method of learning by experience oriented towards natural objects, had been applied by some English philosophers a hundred years later, with Locke in the forefront, to mental objects. The timespan of a hundred years was not atypical, he said; a century was also the period that separated Thales from Socrates. By drawing this bold parallel with the venerable origins of the European sciences of man and nature (and of the formation of concepts), Hume was demonstrating self-confident pride in the British tradition. The far-reaching effect of British Empiricist philosophy and experimental science on continental Europe shows that this pride was not misplaced. Locke's *Essay* was translated into several languages, and was for a time probably the most important current work of philosophy published in Europe.

Locke's goal was a reasonable, one might even say, common-sense analysis of the conditions for making meaningful statements. These included testing the statements "against" experience and showing that all meaningful concepts originally arose "from" experience. Both demands were respected in the course of an empirically oriented epistemological shift toward analyzing the functions of the intellect and their effect in the construction of knowledge from experience. Locke investigated the intellect ("human understanding") and the composition of ideas

London, Contemporary engraving, 17th century

Illustration to the *Treatise on the Principles of Painting* by Roger de Piles, 1709

The "Physiology of the Intellect," as Kant metaphorically called John Locke's chief work, was concerned with "simple" ideas, derived from sensory perception, and "reflective ideas," which built on the former. Reflective ideas included for example the distinction between two kinds of ideas of things, which according to Locke related to "primary qualities" and to "secondary qualities." The former were quantitative definitions, for example size, shape, movement and rest, while the latter included color and smell. The secondary qualities were "subjective," and corresponded directly to nothing in the things themselves. In this connection, there was a great deal of discussion in the 18th century about the transmission of sound, the effects of light, and the perception of color. Artists too, of course, were interested in theories of visual perception. Roger de Piles, in his theories of art, dealt among other things with the particular acuity of vision in the center of the field of view, and the way individual things could be brought into focus by the attention of the viewer. All this should be reproduced in pictures, he said, through distribution of light and shade, which should not, as in the bottom illustration, be "scattered." De Piles was concerned with the "unity of the object" of painting, which he also sought to explain philosophically by reference to nature itself, which strove for unities.

in the same way as Descartes had investigated the physical world and its composition. Simple ideas went to make up complex ideas in the same way as atoms went to make up bodies. "Ideas" is Locke's word for all the contents of consciousness, in other words, perceptions, pictures in the mind's eye, words in the mind, fantasies, thoughts, memories etc. Today, the word "ideas" is largely confined to concepts in the sense of a (perhaps still vague) project of action or of a particular thought in an incomplete mental context. In Locke's time, the broader meaning was usual enough. (This could not happen, of course, until Descartes had freed the term "idea" from its Platonic context.)

Locke began his investigation in the second book of the *Essay* neither with explanations of basic metaphysical or logical terms nor with definitions of the terms he used himself to differentiate ideas. His approach in the *Essay* was, in his own words, that of an "historical, plain method." "Historical" is here being used in its older sense of "listing collected facts." What we have is an inventory of the possibilities of the intellect; he was concerned to show how the individual items were arrived at. Classification of ideas and explanation of origin go hand in hand. There is no attempt at logical consistency come what may; the *Essay* provides no conclusive, total, self-contained epistemology or theory of ideas.

The distinction between simple and complex ideas addresses a relationship reminiscent of other notions of elementary analysis and synthesis in the Baroque period. Simple ideas are components of internal or external perception that cannot be sub-divided any further. The solidity of bodies, for example, is one such simple idea of outward perception; it is formed by touch, experiencing the impenetrability of things and the resistance they offer. Individual colors and sounds are also elementary; they cannot be derived from other ideas, let alone ideas from other fields, and thus cannot be described where there is no possibility of experience, e.g. in this case to a blind or deaf person respectively.

Now we do not collect these elements, which are juxtaposed in things, consciously one by one as such. "Though the qualities that affect our senses are, in the things themselves, so united and blended, that

there is no separation, no distance between them; yet it is plain, the ideas they produce in the mind enter by the senses simple and unmixed." The separation into recognizably and denotably different qualities is however in itself an achievement of the mind. For Locke does not mean that the senses manage to separate out the idea of "black," for example, from their total impression of a heap of coal. The senses give us individual qualities, while "blackness" is a general concept obtained by abstraction. But of course the senses react quite specifically, and what we single out in certain sorts of coals as the particular quality of being black must, according to Locke, somehow also be present as sensory data.

"The senses at first let in particular ideas, and furnish the yet empty cabinet, and the mind by degrees growing familiar with some of them, they are lodged in the memory, and names got to them. Afterwards, the mind proceeding further, abstracts them, and by degrees learns the use of general names. In this manner the mind comes to be furnished with ideas and language, the materials about which to exercise its discursive faculty." Simple ideas cannot be multiplied arbitrarily: "The dominion of man, in this little world of his own understanding being much what the same as it is in the great world of visible things; wherein his power, however well managed by art and skill, reaches no farther than to compound and divide the materials that are made to his hand; but can do nothing towards the making the least particle of new matter..."

Alongside the simple ideas of external perception, there are those of reflection, "the perception of the operations of our own mind within us, as it is employed about the ideas it has..." These ideas about internal processes include for example "perception, thinking, doubting, believing, reasoning, knowing, willing." Some of these – it is true – are complex ideas. Of this list, Locke allows only "perception/thinking" and "willing" as "simple."

Complex Ideas, Words, Knowledge

Numerous simple ideas always occur in groups, albeit sometimes with modifications and changes of scale. We then assume that they belong to a thing, that there is a host,

Still Life, Painting by Jean-Baptiste Siméon Chardin, c. 1760, Louvre, Paris

Chardin was doubtless following the recommendations of art theoreticians like de Piles (see illustration opposite) when he varied the sharpness of his objects and focused the beholder's attention on to centers of brightness against a fuzzy background. But he was also reflecting on sensory perception and its capacity for gathering knowledge by questioning the reality and objectivity of phenomena. This is done, for example, by means of a strange indeterminacy of distance between vision and the painted object of vision. On the one hand, the things seem to be far away, and thus spared the distortion resulting from close-up perspective. On the other, they come across as though they were being, in a sense, directly palpated by the eye. Thus here we have on the one hand a view of "primary qualities," as best expressed through ground-plans and sections (as for example in scale plans for buildings, where there is no central perspective), while on the other hand, we have the subjectivity of a momentary aspect.

in which they exist. This host, according to Locke, we call substance. An idea of substance is, although it might seem so, not a simple idea, because it arises only in connection with a group of qualities. The qualities may derive from internal or external perception, and so the substance may be physical or mental.

The formation of the idea of substance is for Locke a totally non-arbitrary achievement of the mind. But this does not justify positing substance as a fact of experience of something with a real existence. It is only an "I know not what." Thus Locke criticizes the concept of substance which tradition found so indispensable, takes away the ground from beneath its feet, without actually giving it up. Another kind of complex idea is represented by modes. Philosophical language since Descartes had seen modes as existing dependently "in" substances or as particular states of substances. This is also true of what Locke imagined in his "ideas of modes," but to start with, modes are products of multiplications or compounds of simple ideas in the understanding. The simple mode "infinity," for example, is a mode of each of the simple ideas of extension, duration or number. It arises through the constant expansion of a quantity, any quantity, of the kind of one of these ideas. Another of Locke's examples calls the idea of spoken "words" a modification of

the idea of "sound." Mixed modes combine various ideas; these in fact cover all the words that language has to offer for cultural phenomena. Sacrilege, murder, beauty, are concepts from simple ideas taken from different fields. The coining of words in, for example, the fields of esthetics, law or politics, is a manifestation of the development of a society. Language changes, "because change of customs and opinions [brings] with it new combinations of ideas." Words are subordinate to ideas, represent them, and serve the ends of memory and communication. This is how Locke represents them in Book 3 of his *Essay,* devoted to the theme of language.

Having finished his classification of ideas, in Book 4 Locke turns to knowledge and opinion. As in classical logic, he deals with true judgments or statements, in which our knowledge is presented, and thus with the way that ideas are structured in sentences. "Since the mind, in all its thoughts and reasonings, hath no other immediate object but its own ideas... it is evident that our knowledge is only conversant about them. Knowledge is the perception of the agreement or disagreement of two ideas. Knowledge then seems to me to be nothing but the perception of the connection of and agreement, or disagreement and repugnancy of any of our ideas."

Locke goes on to sub-divide the possibility of agreement into classes, recognizing three

Trinity College, Dublin, Interior of library, photograph, 1995

After graduating from Trinity College, Dublin, the young George Berkeley waited for a vacancy to occur among the teaching staff, and in the meantime enthusiastically pursued the studies that were to form the basis of his entire later work. The college curriculum consisted of a mixture of traditional and modern studies. Among these were the works of Newton and Locke. After studying the latter's *Essay Concerning Human Understanding,* Berkeley sought to draw the consequences from Locke's views. He agreed with Locke that all knowledge derives from sensory perception, but unlike Locke, he did not believe that anything existed independently of experience ("To be is to be perceived").

degrees of knowledge. "Intuitive" knowledge is the immediate and indubitable insight into the agreement or disagreement of ideas; with "demonstrative" knowledge the insight is indirect, recognized through deduction in a number of steps. Finally "sensitive" knowledge consists in the certainty of the existence of individual data of perception in the external world.

In conclusion Locke remarks on the classification of the sciences into (natural) philosophy, which investigates the material and intellectual world, practical philosophy, which deals with correct behavior and the path to happiness, and semiotics or logic, which have to do with the signs which we use when thinking or communicating.

George Berkeley

"Esse est percipi"

George Berkeley, later to become Bishop of Cloyne in Ireland, was still a young man when he formulated his central philosophical thesis, which is now always associated with his name. It states that *esse est percipi aut percipere* ("Being is being perceived or perceiving"). According to this thesis, there can be no existence outside perceptual relationships.

A "something" that only exists through being perceived might be a pain, for example. In such a case, the thesis is altogether plausible. Apart from the person feeling pain, there is no pain. My toothache or, for example, my

hunger and the associated incitement to go to the larder, belong entirely to me; they take place within my consciousness. For Berkeley, all sensations were in principle of this kind – colors, sounds, heat and touch perceptions for example, and as such, they too are in the consciousness of the perceiver. Galileo, Locke and others had understood the so-called secondary qualities (including colors and temperatures) as characteristics which we attribute to things by virtue of merely subjective sense impressions. The primary qualities (e.g. spatial measurements or movements), which are expressed in geometrically and mathematically constructible quantities, were by contrast regarded as objective data of the material world. Berkeley abandoned this distinction; for him, all qualities are "secondary." For this reason, in Berkeley's thesis, the existence that only results from being perceived also extends to the objective reality of the "external world."

This is initially confusing, for normally we are convinced of the independent existence of the things which are accessible to us through our senses. We do not see them as dependent upon our or other people's perception. Berkeley however awakens doubts about this conviction when he rightly notes: "It is curious to think of a world emptied of rational beings." In this thought experiment, the attempt is made to describe the world or anything in any possible world without respect to at least possible, if not perhaps practically realizable, perception. It is also necessary to specify this something without reference to our capacity to perceive colors, shapes etc. For Berkeley, what emerges from this exercise is – nothing. Anything that exists, deprived (in thought) of all the qualities which we only recognize through our specific sensory perceptions, must be regarded as totally without qualities and abstract. Descartes had understood spatial extension *(res extensa)* as the real equivalent of such an idea. Berkeley by contrast denies the possibility of imagining an abstract X, a thing without sensory qualities.

In his critique of the concept of abstract ideas, Berkeley was aiming particularly at Locke. Initially, their philosophical approaches have much in common. Berkeley too thought that all knowledge derives from sensory experience. Along with Locke, he stressed that our consciousness only ever has to do with ideas (which are, or are based on, perceptions). But in respect of general ideas, e.g. that of the triangle or of the human being, Locke believed that they carried their generality, thanks to which they could in principle encompass infinitely many individual things, within themselves. Ideas or perceptions of concrete individual things are accordingly distinguished by their character from general ideas. Thus for Locke, the general idea of a triangle contains neither the definiteness of an actual size nor the quality of acuteness, obtuseness or right-angledness as the case may be. Since Locke, Berkeley, and later Hume regarded ideas as a kind of mental image, a general idea must accordingly be a totally formless, colorless and immaterial image, and understandably Berkeley regards such a thing as impossible. According to him, there are only ever concrete ideas; if one can imagine anything by the word "triangle," then it must be a series of different, but in each case specific, figures. That the word can be applied to all the different triangles is due in this case, as in others, not to the fact that the word corresponds to a general idea, but exclusively to the existence in every language of general names (i.e. all predicators, e.g. adjectives and common nouns, as opposed to proper nouns, which refer to particular things or people). Therefore no abstract or general existing thing is imaginable as the

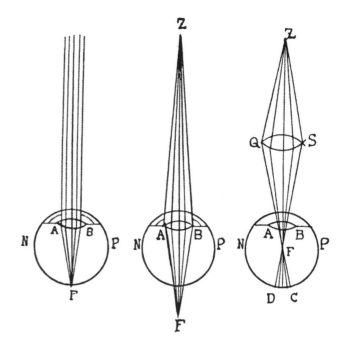

cause of such an idea. In particular, there is no "material," no "substance" in the sense of quality-less "thinginess." For Berkeley, it is meaningless to talk of the material world. Only the perceptions of the immaterial mind are real.

In the next stage of his considerations, however, Berkeley retains a multiplicity of minds whose perceptions and thus whose worlds entirely correspond one with another, in the everyday sense, and who therefore do not "produce" their ideas arbitrarily. Rather, it is God from whose mind all ideas spring, and who harmonizes the – in a sense,

Illustration for: *A New Theory of Vision* **by George Berkeley**

Berkeley's *New Theory of Vision* (1709) was for a long time an influential standard text on perceptual psychology, and represented significant progress compared to the relevant theories of Descartes and his successors. They, for example, explained visual judgment of distance by analogy with the triangulation procedures used in surveying. Berkeley by contrast showed that in the visual field there is only a juxtaposition of color impressions; the perception of distance, size, and shape is only possible because experience provides us with a known relationship between our sense of vision and our sense of touch.

The Experiment with the Bird in the Air Pump, Painting by Joseph Wright of Derby, 1768, Tate Gallery, London

In England, natural philosophy and physics were studied not only in the ancient universities, but also in numerous smaller academies such as the "Lunar Society," attended by deistically oriented and progressively minded members of dissenting Protestant communities outside the established Church. Here, discussions and experiments took place in private circles to which Joseph Wright had links. This is the context of this picture. In the spirit of the Enlightenment, Wright combined physics, anthropology and psychology; he depicts people of different ages, and shows different emotional reactions to the experiment, in which a vacuum is produced in a glass vessel. The bird consequently loses the ability, for a short time, to fly and breathe. In his light effects, the painter was presumably alluding to representations of the Nativity, and was thus staging a field of tension between religion and modern science.

telepathically transmitted – ideas in every human mind. For Berkeley, who was after all a Christian philosopher, this metaphysical construction, from which everything non-mental and un-godly had disappeared, certainly represented a great success for his refutation of "materialism" (by which he meant nothing more than the standard assumption that material existed), and may indeed have been the motivation for it in the first place.

How can "immaterialism" be reconciled with a basically Empiricist attitude? Berkeley repeatedly emphasized that the epistemological thesis *esse est percipi* in no way affected whatever the reality of the perceptions on the basis of which we form our ideas of things. "According to the immaterial thesis, the wall is white, the fire hot etc." The point is that the things of the world of perception, a sensory unity now that the distinction between primary and secondary qualities has been done away with, can only be understood as phenomena, as complexes of perceptions. The task of empirical researchers is to formulate their regularities in laws and to reconstruct how they originated from the processing of simple impressions.

David Hume

The Science of Human Beings

As one of the great thinkers of the Enlightenment to owe much to Locke, David Hume actually belongs both thematically and chronologically in the next chapter. However, on account of the many common features

shared by Locke, Berkeley and Hume, and the fact that all three came from the British Isles (an Englishman, Irishman and Scotsman respectively), we shall deal with all of them here.

Hume's major philosophical work was entitled *A Treatise of Human Nature. Being an Attempt to Introduce the Experimental Method of Reasoning into Moral Subjects* (1739 – 40). By a science of "moral subjects" he meant approximately what is meant nowadays by the humanities. The three books of the *Treatise* deal respectively with understanding, the passions, and morals (including constitutional theory).

The human being, Hume decided, is the subject of many individual sciences, but above all of course it is always man who pursues science. For this reason, basic scientific research in the most general, but yet precise sense should consist in the investigation of the psychological nature of man, i.e. above all in the analysis of his potential to form meaningful concepts, to feel emotion, to will, and to evaluate actions. This basic research, which Hume judged to be the task of philosophy, should, in accordance with the sub-title of the *Treatise,* be strictly based on experience, eliminating all speculation and any reference to the transcendental.

It is quite unusual to understand philosophy in this way as empirical research and thus as an individual science. Hume's ambitious goal was to do for the humanities what Newton had done for natural science. Admittedly,

Reflecting Telescope
by Sir Isaac Newton

In the introduction to his major work, David Hume describes a line of intellectual development, starting from Francis Bacon's method of learning, which was oriented to natural objects, and then applied a hundred years later by certain English philosophers to mental objects. And indeed, British Empiricism attracted great interest, as did the scientific research pursued by the Royal Society. This body, which included Locke among its fellows, acknowledged its debt to Bacon and institutionalized the modern research procedures which had been introduced in the Renaissance, whereby new hypotheses were obtained by experiment. Sir Isaac Newton, who was a long-serving President of the Royal Society, carried out a number of experiments in the field of optics. He built a reflecting telescope (1671) and proved that white light was made up of the colors of the spectrum.

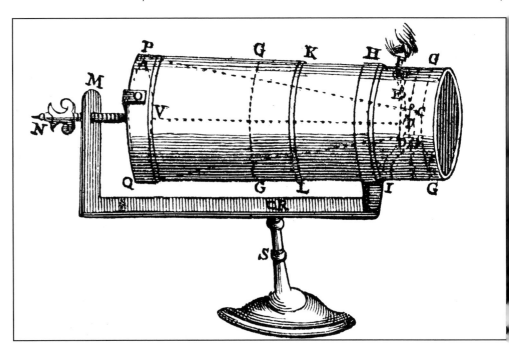

Public Billiard Room in Paris, Painting by Jean-Baptiste Siméon Chardin, Musée Carnavalet, Paris

It was not only the great popularity of the game depicted here that led Hume to use the collision of two billiard balls as his example of the sequence of cause and effect. The transmission of momentum by elastic impact, the laws governing which had been precisely investigated by the physicists of the 17th century, was an important foundation of the mechanistic picture of the world, according to which everything is causally determined, and according to which, also, many phenomena can be explained by the collisions of tiny particles of matter. Hume showed that the causality principle had no objective validity. There was no empirical reason for the view that a particular cause must necessarily be followed by a particular effect, he said.

experiments and mathematical methods were of no help here. "We must therefore glean up our experiments [...] from a cautious observation of human life, and take them as they appear in the common course of the world, by men's behavior in company, in affairs and in their pleasures." Anyone expecting a leisurely philosophical tour after this introduction will be disappointed by the frequently specialized and almost always complicated issues dealt with in the *Treatise*. But in many passages, and in particular in other writings, Hume does indeed turn out to be a serene, accessible thinker, who also understood philosophy in one of its modern senses as "philosophy of life."

Empiricism and Epistemology

Hume's empiricism follows the basic assumptions set out by Locke, and, in this connection, Berkeley's critique regarding the concept of abstract ideas. This means that for Hume, all our ideas and concepts come from sensory perceptions, and they all possess to a greater or lesser degree the concrete "fullness" and the qualities of sensory perceptions. These qualities include, for example, spatial and/or temporal localization of the thing perceived; in perceptions of the external senses (which Hume follows Locke in calling "sensations") these include color, hardness etc., while in perceptions of the inner sense ("reflections") they cover references to other perceptions. Hume divides perceptions into "impressions" and "ideas." The former are direct and immediate, the latter their images,

which can be reproduced in a more or less faded version, for example in the memory. Locke had still called all contents of consciousness "ideas," and, insofar as they were, or stemmed from, external perceptions, understood them as representations of things. For Hume, the relationship of representation was only between impressions and ideas; things were excluded. The freshness and strength of impressions, which cannot be reproduced in the imagination, is at the same time the characteristic feature of the non-arbitrary availability (which for Locke had been anchored in represented reality) of the information gained by experience.

Here we see that Hume was continuing the tradition of consistently not going beyond the experiences of consciousness, and surpassing Locke in exposing all transcendence. This term derives from the Latin *transcendere,* "to go beyond," and in philosophy usually means going beyond conscious experience to some objective reality independent of consciousness. Conscious experience includes perceptions, for example seeing and hearing. We hear steps on the street, and take it for granted that someone is walking past. Descartes had already pointed out that sensory impressions like these, and the often unconscious attribution of their cause, not infrequently involved errors and illusions, and that it is not absurd to doubt the existence of the outside world altogether. Hume follows neither Descartes in his laying aside of this doubt via the proof of the existence of God,

Adam Smith, Portrait by Charles Smith

Hume is doubtless the best-known, but by no means the only important Scottish philosopher of the 18th century. There was indeed a "Scottish School" based on what was called "common-sense philosophy," which sought to give due emphasis, in opposition to Berkeleyan idealistic immaterialism and Humian skepticism alike, to the everyday conviction that we have direct access to an outside world independent of the consciousness. The ethics, and above all the economic theories, of Adam Smith (1723–90) achieved far-reaching importance. A friend of Hume's and influenced by him, Smith saw the foundation of moral action not in norms and rational insights, but in emotions. Self-love on the one hand and sympathy for others on the other combine in the need to see the feelings underlying one's actions approved by other people. In his economic theory, which founded the science of economics, Smith traced the wealth of a nation not to its balance of trade or natural resources or agriculture, as earlier opinions had done, but to the total quantity of work engaged in producing goods for exchange.

nor Berkeley in his dogmatic rejection of the existence of the material world and his anchoring of conscious experience in the mind of God. Instead, Hume leaves open the question of the origin of impressions. We have a steady stream of perceptual experiences, he says, but why this is so, and where they come from, or indeed whether it makes sense to speak of "causation" at all, are questions we simply cannot answer. For we are always enclosed in the "little world of our mind," external things are never given to us in themselves. If we are nevertheless firmly convinced of the existence of these things, and of objective existence generally, this is to transcend our sense-impressions, and no more can be said.

What is Meant by Causality?

Even though our knowledge and thought has to do with perceptions and ideas, and not with things in themselves, there nevertheless exists for us a world in which there seem to be objective facts. For the Empiricists it was just as important as it was for Descartes to determine about what we can say anything with "certainty," and why. What constitutes certain truth about statements of fact? Hume, like Leibniz, distinguished between rational truths and factual truths. The first dominate in mathematics and other calculation systems based on absolutely clear rules. Here, anything is true that follows logically from the rules (in the case of mathematics, these are the definitions and axioms). Hume agrees with the Rationalists that rational truths are demonstratively certain. "Factual truths" are based on sensory data, for which there are no intrinsic rules and which cannot therefore be subject to any logic as rational truths are. In this case, something is true if it can be empirically verified. The opposite of "rationally true" is "illogical," whereas the opposite of "factually true" is not. All the same, we do set up rules in the field of empirical facts, and draw conclusions similar to those of logic. Hume now asks the decisive question for natural science: upon what is this non-demonstrative drawing of conclusions based, and can it ever lead to certainty about objective states of affairs?

Let us assume that one observes on a number of occasions the following: (a) the rolling white billiard ball strikes the motionless red ball; immediately this event takes place, we observe every time (b): the red ball starts rolling. We "conclude" that given identical conditions, (a) will "always" be followed by (b). This is an inductive conclusion, which proceeds from a number of individual cases to a rule, a universally valid law, and thus asserts a factual truth. But such an induction, Hume maintained, is circular. In other words, the proof rests on a precondition, which in turn is only proved by the proof. In the case of our induction, the circularity is as follows. (1) A regularity observed in the past – (b) follows (a) – must also be a future regularity because there is a regularity in the total course of things. (2) But this necessarily presupposes a general regularity in physical processes. (3) But this itself has only ever been observed in the past, and it could only be extended to all time if the conclusion was valid. (4) But this is precisely what we are seeking to prove.

We believe nevertheless that we can predict the behavior of the billiard balls with certainty without recourse to induction. For we see in the transfer of movement through impact a "causal relationship," and know, or presume, that it can be described by the laws of physics. We believe that this relationship of cause and effect, for which apparently we can even provide a precise explanation, means that (b) "must necessarily" follow (a).

Hume says, reasonably enough, that the principle of cause and effect is one of the decisive foundations of our orientation on the world. All our plans and actions are based upon it, and so too is science. The facts that science establishes are not isolated but stand alongside other facts which explain them. Without the tissue of cause-and-effect relationships, there could be no objective world of experience at all. For individual experiences only fall into a total context through thinking in the aforementioned non-demonstrative conclusions, which largely rest on the principle of causality. If we cannot provide causal explanations for everything, and thus also produce effects, we would be faced by chaos.

But Hume also says, in a central and very famous argument, that the epistemological foundations of causality are no firmer than those of induction. For wherein consists this "necessity" which we attribute to the causal relationship? It cannot be a "logical" necessity, for we are in the sphere of factual truths. Nor is this necessity anywhere to be found in "experience." "The impulse of one billiard ball is attended with motion in the second. This is the whole that appears to the outward senses. The mind feels no sentiment or inward impression from this succession of objects: consequently there is not, in any single, particular instance of cause and effect, any thing which can suggest the idea of power or necessary connection." This is convincing. While we say that (b) happens "because" (a) has happened, we cannot explain this "because" by any internal necessity of the situation, but only ever paraphrase it by reference to the primary data: the spatial and temporal vicinity of (a) and (b). The physical subdivision of the process into smaller elements alters nothing in this; it merely postpones the problem.

Necessity, which is part of the concept of a causal relation, was, according to Hume, no more than the projection of a customary association on to an alleged state of affairs in the external world. Because we have always experienced (a) and (b) in sequence, we always associate (b) with the perception of (a), and we then assume this connection to be a substantial necessity of the sequence itself.

Skepticism and Human Nature

According to this train of thought, the "certainty" of factual truths dissolves into mere "custom." Hume thus became a true Skeptic, and was forced to deny the possibility of objective scientific knowledge. However, he realized that this had few consequences for everyday life. We go on playing billiards as before, and we never consider the possibility that causal necessity is unreal and that maybe a ball will stay where it is when struck by another.

So we are faced with a contradiction, which is known in the history of philosophy as the "skeptical paradox." A watertight argument falls down flat, so to speak, because while it cannot be disproved and thus by all the rules of argumentation ought

to be convincing, yet it is rejected on grounds of a fundamental human attitude which is emotive (though not randomly subjective). Hume solved this contradiction on the side of skepticism against reason. From the point of view of philosophical tradition, this was shocking, and at first Hume also found it so: reason was no longer mistress in her own house. She "is" and "ought to be" a slave of the "passions."

Thus Hume arrived at what has often been called a naturalist standpoint, by which any assertion of the autonomy of reason vis-à-vis a world which is itself rationally structured is nothing but rationalist superstition. Rather, thought is embedded in human nature; it does not so much control sensations and passions as accompany them. Hume did not view this conclusion pessimistically, however, because the senses have their own kind of practical reason; in a manner of speaking, nature regulates herself.

Charles I, King of Great Britain, Painting by Anthony van Dyck, c. 1635, Louvre, Paris

David Hume is best known today for his philosophy, but to contemporaries he was probably familiar above all as a historian. Alongside his epistemological writings, he was also the author of a comprehensive *History of England*, which caused a major scandal, largely because he aimed for a totally unprejudiced and impartial depiction of events. The main criticism was directed at Hume's assessment of the fate of King Charles I, who had been tried and executed in 1649 for transgressing the customary and statutory rights of the people. Hume considered his execution barbaric, and thus earned himself the displeasure of the governing Whigs, who regarded it as justified. He was heavily criticized on other points too. The result was that the "History" soon became a best-seller, and was used as a standard textbook in history lessons in England until the early 20th century.

Reason and Freedom

The Enlightenment

RATIONAL HUMANITY

The Light of Publicity

Probably the most famous definition of what "enlightenment" means was not restricted to any particular "era": "Enlightenment is Man's emergence from his self-imposed immaturity. Immaturity is the incapacity to make use of one's intellect without the guidance of another. This immaturity is self-imposed when its causes are to be found not in a lack of intellect, but of the determination and courage to use it without the guidance of another. Have the courage to know – that is the motto of enlightenment."

Many modern writers have come up with general definitions of "enlightenment" in the broad sense, seeing it as a process which is constantly taking place in history or is particularly noticeable at certain periods, for example the age of Socrates and Plato, or the modern age. This process includes the abandonment of prejudices, the destruction of myths, the will to liberate oneself from natural or social fetters, and, on the part of enlightened pioneers, an actively emancipatory attitude to education.

However, more than other periods, the Enlightenment in the historical sense has a definite article and a capital "E," and denotes a particular era, namely the 17th and 18th centuries - more particularly the latter. Indeed in the period between the English Revolution of 1688 and the French Revolution of 1789 – and these two dates provide a useful frame for the period of the Enlightenment in the narrower sense – people were growing increasingly aware that they were living in what was, scientifically and philosophically, a new era. In France, Italy and Germany, the talk was of an enlightened century; the first concern was to cast light on "dark" and confused ideas and spirits. During the course of the 18th century, the noun "Enlightenment" came to be used. For Immanuel Kant, with whose definition we opened this chapter, independent thought and the questioning of traditional patterns included the "freedom to make public use of one's reason in all fields." By this he meant the reason "which someone makes use of as a scholar, before the whole reading public." This kind of "use of reason" had, together with the "reading public" itself, expanded enormously in the course of the 18th century to reach undreamed-of heights. Throughout Europe, the public were informed by the press about wars, disasters, exotic discoveries and day-to-day politics. Above all, though, there were also "moral weeklies," "intelligence sheets," and scholarly journals, in which the talk was time and again of that "reason" of which Kant had spoken. This buzzword of the Enlightenment gave a name to what all men had in common, in whose sign a newly awakening "world citizenship" was to take shape. While there was no demand for the abolition of national borders, and rarely for radical change in the forms of government, the motto of the French Revolution, "Liberty,

THE ENLIGHTENMENT

Toward the end of the 18th century, Thomas Paine, the best-known political writer of his day, who was actively involved in the **American Revolution (1773–83)** and the **French Revolution (1789–92),** wrote two books: **The Age of Reason** and *The Rights of Man.* The first title can be used as a description of the century as a whole, while the second states one of the major themes of this period.

In his work *The Spirit of the Laws* (1748), the central work of constitutional theory of the Enlightenment, Charles de Montesquieu analyzed **types of civil and political law** and their dependence on the age and the society in which they were made. One of his influential theses was that a precondition of political freedom was the separation of powers and mutual checks and balances.

In the "enlightened despotisms" **reforms** were implemented in the fields of **law, education and the economy.** Frederick the Great in Prussia and Catherine the Great in Russia intently followed the philosophical and literary developments taking place in France.

In his *Persian Letters,* Montesquieu satirized the society of his day, describing it from the point of view of a non-European. This relativization of prevailing morality

Frederick II ("the Great"), King of Prussia, Painting by Franz Dudde, c. 1900

and conditions was typical of the Enlightenment, and went side by side with the comparative **study of other cultures.** Thoroughgoing Enlightenment philosophy was pursued mainly in France.

The central features here were the **rejection of all traditional authority,** the exaltation of reason (while rejecting Rationalist metaphysics), the drawing up of the foundations of a non-theological morality, the **conviction that scientific development would bring human progress,** the belief in the explicability of the soul (or the apparatus of knowledge and sensation), and the possibility of using the characteristics of matter to explain all phenomena.

In the 1780s, Immanuel Kant criticized previous epistemological theories and also rejected Enlightenment theses on this topic. His philosophy combined the opposing attitudes of Rationalism and Empiricism.

Equality, Fraternity" was already to be heard, and after that *fait accompli* it found its echo outside France's borders.

Open exchanges of opinion with revolutionary undertones took place naturally enough not just in print. Milan in 1764–65 saw the publication of a progressive literary magazine entitled *Il caffe* – and this reflected a new institution in Europe. Coffee was the fashionable beverage of the age; coffee-houses were places to debate and philosophize, where you could read about the latest news and ideas, venues for communication which transcended class barriers. These were the meeting places of independent men of letters, connoisseurs of arts and science, who, in view of the increased demand for reading matter, were able to make a living from writing, and as witty conversationalists also had access to the salons and tables of the nobility.

In France, these 18th-century intellectuals called themselves *philosophes,* which in this context can also be translated as "enlighteners." Their lifestyle and manners set the tone, but their more or less soundly based *esprit* could also become an end in itself. A fictitious hanger-on and parasite of this *philosophe* society, "Rameau's nephew" (the eponymous hero of a dialogue by Diderot), already resembles the psychologically perspicacious and occasionally nihilistic Bohemians of the 19th century. He embodies the cynical reverse side of a progressive, enlightened investigation of traditions and values, of a general tendency to relativize, which had aimed progressively and optimistically at a practical change in conditions. This critical, "popular" practicality and an ideological polemicism in the rhetorical points of their theses were more notable in many of the *philosophes* than the stringency of their philosophical solutions to problems. For this reason many professional philosophers have, in retrospect, spoken disparagingly of the *philosophes*. Nevertheless, one can still say that at no time, either before or since, has European culture been so strongly marked by philosophical debate as it was in the 18th century.

The Bourgeois Culture of Sense and Sensibility

One class of society that could never have whole-heartedly accepted the motto of freedom and equality did nevertheless contribute more than a little to the progress of the Enlightenment. Sections of the European nobility freely debated atheism, materialism, religious toleration, and the law of nature. A publishing project central to the dissemination

of enlightened knowledge, the *Encyclopédie* or Encyclopedia which appeared in France in many volumes, could not have been implemented had it not been for a large number of wealthy and mainly aristocratic subscribers. However, "encyclopedic" interests also extended to members of the traditional commonalty (e.g. master craftsmen), and in particular the upper middle class, consisting of, for example, professional people such as lawyers, clergymen, civil servants and academics, but also including the new class of capitalist entrepreneurs. In Great Britain, with its constitutional monarchy, this class had played a self-confident and unopposed role since the mid 17th century, and it was Britain that provided the major impetus toward political and religious liberalism (not to mention technical and practical innovations in the commercial and industrial sphere). But in other countries too, the middle classes were growing in importance in a decisive fashion. In spite of their disproportionately small political influence, they were becoming the driving force behind social change and the standard-bearers of Enlightenment culture.

A major contribution was made by the emergence of a public for new forms of literature and drama. In a flood of novels, the swashbuckling or maybe melancholic adventurers of Baroque literature were transformed into thoughtful, rational, far-sighted, yet emotional and passionate fellow human beings. They underwent minor, private experiences, the description of which was nonetheless a demonstration of typical humanity appropriate to citizens of the world; or else they suffered devastating blows of fate, which nonetheless did not prevent them from cultivating an attitude of human moral sensibility towards the non-human. In the theater (and in painting) there were on the one hand historical heroes doing their civic duty by sacrificing themselves for the republican cause, while on the other, contemporary bourgeois heroes were destroyed by the contradictions, injustices and anachronisms of a society which preserved many of its feudal characteristics. Parallel to the part courtly, but also part bourgeois art of the Rococo, so-called "sensibility" in literature formulated a self-awareness of "silent" bourgeois individuality, a self-awareness which was derived in no small measure from the Protestant search for direct, personal, contact with God. This sensibility was not exhausted in what Hegel later described as a "fading of the beautiful soul into itself," but

rather the "beautiful soul" (in Germany at least a much-used expression at the time) could also realize itself and enter into conversation through the art of rationally sensitive argumentation. This can be seen in numerous epistolary novels, a form which came to enjoy particular popularity and was especially appropriate to a subjectivity which was already taking on Romantic aspects. Other forms of writing also reflected the importance attached to addressing the person, to emotion and spontaneity; thus countless classroom textbooks and philosophical treatises were composed in dialogue form.

Mind and Matter

In his preface to the French Encyclopedia (1750) and his *Elements of Philosophy* (1759), Jean Le Rond d'Alembert set up a genealogy of knowledge. He began with the end of the Middle Ages, which is represented as a Dark Age in contrast to the coming Enlightenment. The Renaissance, according to d'Alembert, was when minds began to be revivified with literary and artistic scholarship and enthusiasm for the ancient world. In the 16th century, the Reformation split the closed religious world of the Middle Ages asunder. The 17th century saw the renewal of philosophy by Descartes and his placing of science on a firm philosophical foundation. In the 18th century, scientific knowledge of Man and nature took a giant leap forward, largely as a result of Newton's discoveries and his "philosophical" method (no speculative, but empirical, hypotheses). It had thus reached its "modern" stage.

The 18th-century Enlightenment saw itself as the culmination of a line of enlightened thinking in the broader sense, namely the abandonment at the dawn of the modern era of the Christian Scholastic world image. At the same time, there were discontinuities in this line, and clear signs that the Rationalism of the Baroque was not always accepted. Thus d'Alembert and his contemporaries followed Descartes where he replaced Scholasticism, and a hotchpotch of scientific explanations often based on mere analogy, by methodical reasoning and the analysis of physical processes. But they did not follow his "idealist" understanding of reason, according to which the "system" of the

mental and the material worlds can be constructed according to pre-existing possibilities of thought, and the essence of the *res extensa* was revealed by the essence of the *res cogitans*. Like David Hume, the continental enlighteners denied the possibility of metaphysical knowledge of essences, and like Hume, they built on Locke's Empiricism. Descartes' dualism of mind and matter, according to which Man, thanks to his being part of "thinking substance," is separate from nature, was also rejected. The attitude of the materialists among the *philosophes* was, however, precisely opposite to that of Berkeley. He had abolished dualism in favor of mind alone, by declaring the concept of "matter" empty. Diderot, Helvetius, La Mettrie and d'Holbach by contrast allowed mind no independent existence, declaring all mental phenomena to be effects of matter. Thus La Mettrie: "I am so far from considering thought incompatible with organized matter that thought seems to me to be one of matter's characteristics, like electricity, mobility, impenetrability, extension etc." In his book *L'Homme machine* ("Man a Machine"), published in 1748, La Mettrie demanded that all psychological processes be traced back to physical processes, and explained Man entirely in mechanistic terms. The Baroque mechanistic view, oriented as it was toward the basic physical theory of motion, was however losing its persuasiveness. After all,

Etienne Bonat de Condillac,
Chalk lithograph after a contemporary portrait, first half of the 19th century. Bibliothèque Nationale, Paris

The founder of Sensationalism, Etienne Bonat de Condillac started from the assumption that all knowledge was based on sensory experience and that there was no essential difference between thinking and sensing. John Locke, on whom the Sensationalists based their theories, had distinguished between simple and complex ideas. Simple ideas came from external or internal perception, i.e. from the perception of external objects and the activity of the soul that this provoked. Locke in other words presupposed some creative activity on the part of the soul. It was precisely this aspect that Condillac doubted. For him, all simple impressions came from outside. Only when a number of sensory impressions had come together in the consciousness was the soul provoked to act, in other words its activity was not independent.

except for example in the case of Hobbes, it had not been invented to explain physical and psychological phenomena, and left open all questions relating to "life." Diderot and others supplemented the mechanistic picture of nature with the concept of organic units, whose possibility rested on a kind of basic sensibility and readiness to organize on the part of matter.

Sensationalism

Epistemologically, Materialism found its parallel in a strict Sensationalism (in the psychological sense to be outlined below). It was demonstrated by Etienne Bonat de Condillac in his *Treatise on Sensations* (1754) by means of a thought model very much in the spirit of the age. The lifeless statue of a human being is given just one of the five senses to start with, and thus, through the appearance of traces of memory (which are to be imagined as linked with the mere possibility of human sensation) and the resulting distinctions etc., develops a complete psychological apparatus.

Sensationalism differs from Lockean Empiricism in that it allows perceptions of things and relationships, as well as the foundations of the mental conceptual apparatus, to arise without any activity on the part of the intellect. For Locke, the "reflections," or perceptions of the internal sense, revealed such activity and were not bound up quasi-automatically with the passive uptake of the external sensations. For Condillac there were no "reflections" as Locke understood them;

all original simple impressions came from outside. This did not mean that we operate unthinkingly: no one could assert that. But the material and the capacity for these operations were formed, to use a modern expression, by environmental stimuli.

Deism and Critiques of Religion

"Man is only unhappy because he misjudges nature." The opening words of the *System of Nature* by Paul Henri, Baron d'Holbach, published in 1770. What he meant was a misjudgment which lay in empirically unfounded expectations of a future life and assertions of transcendental norms, along with the false ideas of happiness these gave rise to. D'Holbach wanted a morality geared to this world, based "physically" on bodily sensations and social utilitarian demands.

Here we see a mechanistic Materialism which has not only finally broken away from Rationalism and its autonomous mental processes, but which also rejects all theology and religion. One can see it as the provisional end to an emancipation process in philosophy (and science), which had already begun in the Middle Ages with the cautious assumption of a dual truth represented by rational knowledge on the one hand and revealed religion on the other. In the 17th century, Descartes and Leibniz, conscious of this division, had attempted to uphold the compatibility of science and theology, albeit a theology with a strong philosophical strain. Hobbes by contrast had rejected this connection. Spinoza separated the central

Feast of the Supreme Being on the Champ de Mars in Paris, June 1794,
Contemporary painting by Pierre-Antoine de Machy, Musée Carnavalet, Paris

In connection with the Enlightenment, the 17th century saw the rise of Deism (Latin *deus*, "god"), a form of religious belief which saw God as the creator of the world, but not as intervening in the world thereafter. The cult of the Supreme Being as the Creator of the universe was inaugurated by Robespierre in order to stabilize the achievements of the Revolution and replace Roman Catholicism as the state religion. The Feast, staged by the painter Jacques-Louis David, began with a procession led by Robespierre and members of the Convention. It ended at an artificial mound, on which hymns were then sung in praise of the Revolution, and oaths of hatred of the monarchy were sworn.

necessities of faith, which he linked to a not exactly traditional Christian concept of God, from the sphere of opinions and detailed articles of faith, and he emphatically demanded toleration in this sphere. This made him an exemplary figure for the *philosophes,* who demanded the toleration of free research, and after Newton's successes sought to exclude God entirely from science. However, the extreme Materialist position remained the exception; it not only met with vehement reactions from the authorities of the Roman Catholic French state, but was also opposed by many *philosophes* themselves. Nevertheless it did give expression to a conviction which in milder form also reflected other Enlightenment tendencies and which can be summed up in a simple formula: Man is nature, and nature is not the image of a timeless world of ideas or the realization of a completed plan of creation. However, human nature could still occupy a special position, and the mental and moral world could still be a sphere in its own right in spite of being anchored in the physical world; nor is the idea of creation totally rejected. Thus the philosophy of the Enlightenment was practically always linked to a direct or indirect critique of religion, but only very rarely with d'Holbach-style atheism.

The ubiquitous and constant questioning of, doubts about, and attacks on religion centered not so much on the existence of God or the religious relationship to a God, but more on what was called positive religion, which, like Roman Catholicism for example, strictly demarcated itself from other religions by setting up a canon of specific articles of faith and supporting itself on revealed evidence like the Bible.

Positive religions in this sense had already found themselves challenged in the 17th century by the assumption that there was a "natural" religiosity (attested even earlier from a Christian Scholastic point of view), resting solely on Man's intrinsic mental or moral qualities, and not on any historical revelation by some prophet or Messiah. By this criterion, natural belief in God, first promoted by English freethinkers, arose – and indeed this criterion had arisen long before Christianity and older religions – from inevitable questions concerning the reason for all things, from a feeling that the individual soul was immortal, and

from the need for a basic foundation of justice which was not subject to any human arbitrariness. These grounds of faith, unlike the beliefs of traditional religions (miracles, specific and often anthropomorphic attributes of God etc.), could, it was thought, be reconciled with reason and science. Thus, natural religion could also be called the religion of reason, and as *the* "religion of the Enlightenment," it was often called Deism. This word was coined from *deus,* the Latin word for "god", and refers simply to the belief in a god which a religion without cult or tradition has in common with traditional religions. Often Deism is held to include the view that God created the world and the laws of nature, but no longer interferes in the operation of the cosmic "clockwork."

Voltaire

Compared with Hume and Kant, Voltaire was not one of the great philosophers of the 18th century. But he was a phenomenon of the philosophical spirit, the greatest intellectual

Company at Table at Sanssouci
(from left: Marishal, unknown, Voltaire, von Stille, Frederick the Great, d'Argens, Keith, Algarotti, Rothemburg, La Mettrie), Painting by Adolph Menzel, 1850, formerly in the Nationalgalerie Berlin, destroyed in 1945

Voltaire went to Berlin in the summer of 1750 at the invitation of King Frederick the Great of Prussia. The invitation followed a wide-ranging correspondence between the two, in which Frederick expressed his admiration for the writer, while Voltaire for his part gave voice to his enthusiasm for the "philosopher-prince". Unlike Paris, where Voltaire was exposed to calumny and engaged in a perpetual battle with the censors, Berlin welcomed him as a leading writer and thinker. But the good relations between the King and the intellectual did not last long. Voltaire felt dependent on the King, who laid claim to his time whenever he felt like it. Those pictured here at table in Sanssouci Palace in Potsdam all had the reputation of being freethinkers. Among them, Voltaire was the most prominent guest. He occasionally allowed himself critical utterances, which Frederick did not like. After almost three years, they parted acrimoniously in March 1753.

The Sleep of Reason Gives Birth to Monsters, Graphic by Francisco de Goya, c. 1797, privately owned

Goya was close to liberal circles in Spain, and certain aspects of his work reflect the spirit of the European Enlightenment. In a number of series of graphic works, he depicts the horrors of war and the fantastical products of unreason. The mysterious thing about these graphics is their depiction of the irrational. It is not revealed, but presented with a persistent remnant of the incomprehensible. Entirely in keeping with this spirit is the ambiguous title of the illustrated work from the series *Caprichos* ("Fantasies"): where no reason prevails, monsters appear and command – that would be the purely "enlightened" reading; but according to the other reading, it is reason itself that cannot always remain awake and, dreaming, releases the monsters from itself. Herein one can see doubt regarding the Enlightenment's optimism on the subject of reason.

Emile, novel by Jean-Jacques Rousseau, Copperplate engraving from the 3rd book, after Jean Michel Moreau

With his educational novel *Emile* Rousseau underlined his thesis that Man was naturally good and morally corrupted only by society. For Rousseau, one of the reasons for this development was a wrong approach to education, hence his demand for reform in the sense of replacing traditional educational methods by a "natural upbringing." Exact knowledge of the childlike character constituted the basis of this reform. Everything depended, said Rousseau, above all on furthering the natural aptitudes and instinctive reactions of the child instead of forbidding them. Thus he turned against the opinion, widespread in the 18th century, that children should be instructed in adult duties at an early age.

writer of the age, an enormously influential man of letters, and the archetypal "enlightener." In spite of enormous and undisputed success as a playwright and novelist, he was arrested several times and expelled from France, and many of his critical philosophical writings could only be printed with the help of courageous printers and complicated tricks (for example the use of no less than 175 pseudonyms). Often enough the books were quickly banned and confiscated all the same, a copy being ritually torn up and burnt by the public executioner on the steps of the law courts in Paris, in accordance with the custom of the age.

Anything but arid, Voltaire's critique was invariably presented with wit and brilliant irony; it is peppered with learned quotations of classical and exotic examples, and lively opinions. It was aimed at conditions in an absolutist state which had become absurd in view of an awareness of human rights; this awareness had long since spread beyond a few utopians. But the chief target of Voltaire's attacks was the absolutist Roman Catholic Church. He charged it with repressive dogmatism, anti-human fanaticism, and imprisoning the people in a state of superstition (which was how he saw most aspects of religion). *Écrasez l'infâme!* ("Crush the vile thing!") was his battle-cry.

Not that Voltaire was an atheist. On the contrary: "If God did not exist, we should have to invent him. But the whole of nature cries out to us that God does exist." And why would God

have to be invented if necessary? Not least because Voltaire believed that Man's virtue or simply his humanity needed a center, a foothold, or, as he said, a bridle. The second sentence of this quotation shows however that he did not just think religion was needed for reasons of expediency or utilitarian social considerations, but that his liberal, and even in comparison with enlightened Christianity, easy-going Deism was based on real conviction. By incorporating a wealth of contemporary and historical thought experiments into a literary framework, and individualizing them by presenting them in dialogue form, Voltaire created a climate in which philosophical systems could be put across as literature, capable of capturing superstition and reason, optimism and pessimism, in parables sublime or else ridiculous as the case might be. In so doing he released a potential for critical detachment, which made a major contribution to the relativization of fossilized and irrational values.

Jean-Jacques Rousseau

Immanuel Kant once described himself in retrospect as a young scholar who knew nothing but books, a thirst for knowledge, and science. "Time was when I believed all of this could constitute the honor of humanity, and I despised the rabble who knew nothing. Rousseau put me right. This blindness disappeared, I learned to respect people, and I would find myself far more useless than a common worker if I did not believe that this consideration could give value to all others to establish the rights of mankind."

Kant regarded Rousseau as an "enlightener," for Rousseau demanded recognition of the "rights of man" more energetically than most of the *philosophes*. While their political goal was mostly a liberal constitutional monarchy, Rousseau drew up a democratic ideal. In the course of the French Revolution, he was venerated almost as a cult figure. His novel, *Émile, or Education* asserted individual rights for children and young people too, and provided an impetus for educational reformers until well into the 19th century. He was in fact the first to "discover" childhood, just as the Enlightenment discovered a sometimes transfigured counterweight to civilization in the "noble savage." The impression

Rousseau made on Kant was matched by an equally strong impression on the thinkers and poets of the Romantic movement, but in their case what made the impression was an aspect of his work which was barely compatible with the Enlightenment. Rousseau was the first to conjure up the abyss which at the same time lay, never quite concealed, at the bottom of Romantic reconciliation and unity: the hopeless division between Man and his nature (which is also a social nature), and the ecstatic emotions of an ego that seeks to say everything and in the process threatens to lose itself. For Rousseau, Man was originally free and good. He lived in harmony with his environment and was relatively independent. (In principle, Rousseau was drawing up the blueprint of a free peasant existence). His feelings sprang from a positive self-esteem which united him with himself and at the same time with others. A social organization which had taken a wrong path had turned this self-esteem into a negative, self-seeking egotism which divided each man from himself and from others.

Rousseau describes this organization in similar terms to Locke, whose own idea of the social contract, however, was designed to safeguard private property, in other words were completely the opposite – because for Rousseau: "The first person who, having fenced in a plot of land, ventured to say: 'This is mine,' and found people simple enough to believe him, was the true founder of civil society. How many crimes, wars, murders, miseries and atrocities would humanity have been spared if someone had pulled out the fence-posts and said to his fellows: 'Do not believe this fraudster! You are doomed if you forget that the fruits belong to all and the earth to none.'" Property led to the division of labor, dependency and alienation. It was a similar story on the mental plane: the transition from nature to civilization dissolved the direct relationship between the world and the psyche, and Man began to brood. Rousseau was using strong language here, which isolated him from the mainstream of the Enlightenment. "The state of thought is unnatural" – "The reflecting man is a degenerate animal."

In his *Du contrat social* (1754–62) ("The Social Contract"), Rousseau drew up a picture of a state in which – to use Kant's words

Allegorical painting in honor of Rousseau from the time of the French revolution, Musée Carnavalet, Paris

Jean-Jacques Rousseau is regarded as one of the intellectual forerunners of the French Revolution. The illustration shows an allegorical representation of his theory in the context of the new republic. Above the crossed Tricolors is the portrait of Rousseau; below them an ancient Roman lictor's bundle of sticks promotes the striving for strength, truth, justice and solidarity. It is crowned with the Cap of Liberty of the *sans culottes*, and alongside, on the trunk of the tree, is freedom as the natural right of Man. Rousseau's *Social Contract* was the model for the first constitution of the French Republic. The maxims of "Liberty, Equality and Fraternity" anchored in the rights of Man and the citizen are likewise based on his ideas.

– civilization had "become nature once more through total art, which is the final goal of the moral destiny of the human race" (by "art" here Kant simply meant what is "made," in contrast to what has arisen naturally.) It is a state in which the people is sovereign, deciding issues by vote, and in which "the individual, although united with all, nevertheless obeys only himself and remains as free as before." This last is a virtually impossible trick to pull off, and Rousseau's concept is not entirely clear. In any case, this freedom consists in a voluntary subjection to understood laws which derive from the "general will." The "general will" is not the same as the "will of all" (which is the sum of all the decisions of all the individuals, e.g. the result of a unanimous vote). Rather, it is directed toward the general good in the same way that the individual will is directed to the good of the individual, and can never be wrong (unlike the will of all, which can be led astray, just as the will of the majority can, by partiality or

Immanuel Kant,
Anonymous portrait, c. 1790

Kant's epoch-making *Critique of Pure Reason* (1781) subjected the human faculty of cognition to a serious examination and came to the conclusion that there were certain conditions anchored in the subject himself which determined our view of the world. He argued that no statement was possible about what the world "in itself" was like (i.e. independent of the construction put on it by the subject), because Man could never see things independently of this construction. Therefore knowledge was not oriented to objects; rather, it determined the properties of objects.

misjudgment etc.). Thus the general will resembles a pantheistic God-Nature, which is One and All, projected on to society. The individual is free, in that he recognizes his own fully individual will to be subsumed in the general will and identical with it. Man is a citizen, and yet once again an individual.

Immanuel Kant

The Critique of Pure Reason

Along with David Hume, to whom by his own acknowledgment he owed much, Kant jettisoned metaphysics as an alleged science of the supra-sensory, in other words as the seemingly logical and factual theory of what lies beyond experience. And yet Kant admitted to being in love with metaphysics. He was convinced it was indispensable because questions concerning the most general definitions of reality, the knowability of nature, God, freedom and the immortality of the soul cried out for an answer: "Human reason goes forth inexorably to such questions as cannot be answered by any experiential use of reason or principles based on it." Questions which cannot be answered *a posteriori* ("from what comes after"), i.e. from experience, require knowledge *a priori* ("from what came before"), i.e. on the one hand independent of experience, and on the other not consisting of statements which are true by definition (e.g. "Triangles have three sides"). Kant regarded such a sentence as this last as an "analytical judgment": the predicate ("three-sided") derives from an analysis of the subject ("triangle"). This sentence does not extend

knowledge, in contrast to a "synthetic judgment," e.g.: "Some dogs are dangerous to people." This statement is based on experience, a synthetic judgment *a posteriori*. Now metaphysics is concerned with "synthetic judgments *a priori*." Only when it speaks in such judgments about the principles of individual sciences or about certain conditions or even leitmotifs of knowledge, for example about the "idea" of the infinite (but without asserting any knowable infinite), is metaphysics possible as a science, and then as a "science of the limits of human reason."

In this demarcation exercise, Kant did not follow the skepticism of Hume. In opposition to Hume, he believed that experience, which arises from the mental processing of perceptions, could not in its turn draw its principles from experience. Unlike many Rationalists, on the other hand, Kant was of the opinion that all knowledge begins with experience, and must make reference to experience in every case. It could, however, be concerned with merely "possible" experience, examining through mental processes alone the subjective acts of obtaining knowledge whose possibility precedes experience, and which are definitive for everything which could possibly become the object. This examination is the task of the "transcendental philosophy" which Kant developed. "Transcendental is the name I give to all knowledge which concerns itself not with objects, but with the way we recognize objects, to the extent that this is possible *a priori*." Transcendental philosophy is thus the formal basic structure of everything that can be reality for us. As it makes *a priori* and generally valid statements relating to necessary features of reality, Kant continued to call it metaphysics in this respect.

Space and Time as Pure Conceptions

The Rationalists were of the opinion that theorems derived mathematically or logically from definitions or from basic original concepts could be applied to the objects of perception, and at the same time say something about the world in itself as independent of our perception and thought of as a supra-sensory whole. This was possible, they thought, because thanks to the disposition of God, who does not deceive us, or for other metaphysically derived reasons, certain simple proofs and basic concepts of thought applied to (mentally recognizable) true reality. Like Hume, Kant rejected this position.

In a dissertation written in 1770 on his appointment as professor *(Of the Form of the World of Senses and Intellect, and its Principles)*, Kant discovered a foundation for the applicability of a science independent of experience (in his own terminology: "pure"), namely geometry, to the world of experience. This foundation was new compared to the assumptions of the Rationalists, and pointed the way forward to his own transcendental philosophy. According to Kant (as also to Descartes), space is not an idea abstracted from the perception of spatial objects. For three-dimensional extension is not a quality of things which is distinguishable by the senses, but an actual precondition for our being able to perceive something as something in a place "outside" ourselves, as an object apart from us, so to speak. Nor is "space" what Descartes would have called an innate concept; indeed it is not a concept at all. Concepts are "general" ideas, embracing many instances. "Individual" or "particular" ideas, which "relate directly to objects," in other words, sensory perceptions, Kant calls empirical *Anschauungen*. (This German word, as used by Kant, is conventionally translated into English as "intuitions," but as Bertrand Russell has said, the translation "is not altogether satisfactory.") According to Kant, the idea of space, although not derived from experience, is an intuition in this sense, "an individual idea, for what one would call

several spaces are only parts of the same immeasurable space" of our imagination, in other words, these parts do not relate to the idea of space as, for example, individual rooms relate to the general concept of "room" or as "room" to the concept of "house." And besides: "The fact that there are no more than three dimensions in space, that between two points only one straight line can be drawn, that from a given point on a plane only one circle can be described by a given straight line etc. – none of this can be concluded from any general concept of 'space,' but can only be 'viewed' (or 'intuited') in it, so to speak in the concrete." But as space is not an object of perception, it is not an empirical intuition, but rather a "pure" intuition, that is to say, preceding all experience, a part of the human sensory and intellectual apparatus, something that in a certain way resembles the data of perception and in any case has important characteristics in common with them. In short, space is "not something brought together by our sensations but the basic form of all our external sensations."

But what is this thing from which we receive external sensations, i.e. sensory impressions, which according to Kant's plausible conviction do not arise spontaneously in our organs or in our mind? According to Kant, we cannot say anything at all about it, and here he is in agreement with Hume once more. Our knowledge is related only to things as we perceive them, and in Kant's terminology, these are "phenomena," but not

Kant mixing mustard, Drawing by Friedrich Hagemann, 1801

Kant and Friends at Table, Painting by Emil Doerstling, c. 1900

Kant led an extraordinarily regular life. He always got up at five, and his day consisted in a regular alternation of work at his desk, lectures, and walks. In the evening he went to bed punctually at ten. Even minor irregularities disturbed him. After being invited for a carriage-ride one day, and only taken home at about ten o'clock, he was very angry. In spite of his intense need for peace and quiet, he was not a recluse. He regularly invited friends to dinner. The conversation would range from "roast veal to comets." He did not like talking shop, however. He preferred to deal with philosophical topics alone, and maybe it was this peace and discipline which allowed him to create works which are among the most important in the history of philosophy.

"things-in-themselves" independent of our intuition. But as space, being the "basic form" of all external phenomena, is part of our own sensory recognition apparatus, it would be meaningless to say that things-in-themselves have extension or exist in space. That would mean confusing the conditions of our knowledge with unknowable conditions; these might include the reason for the recognized phenomena, which can be imagined at most as the limiting concept of material objects. Therefore Kant definitively disputes that space is a real definition of things-in-themselves. (He repeats the whole argument in a parallel fashion for the likewise pure intuition of "time".)

The "Copernican Revolution" in Philosophy

The synthetic judgments *a priori* addressed previously are to be found not only in metaphysics, but first and foremost in natural science and pure (experience-independent) mathematics. The initial question in the *Critique of Pure Reason* (1781), Kant's earliest well-known major work, is about the possibility of such judgments, which are what make a science a science in the first place. For geometry and arithmetic, this question is largely solved by the theory of time and space sketched out above. That the sum of the internal angles of a triangle is 180°, is for Kant a "synthetic" statement like the other theorems of geometry. It does not arise, he thought, by simple logic from definitions and axioms; rather, as we said, we have to construct it in our minds, so to speak. This takes place in space as pure intuition, and is thus *a priori*. The same is true of

arithmetic: according to Kant, when adding, we have to put something together in time. But what about "pure" science? To start with, is the basis of what we know from experience by its regularity, namely the causality principle, valid *a priori*? According to Hume, this principle is purely a conclusion drawn from experience. The fact that it might look like an *a priori* concept, that there might appear to be a logically necessary connection of cause and effect, was, for him, something to be explained psychologically. According to Kant, however, it really was an *a priori* concept: the fact "that" it is necessarily applicable to every possible physical process which can possibly be present in experience, is something of which Newtonian physics had convinced us. "Why" this should be possible must however be demonstrated. The argumentation is similar to that which illustrates why Euclidean geometry is in accord with the "external world." While perceptions are determined by the forms of sense registration (space and time), cognition, which relates perceptions to objective contexts by means of thoughts and concepts, is determined by the "form" of the intellect, by "purely intellectual concepts." "Experience is a form of cognition which requires intellect, whose rules I must presuppose in myself even before objects are presented to me, and thus *a priori*; rules which are expressed in concepts *a priori*, toward which therefore all objects of experience are necessarily oriented, and with which they must be in accord."

This insight has "similarities with the first considerations of Copernicus, who, after making no progress with the heavenly movements when he assumed that the whole host of stars revolved around the observer, tried whether it might not work better if he made the observer revolve, and left the stars at rest." Just as the (apparent) movement of the stars is a "phenomenon" due to the (actual) movement of the observer, the objects of experience are "constructed," i.e. generated, as phenomena by our cognitive faculty. In this process the receptivity of our sensory perception and the spontaneous activity of the intellect always work together. These two "stems" of our cognitive faculty are each, taken by themselves, in a sense useless: "Intuitions without concepts are blind; concepts without intuitions are empty."

Königsberg Castle, Engraving, 19th century, with Kant's house in the left foreground

Kant never left the city of his birth, Königsberg in East Prussia (now Kaliningrad in Russia). He did not regard it as necessary to go on long journeys, and he obviously felt very much at home in his native city. In the preface to his *Anthropology* he wrote of Königsberg: "A large town, the center of a kingdom in which the state institutions of the government thereof have their seat, it has a university and in addition its location allows it to carry on maritime trade, favoring commerce with the hinterland by means of rivers, and with neighboring countries with different languages and customs. A city like this, where knowledge of people and the world can be gained without traveling, can certainly be an advantageous place from which to gain both."

Intellect and Reason

How are purely intellectual concepts or "categories" to be discovered? As they represent the conditions for the possibility of knowledge, they must, in "judgments" (statements) combining various ideas into the unity of a single cognition, and in turn leading to the formation of concepts, allow precisely this combination to be made. Now there are various forms of judgment which differ according to the way in which subject and predicate are combined. The predicate (e.g. "shabby" or "bowler") can be either attributed to the thing described by the subject of the sentence (e.g. "hat"), or the attribution can be denied. It can be attributed to a singularity or plurality; several predicates can be combined disjunctively (with "or"), etc.. Traditional "formal" logic had already classified these forms, but had not traced them back to original synthetic actions of the intellect in a transcendental logic which also investigates the very possibility of the "substantial" reference of true statements to things themselves. From the table of judgments, Kant now derived the table of categories. The category of causality, for example, is assumed as the condition of combination in hypothetical (if/then) judgments.

Kant now went on to undertake the "transcendental deduction of purely intellectual concepts," which uses the "Copernican revolution" mentioned above to explain the "legal claim" of the categories in their reference to things: knowledge is not geared to things, but vice versa. Kant showed in detail how the synthesis of the variety of perception to the unity of the judgment and the concept cannot arise from the object, but only from the subject.

In the *Critique of Pure Reason,* critical metaphysics as the "science of the limits of human reason" was developed above all in the "transcendental dialectic." What Kant deals with here is the "cosmological idea" of a world-whole, the question of a possible beginning of the world in time, the thesis of the immortality of the soul, and other metaphysical questions. These questions were asked of "reason;" reason transcends the intellect (which enables us to form concepts and recognize regularities) in the direction of the unconditional, and can prescribe the goals of knowledge for it. Here, "reason" is understood as a particular "faculty," while in the title of the work it signified the epitome

of all human psychological or mental faculties. While the senses constitute the "faculty of intuitions" and the intellect the "faculty of concepts" and rules, reason constitutes the "faculty of ideas."

The "reason-based ideas" of the unconditional and the absolute unity of all knowledge give rise to metaphysical theses which impose themselves inexorably and yet only have the appearance of truth; they can never become knowledge. Thus out of the idea of the totality of things and conditions there arise "antinomies," in other words contradictions which arise from the (in each case) apparently valid proofs of two opposite assertions. Kant resolved the antinomies by saying they could be traced back to asking the wrong questions. But he did not, nevertheless, regard the arguments and proofs as worthless. Metaphysics generates "transcendental appearance" and "necessary illusions," which are, it is true, seen through by pure reason itself, but, like a optical illusion, continue to exert their effect. Nor should this be seen as something negative, for only through the regulatory idea of the unconditional does experience attain systematic unity.

Critique of Practical Reason

In his *Groundwork of the Metaphysic of Morals* (1785) and the *Critique of Practical Reason* (1788), the latter being his second major work after the *Critique of Pure Reason,* Kant turned to the subject of ethics.

Vesuvius by Night, Painting by Jakob Philipp Hackert, 1779, private ownership

With his *Aesthetica* ("Esthetics"), written between 1750 and 1758, A. G. Baumgarten laid the foundations for a philosophical discipline, which, according to Kant's *Critique of Judgment*, was concerned with the formal and general analysis of the "judgment of taste," directed toward beauty, and the "judgment of mind," directed toward the sublime. This "sublime," widely discussed in the 18th century, extended not only to the incredibly great, but also to the terrible, e.g. "volcanic eruptions in their destructive violence, hurricanes with their trail of devastation, and the boundless oceans in a state of rage." All this demonstrated our powerlessness in the face of nature, and yet (as long as no actual danger blocked the esthetic view) "at the same time a capacity to see ourselves as independent of it," to see ourselves as moral beings, and to "sense humanity in ourselves."

Practical reason, in other words the reason that guides our actions, is identified with free, self-determined, will. It is not different in principle from theoretical reason, but evinces a different use of reason and a different field of operation. The first sentence of the *Groundwork* states: "It is impossible to imagine anything anywhere in the world, or indeed outside it, which can without qualification be regarded as good, except for a good Will alone." Here, Kant starts out from the ethical idea of the Good, and asserts that there is a Good "without qualification," i.e., unconditional. Anything which is not good in itself, but only for a particular purpose or in a particular context, in other words "qualified" by circumstances, is useless as a criterion of morality. He thus dismisses utilitarian ethics, according to which we call something good if it serves the ends of humanity or some purpose formulated in some other way. For Kant, actions cannot be judged by their consequences, which are ultimately never predictable. But how then can good will be judged? By what is it characterized? Not least by its independence of personal inclinations and needs, and in addition by its independence of inclinations in general, even though they may be free of obvious self-interest and, viewed pragmatically, seen to be of general use, such as for example philanthropy.

A will undetermined by inclinations subordinates itself to "duty." The commands of duty express themselves in imperative rules of action ("Do this and this.") Any command or law which would be morally binding on any reasonable being at any time, Kant calls a "categorical" imperative (in other words, unconditional, context-free). If there is a supreme practical or moral principle which can be derived *a priori* and not from experience, it must be in the form of a categorical imperative in this sense. In its generality and freedom from prior purposes, it must not contain any specific injunctions, but must only relate to the "form" of rules of action. It states (in one of the various versions in which Kant formulated it): "Act in such a way that the maxim of your will could at all times be the principle of general law." By way of explanation: maxims are an individual's subjectively self-imposed rules of action, such as for example: "Always tell the truth;" by "law" in this context is meant not civil law and legislation, but law which has the necessary validity of natural laws.

For Kant the categorical imperative, the law that makes the will which obeys it unconditionally good, is perfectly familiar to all of us, albeit not necessarily in any explicit form. The awareness of the law is thus a fact, and indeed "the only fact of pure reason which proclaims itself as legislating from the beginning." Kant celebrates this fact in a famous sentence: "Two things fill the spirit with ever new and increasing wonder and awe the more often and the more continuously I contemplate them: the starry sky above me and the moral law within me."

Critique of Judgment

In this third major work (1790), Kant concerned himself with the *a priori* principle of the faculty of judgment, which allows us to subsume individual instances (e.g. individual perceptions) under given general concepts, or to discover general rules which cover a multitude of individual instances. This principle is that of "purposiveness," understood in a particular sense. Thus in its search for regularities, natural science – in particular biology, which is concerned with organic relationships – always looks at nature as though it were in a sense "constructed," that is to say, thought up by an intellect which is free to set goals.

The first part of the *Critique of Judgment* is taken up by Kant's epoch-making esthetic theory. Beauty in art and nature is the subject of "judgments of taste," in which the function of reflective judgment is revealed particularly clearly. When we perceive something beautiful as such with "disinterested pleasure" (i.e. without an all-consuming interest in the beautiful "object"), our reflective judgment seeks a general rule of the unity of the manifold, a concept, in a sense an "explanation," for the special quality of this particular spectacle, albeit without ever conclusively finding anything of the sort. In the process, a "free play" of the two faculties of imagination and intellect unfolds. Both must co-operate in a particular way in every objective act of cognition, which judges an object perceived in context by means of thought (whereby the imagination has the function of putting the "sensory data" of perception together to form a whole). The judgment of taste, however, does not express any act of cognition; beauty is not an objective quality of the thing perceived. However in this judgment there is certainly an "awareness" of a harmonious, in itself purposive, albeit inconclusive interplay between intellect and imagination. This "interplay" – which is what "generates" the object as an "esthetic" object in the first place – is based in a purposiveness of what we perceive as beautiful. But this purposiveness only exists in respect of our judgment; the beauty itself has no purpose. What we judge therefore is a "purposiveness without purpose," in other words the mere "form" of purposiveness, and this process of judgment is related to our "faculty of desire or lack of desire." Something is beautiful when its perception induces pleasure indirectly, namely by triggering off this "interplay." To be precise then, the judgment of taste judges the pleasure we take in judging.

The critique of esthetic judgment concerns itself in addition with the "sublime," with "esthetic ideas," with "genius" and with "beauty as a symbol of morality." The last-named theme brings out once more the determination with which Kant sought to unify the "faculties of the psyche" and thus, starting from the critique of metaphysical explanations of the world which sought to set up a spurious unity, nonetheless to present the world of experience as a meaningful interconnected whole.

From the Modern Age
to Modernism

The 19th century

GERMAN IDEALISM

The Beginnings of Modernity

The following chapters on German idealism take up the story directly from the preceding chapter on Kant. Nevertheless, to give the book a clear structure, a new main section is needed at this point, so the following paragraphs will comment on the transition from the 18th to the 19th century. In recent historical research, including the history of art and literature, this transition is seen as an important threshold between the eras of the "modern age" and "modernism" in its broader sense (whereas "Modernism" in its narrower sense refers rather to the 20th century).

In the second half of the 18th century, up to the Romantic period around 1800, changes in art and science came to a head which may be termed "secularization" and "humanization." Secularization meant the opening up in biology and cosmology of new dimensions of natural history by way of evolutionary perspectives. Thus, for example, a theory developed by Kant concerning the origin of solar systems in gaseous nebulae, which also implied a theory of the formation of the earth, required the assumption of a period of time for this formation out of all proportion to the younger age of the earth that was generally assumed at the time. Also – long before Darwin's theory of evolution – the great diversity of biological species was gradually being seen in historical terms, that

is to say it came to be understood as the result of long-term changes, as opposed to the assumption of a fundamentally unchanging number of species and varieties. The world became the product of a process extending back into in the unimaginably distant past. In philology, semiotics and the theory of art, secularization is to be seen in the assumption that meaning is created by means of an individual interpretative process which necessarily proceeds by way of the synthesis of diversity as a temporal process, and, moreover, presents a different appearance at different times. Thus meaning is in a double sense not timeless.

The Baroque idea of letting the world represent itself objectively, so to speak, on a vast panel of signs, disappeared altogether. Humanization – not to be understood here as the creation of humane conditions – is to be seen in a boom in anthropology, the science of man, in medicine and philosophy, and in the beginnings of sociology.

Johann Gottlieb Fichte

The first version of Fichte's *The Science of Knowledge* appeared in 1794, 13 years after Kant's *Critique of Pure Reason*. In his own way Fichte continued Kant's transcendental philosophy, that is to say the investigation of the preconditions that are given in the faculty of knowledge itself prior to any experience, and that make objectivity and an epistemological relationship to

THE 19TH CENTURY

After the wars of liberation against Napoleon the **age of European nation states** began, in which a strong awareness of national identity came into being helped by an increased awareness of the conditions determining any particular historical moment.

German idealism, the most important philosophical movement at the beginning of the 19th century, is linked to historical awareness inasmuch as it reduces nature and mankind, so to speak, to history. In this conception history is the self-unfolding of the supra-individual subjective spirit.

Karl Marx's **materialism** was a response to idealism. His critique of the capitalist economic system was at the same time

philosophically significant as a cultural critique relating to the sphere of fundamental labor and property relations.

Marx turned his attention above all to the **consequences of the industrial revolution,** which began in England in the last third of the 18th century, advanced rapidly and led to the emergence of the proletariat.

New forms of the division of labor also arose in natural science, which began to break down into separate sciences and to shed its links with philosophy. The as yet young disciplines of **biology** and **chemistry** altered the image of inanimate and animate matter. **Darwin's theory of evolution** constituted a revolution in the image of man.

Philosophy adopted various attitudes towards the triumphs of science. **Positivism** (Auguste Comte), continuing the Enlightenment's belief in progress, saw the only remaining role for philosophy as being the science of science.

Wilhelm Dilthey, on the other hand, introduced the **distinction between "natural sciences" and "human sciences."** Philosophy, as a "critique of historical reason" and an "application of historical awareness to philosophy and its history," was to prepare the way for the "human sciences."

Dilthey's aim was to get closer to life itself through the fluid understanding and experience of "types

of world-view." Hence he also spoke of **vitalism.** Henri Bergson and, to a certain extent, Friedrich Nietzsche are also regarded as belonging to this movement.

**Johann Gottlieb Fichte
Caricature by Gottfried Schadow**

objects possible at all. Fichte spoke of the "theory" or "science of knowledge" rather than transcendental philosophy, because his concern was with the knowledge of knowledge, i.e. with ideas which are accompanied by a feeling of certainty, and with the knowledge of these ideas and their possibility.

Knowledge only exists where something can be stated about something, where a judgment can be made. In judgments (statements) that which is judged is linked with the judgment that is made on it by means of the word "is" (or "are"), as for example in the proposition "A = A," "the object A is equal to the object A" (the incontestable judgment, for Fichte, that a thing is identical with itself). The unity of this link does not derive simply from what is linked but is based on a unity in the activity of judging. Kant had found this in the "I think" which "must be able to accompany" any judgment or idea, i.e. in self-consciousness. Fichte put it thus: "One cannot think anything at all without also adding the thought of one's ego, as conscious of itself." I cannot think anything that is not thought by me, for "one can never

abstract from one's self-consciousness." Kant called self-consciousness the "supreme principle" and the necessary precondition for any use of the intellect. For Fichte it was simply the supreme principle and not merely a precondition, but also the sole and ultimate source of all ideas. Kant's "thing in itself," which somehow affects the faculty of perception, was a contradiction in terms for Fichte and some of his contemporaries, for the cause-effect relationship is, according to Kant's own teaching, a purely intellectual concept which cannot in any way be related to things in themselves (nor, therefore, to their relationship to our ideas). But if the assumption of things in themselves is abandoned, all reality must be derived from the ego (Fichte) or the absolute idea, the spirit or the world-spirit (Hegel) themselves. The term "idealism" is used to describe this view. The opposite view, according to which things which are independent of ideas are posited as real, Fichte called "dogmatism." The first of three principles of the *Science of Knowledge* explains self-consciousness as the result of an "action": "The ego originally

Rain, Steam and Speed,
Painting by J. M. W. Turner, 1844, National Gallery, London

Turner's visionary late landscape paintings depict the elements as the expression of the sublime and mighty forces of nature. Man and his works are wholly at the mercy of natural forces. Any attempt to change the way of the world is doomed to failure. Turner's pessimistic view of the world and the opposition of nature and technology can be seen in this picture with particular clarity: steam and water engulf the railway train, making it appear the plaything of the elements. The atmospheric dissolving of objective reality creates an effect of diffuse light which makes color the real bearer of meaning. In this way Turner succeeds in building a bridge to the modernist aspirations towards autonomy.

Morning (small version),
Painting by Philipp Otto Runge, 1808, Kunsthalle, Hamburg

Runge had intended to rework his series of pictures *The Times of the Day* as a cycle of paintings illustrating his theory of color. Taking Newton's spectral color rings as his starting point, Runge had been the first artist to create a diagrammatic analysis of color, the color sphere *(Farbenkugel)*. In Runge's view color and light had their origins in God; hence the three primary colors blue, red and yellow, of which all other colors are composed, symbolized the Trinity. For Runge, morning was "the boundless illumination of the universe." At the center of the picture is Aurora, the goddess of the dawn, embodying the eternal rhythm of the cosmos. Above her floats a chalice in the shape of a white lily in bloom, a symbol of creation, with children sitting on it who symbolize seeing and knowing as the beginning of all things.

simply creates (or posits: *setzt*) its own being." For Fichte no general statement of identity A = A is possible without an original "I am I." This "I" is not, however, the empirical ego which we assume to be known to ourselves and of which accordingly we speak when we say, for example: "that is just the way I am" or "I recognize that as correct." It is a "transcendental I," the precondition of the possibility (and a structural determinant) of all knowledge, and as a principle of reason it is not individual. Fichte's idea was, by progressing via the two following principles (see below) and further developments of the absolute ego, to derive all categories of thought such as substance, reciprocal effect, reason and consequence, from this very ego, or to explain them by reference to their genesis, that is to say not to derive each one separately, as Kant had done, from pre-existing forms of knowledge.

What does Fichte mean by his word *setzt* in the principle quoted above? If it were to mean "creates," then the ego would be its own cause. This would be a revival of the old metaphysical concept of *causa sui*. But *setzt* can also mean "posits." In the case of a supposition, for example, something can be posited as a hypothesis and its consequences then reflected on. However, the self-creation of the ego in the judgment I = I cannot be a matter of a supposition and a merely logical formula, in which nothing is said about the actual existence of the ego. The ego "necessarily" creates/posits itself, i.e.

as something that cannot not exist (it can quite simply never be "thought away") and it creates itself "unconditionally," i.e. it is not derivable from anything else. This creation is the origin of all other "creations of being": "Whatever is, is only inasmuch as it is created in the ego, otherwise it is nothing." Fichte called the second principle of the *Science of Knowledge* the principle of opposition. The proposition that what is non-identical is not identical, is just as indubitable as the proposition A = A: "As surely as the unconditional acknowledgment of the absolute certainty of the proposition: "Not-A does not = A" is one of the facts of empirical consciousness, so, just as surely, a non-ego is simply opposed to the ego." Nothing but the ego was initially posited, thus everything that is opposed to it, everything that is objective, is initially non-ego.

But this second principle "cannot be expressed in a verbal formula," it is a non-independent antithetical step in the dialectical sequence of thesis, antithesis and synthesis. Synthesis is necessary, for the first two principles create an antinomy: the non-ego is created "in" the ego, for "all opposition presupposes the identity of the ego in which something is created and something is opposed to what is created. Hence the ego is not created in the ego, inasmuch as the non-ego is created in it. Hence the ego does not = the ego, but rather ego = non-ego." The synthetic third principle reads: "In the ego I oppose to the divisible ego a divisible non-ego." The ego and what is opposed to it are not each unlimited, but mutually limit each other. Subject and object are indissolubly linked with each other. Self-consciousness does not exist, on the one hand, without objects to which consciousness is directed and by which it is determined, nor, however, on the other hand, without experience of its own effectiveness in reality, where objects or events, or the conditions for them, can be created.

Friedrich Wilhelm Schelling

"Everything that is, is in itself one." Not only this proposition, but also its context in Schelling's essay *Exposition of my System of Philosophy* (1801) is reminiscent of Spinoza, the 17th-century philosopher who in his main work *Ethics* (1677) had derived a sequence of theorems one from another in the manner of a textbook of geometry. Schelling followed Spinoza explicitly by adopting a similar form of presentation as well as with regard to particular points in his argument. The "One," however, that he was concerned with, is not quite the same thing as Spinoza's one, unique "substance." For the latter is, so to speak, a static unity of all being, whereas the "Absolute," Schelling's unity, is derived from Fichte's "absolute ego" and is the unity or identity of constitutive polarities of thought and self-consciousness. Unlike Spinoza's substance, "absolute identity only [exists] in the form of knowledge of its identity with itself."

Knowledge is not, however, to be understood here in the sense of the knowledge of an empirical "personal" ego: the latter presupposes the fundamental separation of subject and object, of the knower and the known, whereas the former signifies the "absolute indifference," the undifferentiated nature of these polarities. Schelling nevertheless believed that we are not restricted to speculation about the Absolute, but that it is directly accessible through "intellectual intuition." Kant had spoken of such intuition, an intellectual vision, as a construct of the faculty of a conceivable divine *intellectus archetypus*, a primal intelligence which simultaneously creates (and hence also intuits) what it thinks, but

he had regarded it as being beyond the scope of human knowledge. Schelling understood it as insight that depended neither on sensory perception nor on concepts and deduction, and that could not be taught. What this faculty is "cannot be demonstrated by means of concepts. Everyone must find it in himself, or he will never come to know it." (Fichte) We have a "mysterious, wonderful ability to withdraw from all the vicissitudes of the age into our innermost self and there to contemplate in immutable form the eternal in us." (Schelling) The language of this proposition, with its talk of the "Absolute" in which reality and ideal, nature and spirit, being and knowledge and all pairs of opposites are one, perhaps gives an idea of why Schelling may be described as a "Romantic" philosopher. Subjectivity as a principle of the organically conceived cosmos, the transcendence of the dualistic and mechanistic separation of thought from nature, the blending of the finite and the infinite in the contemplation of art, and the infinite freedom and creative power of the imagination: these are the main themes of the poets and theoreticians of German Romanticism – inspired not least by Fichte – including, for example, Novalis and Friedrich Schlegel.

Schelling also saw in art a realization of "intellectual contemplation" and the supreme possibility of unifying the real and the ideal. Thus the "oldest systematic program" of

Friedrich Wilhelm Schelling, 1775–1854, Portrait by Christian Friedrich Tieck, c. 1801–1802

For Schelling all reality exists solely as an idea of an absolute ego. The central idea of his philosophy of identity is the Absolute; all polar opposites such as subject-object, nature-spirit, real-unreal are united in the Absolute and separate in such a way that at various stages of being (potentialities) either one pole or the other predominates. For Schelling absolute identity can be experienced in intellectual contemplation or, especially, in the work of art, "the only true and eternal philosophical document," which in the first instance is created by man but is ultimately the product of an unconscious creative natural foundation. By going beyond the real, not merely copying it, all art reveals the meaning of the world and embodies the truth creatively in the work.

Two Men Contemplating the Moon, Painting by Caspar David Friedrich, 1819–1820, Gemäldegalerie Neue Meister, Dresden

The painting presents the encounter with nature as one of the central experiences of urban man in the 19th century. The desire that arises in the Romantic era for tranquillity, harmony and redemption from a present that is felt to be problematic finds expression in the figures seen from behind in the picture. By contemplating the moon, the persons depicted feel connected with the universe. The infinity of nature, symbolized by the moon, and the finite nature of human endeavor, symbolized by the uprooted oak tree, are revealed to the onlooker by the experience of art. In this way the divine beauty of nature becomes visible in the beauty of art, the handiwork of man. Landscape as an area of emotion and experience gradually reveals the hidden depths of nature via its surface. Thus by means of its subjective symbolism Romantic art conveys to the onlooker a universal understanding of the world.

Hegel (1770–1831) at the lectern, Detail of a lithograph by Franz Kugler, 1828

Like Kant, Hegel investigated the structures of spirituality. He did not, however, see them in the principle of the ego but rather in intellectual reality (art, the state, knowledge, religion). For him, the development of this spiritual reality was the development of the spirit itself (panlogism), which by its nature is in dialectical movement. Each stage (thesis) calls forth its opposite (antithesis), and both are subsumed (aufgehoben), i.e. both negated and preserved, in the resulting higher stage (synthesis). As a science of the Absolute, Hegel's philosophy claims to be itself an account of the perfected reflective consciousness, the final stage in the history of a universal reason which comprehends itself through the human spirit.

Friedrich Wilhelm University (since 1949 Humboldt University), Steel engraving, c. 1860

The Friedrich Wilhelm University founded in Berlin in 1809 became the model for German universities in the 19th and 20th centuries. Its basic principles were academic freedom and the unity of teaching and research. For Hegel it was the special role allocated to the pursuit of knowledge in Prussia, with its desire for reform, which gave him high hopes regarding his own activity. For his inaugural lecture he noted: "Here education and the flourishing of the sciences are among the most essential factors even in the life of the State; at this University philosophy, the central core of all education of the mind and of all knowledge and truth, must also find its place." However, Hegel did not wish his future activity to be tied exclusively to the university; on the contrary, he hoped to be able to give up his work there in favor of a different activity.

German Idealism (1796–1797, extant in Hegel's handwriting but possibly written by Schelling) demands that in a future state of humanity, "poetry" should become once more "what it was in the beginning – the teacher of mankind; for there is no longer any philosophy, any history, only the art of poetry will outlive all other arts and sciences." The philosophy with which both Kant's dualism of the thing in itself and the knowing subject, and Fichte's "subjective idealism" were to be transcended, was described by Schelling as a "system of identity." He declared this to be the "point of indifference" of the transcendental and natural philosophy which he himself pursued. Schelling's transcendental philosophy bases the possibility of experience and knowledge, the subject-object relationship, on the subject. The object of experience, the "real," nature, is seen here as the unconsciously created product of that same absolute Reason which, as conscious production, creates the "ideal," mind, and thought – and is itself these.

Natural philosophy, with what are ultimately the same premises, emphasizes the objective pole and sees in natural history a chain of development moving towards the ideal and creating consciousness. Finally, the system of identity is intended to resolve the contradiction which lies in the notion that something that is created creates its creator. "Nature is to be visible spirit, spirit invisible nature. Thus the problem of how nature outside us is possible, must be solved here in the absolute identity of the spirit in us and nature outside us."

Georg Wilhelm Friedrich Hegel

Rational Reality

Like Schelling, Hegel was of the opinion that everything real, in the boundless variety of its relations with other things by which it was conditioned, was the manifestation of something unconditional, that the – for us essentially knowable – coherence of things was an expression of the purely spiritual, *per se* infinite unity of the "Absolute." Hegel thought, however, that Schelling had seen the "Absolute" too much as a lifeless "substance" and not sufficiently convincingly as an active "subject." The "true," he said, must not only be anchored in the "being" that is identical to itself, it must also be seen in "becoming."

Thus for Hegel idealism becomes to a certain extent historical when the Absolute, or the "idea," the totality of all rational thinking, acquires something like a history and becomes a process, or at least can be represented as a process. The ideal reality, the spirit changes from simple being *per se* or being "in itself" to "other being," or being known as the other, or even being "for itself," and finally becomes being "in and for itself." The spirit is then "an object reflected in itself, for itself." The spirit that knows itself as spirit developed in this way is "knowledge."

Knowledge, which here means purely and simply philosophy, resembles the evolution of the absolute spirit, which has always been what it is, but which nevertheless only finds itself by progressing through division, opposition and difference. Empirical science, therefore, describes the manifestation of the

absolute spirit in the individual mind – as one might paraphrase the title of Hegel's first great work *Phenomenology of the Mind* – a sequence of stages in which insights "dialectically" negate each other and are subsumed in higher unities. "Truth is the whole. But the whole is merely the entity that completes itself by its development." That does not, however, mean that the individual stages in the process of development, seen for themselves and in relation to previous stages, can simply be described as "untrue" or "irrational." This is also the case as regards nature and the history of mankind, which are likewise manifestations of the Absolute on its path to self-transparency, and which give expression to reason in its process of "becoming." Hence Hegel is able to say, emphatically and at the same time very succinctly: "What is rational is real, and what is real is rational." A natural reaction, even for Hegel's contemporaries, was of course to interpret this proposition as a justification and affirmation of all real, existing conditions and to criticize it accordingly. Hegel explained that this was a misunderstanding: much that is possible in nature and history, he said, had only come by chance to exist in its specific form. It could also have developed differently in particular respects, and in its actual form, which was not the product of necessity, it was quite indisputably tainted throughout with irrational inadequacy. "Who could fail to see in his surroundings much that is indeed not as it should be?" But for Hegel "what exists only by chance cannot merit the name of something real." On the contrary, the "reality of the rational" is that of "ideas and ideals." "Philosophical knowledge is only concerned with the idea and thus with a reality of which those conditions (that are not as they ought to be) are merely the superficial exterior." Thus the possible rationality of changing existing conditions is not disputed. The opposite is rather the case, for the "superficial exterior" of the "real" may be irrational.

Dialectics

Determinatio negatio est, "demarcation (or definition) is negation." This proposition, as formulated by Spinoza, signifies that the only reason that we are able to define and denote as a unified object of knowledge everything

that is known by us, is because we distinguish it from something else that it is not. This is, in the first instance, a matter of simple everyday observation: we are accustomed to define and explain things and words by means of distinctions and comparisons which are not statements of identity and hence also refer to differences. We have of course always inhabited an endlessly differentiated network of definitions to which we can refer in order to introduce further distinctions. But how does such a network come into being?

There could be two answers to this question: since no individual object or concept can be defined positively, i.e. solely in relation to itself, but only negatively in terms of its position within the network, that is to say the difference between it and all other individual entities (which are likewise only negatively defined), all individual entities can only come into being through the internal differentiation of a whole. Then the whole, like Spinoza's "substance," in a way precedes all individual entities. Or, on the other hand, an original individual entity is not simple and indivisible in the usual sense, but, as it were, has its "other" or "negative," which sets it apart, as a quality or attribute. In this case the chain of the differentiated diversity would have to evolve genetically from a primal "duality" whose internal relationship is already a third entity, just as for Fichte all basic concepts of thought and hence all objects of knowledge arise from the absolute "I."

But these two alternatives mutually contain each other. The simple entity in the second version is already potentially complex, while

Ludwig Feuerbach, 1804–1872
Wood engraving, 1876

Feuerbach's philosophical development began with a preoccupation with theology. Unlike Hegel, he was of the opinion that philosophy was absolutely independent of religion. At the heart of his philosophical endeavor is man and the science of man (anthropology). Due to the fact that he regarded religious yearnings as a generic characteristic of man, Feuerbach wanted to reduce theology to anthropology. The fundamental idea in his critique of religion was formulated by Feuerbach thus: "Religion is reflection, the mirror image of the human being in himself." Feuerbach's anti-religious materialism had a lasting influence on the teachings of Marx, Engels and historical materialism.

Struggle for the Cross,
Pamphlet, 1842

After Hegel's death (1831) his philosophy was applied and continued by his followers. However, the so-called Hegelian school soon split into Right and Left Hegelians (also known as Old and Young Hegelians). The Right Hegelians were concerned above all with the system of Hegelian philosophy and the synthesis of philosophy and Christianity associated with it. The Left Hegelians, in contrast, were critical of religion and gave particular emphasis to Hegel's dialectical method. In the context of the bourgeois revolution of 1848–1849 the critique of religion expanded into a critique of contemporary politics. This 1842 pamphlet illustrates the dispute between the two groups. The Left Hegelians Ludwig Feuerbach and David Friedrich Strauss pull down the cross while the Right Hegelians try to hold it up.

in the first version the whole could not be differentiated without a "negative," a difference "in" its unity. The starting point for idealistic dialectics is that any thesis or any concept (in this case: the individual entity) becomes reciprocally included in this way in its opposite thesis or opposing concept (in this case: the whole), to the point where each turns into the other. This then leads to a new thesis (synthesis) or a new concept. Here this would be the concept of a whole in the sense of the Hegelian "idea," which does not exist before it has evolved as a series of concepts that are dialectically developed from one another, and which only then are subsumed in this idea. Accordingly, no detail of Hegel's philosophy can be understood unless the doctrine as a whole has been understood, which is, however, only possible if the details have first been understood. For Hegel, whenever an attempt is made to consider something conceptually, a dialectical progression arises from the thing itself. In line with the idealistic conception of the ultimate identity of subject and object, the thing itself is nothing else than the concept.

The early chapters of the *Phenomenology of the Mind* give an impression of Hegel's dialectical procedure. Therefore a brief account of them follows.

Phenomenology of the Mind
The first chapter of the *Phenomenology* deals, under the heading "Sensory certainty or the This and the Meaning," with "direct knowledge," "knowledge of the immediate" or the "existent." The This denotes any datum of the here and now whose existence is for us an indubitable certainty, whether it is a thing or the particular present moment in the existence of the "outside world" in general. "The concrete content of "sensory certainty" makes it appear to be the "richest" knowledge, indeed as a knowledge of infinite richness." However it will be seen that it is the "poorest" knowledge, and that nothing more definite can be said of its object than that it "is."

Let This be night, as in Hegel's example. We say "it is night now" and are sure of this truth; we can write it down. But if we "now, at midday" look again at the truth that we have written down, we shall be obliged to say that it has become empty. The expression "this", or "now" seems directly to denote objects of immediate certainty, as yet quite unreflected, and also not related to any "ego." Nevertheless it fails to match the This that is meant, which is a different one at every moment. The example is intended to show that we cannot express, as such, that which is present to our senses in its concrete plenitude, everything that we "mean" as "real, absolutely specific, entirely personal and individual things, each of which no longer has any absolute equal." "This is impossible because the sensory This which is meant is 'beyond the reach' of language, which pertains to what is general. Any real attempt to say it would cause it to decay." After the sensory plenitude of the ostensibly concrete, as the This, has become "empty," the emphasis shifts, as regards the certainty of existence,

from "objective" being to certainty, to knowledge. Truth "is in the object as 'my' object, or in 'meaning': it 'is' because I know about it." But then again the supposedly concrete plenitude of its meaning cannot be attributed to this ego, it is also, to begin with, general, i.e. only different from the ego of others, for whom the "meaning" of the This is a different one.

Hence what is meant cannot be grasped by isolating the object or the ego. In the next approach, the "whole" of sensory certainty is itself to be posited as its "being," it is "pure intuition" in which an ego has its object. Now, at this stage of consciousness, the general nature mentioned above, of the ostensibly individual reference to the immediate can be consciously grasped. Hegel presents this as a dialectical triadic movement: 1. The Now is shown, "this Now that I mean." But by virtue of being shown it has already ceased to be, and has become something else. 2. It is nonetheless true that the Now "was." It is preserved *(aufgehoben)* as something that has been, it "is" by virtue of the fact that it is "not" (any longer). 3. This is nonsensical, the negation must itself be negated in its turn, thus the second truth is "preserved," and its is once again asserted, that Now is. *Aufheben* thus means both to "preserve" and to "terminate."

But this does not mean that the first assertion is simply repeated; it is now "something that is reflected in itself" and apprehends the Now as a "complex phenomenon" *(Komplexion)* or "simple multiplicity," which "while being different remains what it is, the Now as a simple day that has many Nows, i.e. hours, within itself, which likewise have many Nows within them, and so on. The act of showing is itself the movement which articulates what the Now is in truth, viz. a result or a multiplicity of Nows brought together. And to show this is to experience the Now as something general." Thus the reflective progression that is presented in this manner is one with its object: simple multiplicity. According to Hegel it was clear "that the dialectic of sensory certainty is nothing else than the simple history of its progression or the experience of it, and sensory certainty itself is nothing else than merely this history."

MATERIALISM AFTER HEGEL

Ludwig Feuerbach

As a student in Berlin, Ludwig Feuerbach attended Hegel's lectures for two years. In a polemical essay of 1835, four years after Hegel's death, he was still defending the latter's fundamental assumptions against the objections of a critic. Then, some time later, Feuerbach himself published the very trenchant *Critique of Hegelian Philosophy* (1839). From then on, and particularly following the publication of his principal work, *The Essence of Christianity* (1841), he was seen as one of the Young or Left Hegelians, as they were already being called by then. They were, directly or indirectly, pupils of Hegel, who to some extent continued his ideas and to some extent rejected them. Among other things they did not share Hegel's conviction, which was widely discussed at the time, that the revealed religion of Christianity was compatible with philosophy. They were thus in opposition to a number of Old or Right Hegelians.

Young and Old Hegelians alike sometimes agreed in their reservations regarding the claims – which indeed in some cases they rejected entirely – of that idealistic systematic thinking which, with its tightly knit structure of principles and sequences of stages of being and thought, had attempted to develop everything that existed

View of the Limmat valley from Mount Hotting, Painting by Gottfried Keller, 1842, Kunstmuseum, St. Gallen

When Feuerbach gave his series of lectures "on the essence of religion" in Heidelberg in 1848, the 29 year-old Gottfried Keller was in the audience. Though skeptical to begin with, he came under Feuerbach's influence to such a great extent that he wished to be rid of his own religious ideas. From then on he shared the view that religion was the ideology of the unsensuous person, who squanders on heaven his earthly energies and capacity for happiness. Keller saw this as a vindication of his leaning towards direct sensory apprehension of nature, and gave literary expression to his encounter with Feuerbach and anthropological materialism. In his novel *Green Henry* he wrote: "There he sits, Ludwig Feuerbach, the captivating bird, on a green branch in the wilderness, driving God out of the breast of man with his monotonous, profound and classical song." Man, when he has come of age, has no further need of God: that is what the novel tells us, that is what nature teaches us. For Feuerbach as for Keller, pain was the source of poetry: "Only he who feels the loss of a finite being as an infinite loss, has the power to light the fire of poetry," Feuerbach noted, and Keller makes Heinrich Lee feel the loss of his mother all the more profoundly and intensely because he has abandoned the idea of immortality.

as a self-representation of the spirit. The Old Hegelians made significant contributions in the field of historiography, in particular the history of philosophy, the Left Hegelians urged the progressive political implementation of philosophical insights. Feuerbach was uncommitted in this matter, but he too was explicitly concerned to apply philosophy to the real world.

Hegel had regarded Christian theology as a direct preliminary stage of the "true" philosophy which he himself had outlined, which was to subsume theology whilst dialectically negating it (but without destroying religion in the process). Feuerbach concentrated, critically and from an atheistic standpoint, on Christian ideas of the relationship of man to God, the world and himself. He accepted Hegel's idea in principle but demanded that his system should itself be "preserved and negated" in its turn. He argued that that system, in its negation of theology, had itself become a theology and had not transcended that standpoint. Feuerbach did not wish to explain reality speculatively in terms of the "immaterial being" of God, the idea and the pure spirit, but rather to grasp the concrete datum of man and things in a sensory materialism. Of his work *The Essence of Christianity* he said that "to reveal existence was my sole aim, to see correctly my only aspiration." "Seeing" and "existence" refer here to sensory perception and physicality,

the claims of which Feuerbach emphatically affirmed. He no longer used the term "sensoriness" *(Sinnlichkeit)* only to denote the faculty of sensory perception as opposed to the faculty of thought. "For me sensory perception is nothing else than the true unity of the material and the spiritual, that is not thought-out or contrived, but which actually exists. For me it therefore amounts to reality," and "the real in its reality or as the real is the real as the object of the senses, it is the sensory. Truth, reality, sensoriness are identical." *(Principles of the Philosophy of the Future).*

The subjective and the objective, sensory perception and what is perceived – for Feuerbach these are inseparably joined together in the experience of existence. Intersubjectivity also plays a decisive part here. "The concept of the object is originally nothing else than the concept of another 'ego' – that is how man in childhood conceives all things as free agents. Therefore the concept of the 'object' in general is mediated by the concept of 'You,' the 'objective ego.' Only when I am transformed from an 'I' to a 'You', when I 'suffer,' i.e. am passively the object of another's perception, does the notion of 'an objectivity existing outside of me' arise." The "ego," Feuerbach suggests, had to be a "You" before it could become an "I." More explicitly than Hegel, Feuerbach wanted the significance of language to be taken into account in this connection, for, he said, it makes

A cotton mill in Manchester, Drawing by Hedley Fitton, late 19th century

Taking as its starting point economic conditions in industrialized Manchester, a philosophical movement arose under the name of the "Manchester School," which advocated a liberal economic doctrine calling for unrestricted free trade and absolute economic freedom. It acknowledged only egoism as the sole driving force of economy and society. Their observation of early industrial conditions in Manchester, their visits to working-class areas and factories, along with the contemporaneous decline of the English hand-loom weavers led Marx and Engels to formulate the theory of pauperization. In *Wages, Prices and Profit* they wrote that the entire history of modern industry showed that capital, if it was not kept in check, was ruthlessly and mercilessly determined to plunge the entire working class into a state of the utmost degradation. A little later, in *Wage, Labor and Capital,* they wrote: "Thus the forest of upraised arms crying out for work becomes ever denser, and the arms themselves become ever thinner."

possible "the realization of the species, the mediation between the 'I' and the 'You'." In *The Essence of Christianity* Feuerbach attempted to show truths which in his opinion are to be found in religion even though presented in untrue terms. "The secret of theology is anthropology" was his way of putting it. Anthropology, conceived here as the philosophical determination of the nature of man, in particular of man as a species, was intended not only to transcend both theology and idealistic philosophy, but also to emerge from them as their "negation."

Feuerbach saw in the supposed characteristics of God merely a projection of the characteristics of man, and elaborated specific correspondences between the (false) consciousness of God and the (true, but hitherto unconscious) self-consciousness of the human species. But this is also a matter of individual experience, and of understanding "being" not abstractly, but "being as the object of being," of grasping it as "the object of itself," that is to say of the particular individual human existence.

In this context Feuerbach emphasized unity of sense and intellect in its turn, and it can be seen how, though an atheist, he speaks in positively religious terms. "Being is a mystery for intuition, for emotion, for love. Only in emotion, only in love does This – this person, this thing – i.e. what is individual, have absolute value, is the finite the infinite."

Karl Marx

Labor and the Real World

Looking back, Friedrich Engels, Marx's close friend, co-author and helper in financial need, recalled the enthusiasm which Feuerbach's writings of the early 1840s had aroused in himself, Marx and many of their contemporaries. "We immediately became Feuerbachians." "To have sensory existence, i.e. to be real, is to be an object of the senses, a sensory object, and hence to have sensory objects outside of oneself." In this terse, convoluted sentence, the young Left Hegelian Marx was concerned, just as Feuerbach was in his dialectic of "I" and "You," with superseding a simple opposition of subject and object as the epistemological "realism" of older philosophy had seen it, while at the same time transcending the speculative postulate of the identity of subject and object in German idealism, with its preponderance given to the philosophy of Spirit or Mind *(Geist)*.

It is for this reason that the materialistic stance for which Marx is famous has been somewhat misleadingly characterized by the slogan-like thesis, often quoted in isolation: "Being determines consciousness." This might make it seem as if consciousness confronted a pre-existent Being, perhaps as a kind of epiphenomenon of Being. Marx, however, in his epistemological conception of materialism – which followed on from Hegel – saw reality not as an inventory of

The Fourth Estate, Painting by Giuseppe Pellizza da Volpedo, 1898–1901, Villa Reale, Galleria d'Arte Moderna, Milan

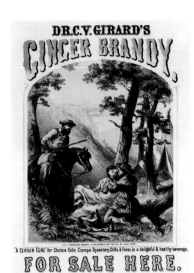

Ginger Brandy, Advertisement, c. 1860

In *Capital*, his *magnum opus*, Marx began by analyzing the dual nature of commodities. They have "use value" and "value" (short for "exchange value"). The latter is associated with the abstract commodity of money and overlays the former, which is determined in living relations with things. From this it ultimately follows that it is not human existence that determines values, but vice versa. The products of labor are like signs which become part of a language that has become unintelligible. They thereby have in their turn an alienating effect on the process of labor. "Value transforms every product of labor into a social hieroglyph."
Hardly anything illustrates this proposition better than advertising and trademarks. They create artificial needs which become ostensibly natural needs and invert the relationship of ends and means.

pre-existing objects, but as a structure of processes in which man and his environment inseparably condition each other, as a product of practical activity *(praxis)*, that is to say as something that is produced.

"The greatness of Hegel's *Phenomenology* and its end result – dialectic as the dynamic, creative principle – is that Hegel conceives the self-production of man as a process, as realization and the negation *(Aufhebung)* of realization, that he grasps the essence of "labor" and understands objective man, who is true because he is real, as the product of his own labor." Hegel was however, as Marx said, principally concerned with processes of consciousness, not with labor as "concrete human activity," *praxis*. But the starting point must, he argued, be the latter, the actual conditions of labor, the relations of production. That was why Hegel's philosophy, he said in language borrowed from Feuerbach, had to be "put from its head onto its feet," because, conversely, its starting point had been the Spirit, from which it had derived all reality.

Marx saw thinking, including the activity of the philosophers, as intellectual labor, "work of the head," which creates products just as does "work of the hands," (be it that of prehistoric man, hunting, cultivating the land and manufacturing tools etc., or of modern industrial labor), and is thus, like the work of the hands, equally subject to the forms in which labor is socially organized at any particular time. This is not realized, according to Marx, by the epistemological realism mentioned

above, according to which a reality that is independent of consciousness is more or less "realistically" depicted in perception and thought. He argued that realism contrasted, in an abstract manner, thinking and the reality which exists *per se*. But this abstraction was a symptom of an "alienation" not only of thought but of the thinkers themselves, vis-à-vis an unalienated state, in which the work of the head and the work of the hands are not separated. Nor could Marx accept Kant's position, although that position made it clear that reality is always something that is produced. In this view, however, the forms of our knowledge and the unity of knowledge and object are rooted in a "transcendental subject", which also makes possible the unity of our ego. For Marx, in contrast, reality arises and exists in "social" conflict, appropriation of nature, and labor. Thus the transcendental ego is replaced, so to speak, by the whole of society as a subject.

Historical Materialism

Marx agreed with Feuerbach in seeing in religion both a reason for and a result of the self-alienation of man, who will not achieve authentic existence if he transfers to God the essential qualities and potential of his own species. Hence Marx wrote: "Religion is the sigh of oppressed creatures, the sentiment of a heartless world, just as it is the mind of mindless conditions. It is the 'opium' of the people." This is not to be understood in an entirely trivial sense: both religion and

Karl Marx in conversation with French workers in 1844, Painting by Hans Mocznay, 1964, Deutsches Historisches Museum, Berlin

Contemplating the history of philosophy, Karl Marx, in his 11th thesis on Feuerbach, came to the conclusion that: "The philosophers have only interpreted the world in various ways. The point however is to change it." His Communist Manifesto, setting out the program of the Communist League, did undoubtedly change the world. In it, Marx defined the proletariat as the class of workers created by capitalism who would resolve the political and economic contradictions of capitalism and bring about the public ownership of the means of production. Class society was to be replaced by a form of association "in which the free development of every individual is the precondition of the free development of all."

Iron Rolling Mill, Painting by Adolph Menzel, 1875, Alte Nationalgalerie, Berlin

From 1870, subjects taken from the world of work appear increasingly in painting, allegorical treatment being abandoned in favor of realistic representation of the process of production. The most famous example of this is Menzel's *Iron Rolling Mill*, which shows what happens at a change of shift on the factory floor. Everything that happens is dominated by the machine, to which the anonymous workers have to be subordinated. The monotonous activity of the industrial process shows up the bad working conditions in the era of industrialization and its disregard for individual human beings. In his search for authenticity based on precise observation, Menzel succeeds in convincingly combining atmospheric and factual depiction.

philosophical systems, on which Marx passes an equally drastic verdict, are not only forms of escape or blindness when faced with harsh, "heartless and mindless" conditions, but in a way the necessary expression, unconsciously created as such, of those conditions. They are part of the "superstructure" of a "material base" which comprises the relations and forces of production. The former are primarily the fundamental property relations from which the organization and distribution of social labor are derived. Their evolution can be traced throughout history, for example in the gradual transition, via intermediate stages, from the feudal medieval order with its fiefdoms, in which among other things the ownership of land and serfs was decisive, to modern capitalism, which is linked to ownership of the means of production (e.g. factories) and the ownership and sale of one's own labor. The "relations" of production (on the more objective side) confront (on the more subjective side) the "forces" of production, that is to say the potential of labor, of technology, innovation and human ingenuity. Then "at a certain stage in their development, the material productive forces of society find themselves in contradiction to the existing production relations within which they have hitherto operated. From being forms of development of productive forces these relations turn into shackles which impede that development. Then comes an era of social revolution." In these revolutions, class struggles are also fought out, for contradictions in the methods of production go along with contradictions in the political class structure of society. Furthermore, the revolutionary upheavals can also arise and develop, for example, in political, economic and philosophical theories, i.e. in the superstructure of the contradictions in the base.

These were Marx's central considerations regarding "historical materialism," which, as a theory of history and society, shows how Marx conceived materialism as a description of reality as process, as opposed to the mechanistic substance-materialism of the Enlightenment. When considering this process, understood in this way, dialectical "movements," i.e. the emergence and resolution of contradictions and antagonisms, are of great importance. In this respect Marx took over decisive elements from Hegel. Nevertheless, he also conceived dialectic as a possible and appropriate "method" for the scholarly reconstruction and "presentation" of history. With philosophical circumspection, Marx avoided seeing history at the same time as an internal law governing the essence and movement of reality. For this leads to metaphysical, or, to put it more correctly, metahistorical assumptions which interpret history as a necessary development, as Hegel, whom Marx also repeatedly criticized, had done. It was not until Engels, and later Lenin, that dialectical laws were formulated, which, in their view, governed history and all material processes (the laws of the dialectical shift from quantity to quality, of the interpenetration of opposites and the negation of negation).

Arthur Schopenhauer,
1788–1860, Painting by
Angilbert Göbel, 1859,
Staatliche Kunstsammlung, Kassel

In the very title of his *magnum opus*, *The World as Will and Idea*, Schopenhauer made the fundamental idea of his philosophy clear. Schopenhauer agreed with Kant's view that man experiences and knows the world only within his own idea of it. That is to say, the world is conditioned by the subject's mode of knowledge. However, there was for him, in contrast to Kant, something on which these ideas are based and which is thus independent of all experience and knowledge, which Schopenhauer called the "Will." The Will is not a goal or an intention but a kind of all-pervading force, the inner essence of things and the driving force of nature. As a "thing in itself", the Will is the basis of reality in its entirety, but it always appears in individual phenomena of the will, which are manifestations of this one Will.

Philosopher, Etching by Max Klinger, sheet 3 of the series *Opus XIII, – Death, Part II*, First impression 1898–1909

With literary virtuosity, Schopenhauer again and again explained the specific goals, aspirations and actions of particular individuals in terms of a few basic drives, leaving events on earth at the mercy of the fateful pull of the supra-individual will, which is not benign. Max Klinger, fascinated by Schopenhauer, adopted this view of things in a series of graphic works, some of which have a dramatic "action." Klinger's "philosopher" arrogantly reaches out beyond the real stream of life and beyond nature, here symbolically fused with the figure of a reclining woman, to a metaphysical foundation of all things. But this is seen to be a mirror, the philosopher finds only himself. The exact location of the mirror (and hence any certainty as to what is reflected and what is directly visible) is left deceptively unclear – a somewhat pessimistic image of philosophy.

Ideology

"The philosophers have only interpreted the world in various ways. The point however is to change it." This famous proposition is the last of 11 brief notebook entries in which Marx formulated his view of Feuerbach and which are known today as the "Feuerbach theses." If philosophy is part of the "superstructure," as was pointed out in the previous section, and merely involuntarily reflects the "base," then it falls short of reality and is unable to change anything. Marx and Engels used the word "ideology" to describe the conviction, which in their view was erroneous, that theories and the changes of consciousness brought about by them, could affect the course of history. (In 1845–1846 they wrote a book, *The German Ideology*, which remained unpublished at the time.) This use of the word does not entirely accord with the way it is used today. But then as now "ideology" included ideas that are put forward in the above conviction: "Ideology is a process which is carried out consciously by the so-called thinker, but his consciousness is a false consciousness. The real driving forces which govern him remain unknown to him, otherwise it would not be an ideological process." (Engels)

Feuerbach, according to Marx, wished to transform the "false consciousness" of religion into a true self-consciousness of man. To that extent his intentions were at one with Marx's own. For Marx "the reform of consciousness consists 'only' in making the

world aware of its consciousness, in awakening it from its dream of itself, and 'explaining' its own actions to it." It is a matter of "the reform of consciousness not through dogmas but through the analysis of that mystical consciousness which is obscure to itself."

But according to Marx, Feuerbach had himself undertaken this analysis in what was still an ideological manner by remaining on the level of reason, of the correct use of the intellect. Marx's concern was to explain the contents of ideologies in terms of antagonistic historical conditions, of class conflict.

NEW QUESTS FOR MEANING – TRANSVALUATION OF VALUES

Arthur Schopenhauer

Like Hegel and like numerous thinkers before him, Schopenhauer developed a philosophy with the ambition of providing an all-embracing account of things. His concern was similar to that of Goethe's Faust: "what holds the world together in its innermost parts." But two of the principal approaches in his thought set him apart from the metaphysical tradition. Schopenhauer neither begins nor ends with God, with Being, with the isolated consciousness or its experiences and concepts, but with man. Man's relationship to the world is, it is true, illuminated philosophically, epistemologically, from the outset, but his knowledge is seen in conjunction with his physical being, his needs and his involvement in the endless mechanisms of life and its relationships. Schopenhauer sees this involvement as vulnerability, as suffering, and with this as its starting point – this too is a breach with the European tradition – his entire doctrine is pessimistic. (Pessimism is here not to be understood primarily as hopelessness regarding the future, but as a negative, critical attitude of rejection towards the world, towards life in general.)

The title of Schopenhauer's principal work *The World as Will and Idea* (1818) expresses, as he himself stated, "the single idea" around which all his writings revolve. The "and" of the title contains part of the point of this idea, for it is a matter of the connection between two aspects of the world, of how we are to experience and interpret it

"The world is my idea": thus Schopenhauer summed up his agreement with the modern critique of the simple realism according to which we see and know the world as it actually is in itself. Against this, Kant had, as Schopenhauer put it, conclusively established that only "phenomena" are given to us, never a "thing in itself." Space, time, and causality determine our world, yet they are determinants which exist *a priori* in us and can only be attributed to us, the subjects of experience. For Schopenhauer "phenomenon" is for the most part synonymous with "idea" and, in contrast to Kant, understood more or less in the sense of "mere appearance": "We are such stuff as dreams are made of, and our little life is rounded with a sleep." For Schopenhauer, these words from Shakespeare's *The Tempest* expressed more than just a poetic idea. It is true that waking life, with its regularity, continuity, and memory, is different from dreams, but in principle the world as idea is dreamlike, even though it is for us a real "veil of Maya" which we cannot pierce. But beyond ideas there is nothing. Here Schopenhauer took issue with Kant's concept of the thing in itself as a kind of wholly unknowable cause which acts on our sensory faculties. The thing in itself, he claimed, is on the contrary something that has no causal relationship (which exists only "in" ideas) to the idea, but to which we do have access in a particular mode of experience. This experience is the physical experience of the self. Epistemologically speaking, the human body is, like everything in the outside world, an idea, yet it is also something quite different, something that is moved according to the will which it itself experiences. What is the actual relationship here between, for example, the impulse of the will to move one's arm, and the movement of the arm as perceived by the self? According to Schopenhauer it is by no means the case that the will comes first and then the movement. The movement and the will to move are "one and the same," but experienced as different data, namely as will and as idea. "The action of the body is nothing other than the act of will objectified, that is to say rendered visible." This can be expressed more strongly by saying "that the entire body is nothing other than the will that has been objectified, i.e. has become an idea."

From this starting point Schopenhauer proceeds to identify an assumed supra-individual universal will with the thing in itself, which, however, as for Kant, cannot be an object of experience and knowledge. Nevertheless Schopenhauer, starting from the analogy with bodily experience, does make metaphysical statements about the will. Just as for Schelling and Hegel, this is a whole, an absolute, that differentiates and objectifies itself within itself. But in complete contrast to Hegel's "spirit," Schopenhauer's will is irrational, blind and meaningless. The will as mindless striving is unfulfilledness, deficiency; that is the reason for its devouring self-movement. It leads to objectifications which in the mode of the world as idea, which originally – i.e. "prior to" man – did not exist at all, take on the form of the inorganic cosmos, then of the organic, animate cosmos, and finally – with man – of consciousness. However, with the emergence of this other aspect, the will has as it were out-witted itself, for consciousness and the ability to reflect entail at the same time the freedom for the will (as embodied in individual men) to negate itself. For Schopenhauer the appropriate form of this negation of what is meaningless was not suicide, which he rejected, but asceticism. However, there is also another way to achieve freedom from the will, at least at special moments. In the "experience of art" all the aims and specific perspectives of life, all involuntary aspirations and needs disappear. Man becomes the "pure subject of

Sigmund Freud, Photograph, c. 1921

Schopenhauer's doctrine of the will had a great influence on Sigmund Freud, the founder of psychoanalysis. Freud called Schopenhauer a forerunner of his theory and described his unconscious will as identical to the "psychological drives of psychoanalysis." Schopenhauer always associated the will with the body (see caption opposite), for in his view man was not primarily a rational being but above all a physical being. There is an inner experience of the subject in which the body is directly present and appears as an expression of the will. The will is thus not known by means of the intellect, but can nevertheless be experienced, for according to Schopenhauer we are much more familiar with this inner entity than with the external objects of contemplation. This account of the will as an inner entity, which eludes the grasp of reason and yet fundamentally determines all activity, shows similarities with Freud's description of the unconscious.

Exotic flowers, Painting by Jean Benner, 1836, Musée de l'Impression sur Etoffes, Mulhouse

Schopenhauer once experienced, as a kind of awakening, his dual notion of being, in other words the "will": "walking about in the hothouse conservatory in Dresden, wholly immersed in contemplation of the physiognomy of the plants," suddenly the very existence of the weird forms of nature (which in some cases had, so to speak, an "instinctual" impact) became a mystery to him. He began to talk to himself, to gesticulate, and when he was cautiously asked for his personal details by the inquisitive attendant, he replied: "Well, if you can tell me who I am, I would be much obliged to you." In his imagination he had evidently become one with the blind energy of the deep source of life, while at the same time losing himself in the lucid multiplicity of individual shapes and forms which confronted that energy, the will, directly and yet were also, albeit ultimately aimlessly, created by it.

Friedrich Nietzsche,
1844–1900, Sketch in oils
by Hans Olde, c. 1899,
Goethe-Nationalmuseum, Weimar

Nietzsche was one of the
harshest critics of traditional
philosophy. Above all, the
overriding themes of his work
are characterized by acute
observation and analysis, powerful
language, a basic skepticism, and
a relativistic way of looking at
things. In his analysis of human
knowledge Nietzsche observed
that man's faculty of knowledge
is marked by a need for
permanence and constancy. In
order to satisfy this need, man is
compelled to think in categories
and unifying structures such as
"Being," "Truth," and "Unity." These
are simplifications which serve to
make the world comprehensible
and predictable. According to
Nietzsche's analysis of all previous
schools of philosophy, the basic
error had been made of dis-
regarding the fictitious and limiting nature of these "postulates."
This observation provided the
basis for his radical critique of
culture, metaphysics and religion,
along with his relativist concept of
values. Values do not simply exist
but are created by human
evaluation. Nietzsche's attempted
transvaluation of values did not
mean that new truths and moral
concepts were to replace the old
ones, but signified the unmasking
of the motives underlying
particular values, thereby making
us aware of their relativity.

knowledge", Ixion's wheel – an allusion to a mythical torture symbolizing both the aimlessly revolving passage of time and at the same time the immutably determined nature of events – is still.

Friedrich Nietzsche
Forerunner of Modernism
In recent writing on cultural and intellectual history it has not infrequently been asserted that as far as anthropological questions are concerned, Marx, Nietzsche and Sigmund Freud, who each in his own way broke radically with intellectual tradition, gave modernism its essential direction. By attempting in their theories to show that reason and the ego were not, so to speak, autonomous masters in their own house, they brought about, independently of one another, an "undermining of the subject." This set them apart from the philosophical tradition which had asserted such mastery – probably more or less in line with our everyday conviction – or had at least conceived it as a possibility and based the belief on that ostensible possibility. In laying the basis for psychoanalysis and a theory of the unconscious, Freud discovered motives and functional mechanisms of human desire, behavior and thought that were not accessible or amenable to self-determination and self-assessment. Marx had earlier tried to provide an analysis of sociological, economic and cultural structures that was in some respects comparable to this, while Nietzsche had represented all values as unrecognized illusions and the product of the "will to power."

In this connection Nietzsche has exerted a great influence on 20th-century thinkers (for example Heidegger and some of the "postmodern" French philosophers, some of whom at the same time date back to Marx and Freud) as regards the evaluation of the subject, the ego, the will and the illusory conception of "Being." It does indeed sound very modern when Nietzsche remarks, for example: "Actually one ought to say 'it thinks' instead of the usual 'I think'," or when he speaks of the "nonsensical over-rating of consciousness" which has been made into "a unity, an entity" and raises the objection that "we are a multiplicity, which imagines that it is a unity," and there must be "a quantity of consciousness and will in any complex

organic entity," but "our topmost consciousness usually keeps the lid on the others."

The "multiplicity" which Nietzsche here sees in the ostensible individual (*individuus* means "indivisible," and hence denotes the opposite of multiplicity) exists for him also in philosophical accounts of the world, which only ever offer differing perspectives, never absolute truth. "Against positivism, which stops short at phenomena – 'we have only facts' – I would say: no, facts are precisely what we do not have, we have only interpretations." The world is open to an infinite number of interpretations. Their implementation always entails a particular mode of existence, and is also bound up with the desire to assert "power." They may also be incommensurable, i.e. neither mutually exclusive nor derivable one from the other. But Nietzsche's work has itself been seen in a wide variety of ways. It was produced in the space of 20 years, between 1869, when he became professor of classical philology in Basel at the age of 24, and 1889, when he became insane. With a few exceptions his books consist of short, more or less aphoristic paragraphs, whilst *Thus spake Zarathustra* (1883–1885) gives an account, in the manner of the Old Testament, of the parabolic utterances of a sage and prophet. Somewhat different kinds of interpretation are required here from those necessary for the understanding of philosophical writings with arguments structured according to strict logic. There are consequently substantial differences between the various interpretations of Nietzsche.

Art
Nietzsche's first book, *The Birth of Tragedy from the Spirit of Music* (1872) put forward, in the form of a treatise in classical philology, the author's completely new image of Greek classicism, an image which was not by any means accepted by Nietzsche's contemporary professional colleagues. It was at the same time a philosophical treatise which concluded, among other things, that: "only as an esthetic phenomenon are existence and the world eternally justified." This proposition echoes in two ways the fact that in his early period Nietzsche was strongly influenced by Schopenhauer. The statement that the world and existence have no justification outside the esthetic sphere links him with Schopenhauer's pessimistic equation of the

meaningless "will" with the world "in itself." Nietzsche was always to remain of the opinion that the will, understood as a non-individual, metaphysical force, was the basis of life, thought and action. The idea that esthetic phenomena, rather than God, reason or ethical principles, for example, are said to "justify the world" dates back to the special role which Schelling and the Romantics, and of course Schopenhauer as well, had allotted to art, and which the early Nietzsche made central to a positively radical degree. He did, however, considerably modify Schopenhauer's notion that in the experience of art the highest form of knowledge is possible and ideas, in the Platonic sense, can be intuitively grasped. For Nietzsche, in contrast, art with its illusions "conceals" the dark depths of the world in itself, but without it being possible to expose this fact as the product of deceptive illusions and false consciousness. It is not only man who needs the appearance of harmony and wholeness in order not to perish from meaninglessness, the meaningless source of life also needs it. *The Birth of Tragedy* posits two opposing poles, which determine art, but also ultimately all forms of life, and which to a certain extent correspond to Schopenhauer's "will" on the one hand and "idea" on the other. The "Dionysian" is pure vital energy which causes the individual to fuse ecstatically with the mass of living things, but which also denotes struggle and suffering. The "Apollonian" signifies form, the ordering mind, detachment, and tranquillity. As regards forms of art, music is ascribed to the former, epic narrative to the latter (with reference to Greek antiquity). The combination of the two poles, according to Nietzsche, produced Attic tragedy. From the composer Richard Wagner, who also published theoretical writings and whom the young Nietzsche admired in the highest degree, he hoped for a renewal of tragedy in music drama, which as a "total art work" *(Gesamtkunstwerk)* would be able, like Greek tragedy, to unite work and audience in a powerful, instinctually confident "tragic spirit" and to take us back beyond all forms of "decadence," which in Nietzsche's view had set in as early as Socrates.

Nihilism and Transvaluation of Values

In Nietzsche's dictum "God is dead," "God" denotes a totality of notions of value, everything that gives closer definition to "the true, the good and the beautiful" and creates a living sense of direction. Nietzsche attempted, in numerous reflections, to trace the historical, psychological and anthropological genesis or genealogy (i.e. the evolution and derivation) of these values and attitudes, and to unmask them as illusory and mendacious.

Dionysus, Greek vase painting, Attic, with red figures, detail from an amphora, c. 490 B.C.

In Greek mythology Dionysus was the god of intoxication, passion, and ecstasy. In Nietzsche's first major work, *The Birth of Tragedy,* his intention was to present the Dionysian principle and the Apollonian principle as adversaries. Nietzsche attempted to show that Greek tragedy grew out of the cult of Dionysus. The Dionysian appears as a primal drive, existing beyond the reach of reason, which finds fulfillment in intoxication and ecstasy. It is opposed by the Apollonian, as the principle of reason, moderation and harmonious order. In the Attic tragedy Nietzsche saw the two forces united, which constituted for him the highest development of art.

The Delights of the Poet, Painting by Giorgio de Chirico, 1912–1913, private owner

In 1903 de Chirico painted his first picture in the manner which he went on to describe as "metaphysical." He noted at the time: "I have begun to paint some motifs in which I have tried to express the intense and mysterious feeling that I have come across in Nietzsche's books: the melancholy of beautiful autumn days, afternoon in the towns of Italy." Along with the mood that he felt in Nietzsche's work and the shadows that play a part in his writings, Chirico may not least have been impressed by a particular passage in *Zarathustra.* In the third part of that work the idea of eternal recurrence appears. According to this idea, every moment has already existed and draws itself along behind itself. This is reminiscent of the strange experience of *déjà vu* (i.e. "already having seen" something), which is not based on any actual recognition, and which is familiar to most people at least from their childhood. If this experience can be represented in painting, then it is surely de Chirico's pictures that do so.

The Philosopher, Painting by Ferdinand Hodler, 1886, Kilchberg, private owner

The painting belongs to a phase in Hodler's work in which he was preoccupied with marginal figures in society. His own depressing material situation is reflected in the way he depicts old men. They are characterized by hopeless submission to an immutable, desolate plight. They thus come to represent a dramatized self-interrogation, which in the painting is intensified in a "literary" mode of expression which gives it a general validity. The self-contained quality of the outward contours and the timelessness of the garment further underline the resigned withdrawal from the world.

"Conscience," for example, he explained as the result of the "instinct of cruelty which turns backwards when it can no longer vent itself externally." He saw charity as egoism in disguise; like humility and pity (and Christian values in general) it was an aspect of "slave-morality," that is to say, of the life-denying and "decadent" reinterpretation by "men of the herd," – i.e. the mass of "weak" individuals – of a "master-morality" which embodied the life-affirming, egotistical natural instincts of "strong" and "aristocratic" individuals. These distinctions, which undoubtedly lend themselves very easily to abuse and which – at least out of context – are more than questionable, are derived from Nietzsche's concept of the "will to power," which the "strong" individual and finally the "Superman" *(Übermensch)* invoked by Nietzsche cannot and must not deny. "This world, a monster of energy, without beginning, without end, this world is the will to power – and nothing else! And you yourselves are also this will to power – and nothing else!"

When Nietzsche described the values (especially those of Christianity), which have of course helped to shape the Western world even outside the religious sphere as "dead," this statement referred not so much to a *fait accompli* as to a process of dying away, which

was still in progress and was bound, Nietzsche believed, to bring about the "rise of European nihilism." This nihilism could, in Nietzsche's view, take on a weak form which merely concealed despair vis-à-vis the total absence of truths or moral values and took refuge in the slogan "Whatever gives pleasure is permitted." But it could also take on a strong form as a necessary transitional stage and transcend itself, thereby bringing about a "transvaluation of all values." Only the few "Supermen" will succeed in this. A touchstone of the Superman, who is surely more of a provocative literary concept than a description of possible individual human beings, is the doctrine of "eternal recurrence" which Nietzsche makes his Zarathustra proclaim. It embodies, in poetic allusions, complex reflections on the problem of time, the experience of time and the conception of Being, but, in brief, says merely that everything that happens repeats itself eternally, without any change or any enhancement. The weak nihilists are crushed by their insight into the meaninglessness of this eternal recurrence, whereas the Supermen "insatiably shout 'encore,' not only to themselves but to the entire drama and spectacle."

Søren Kierkegaard

The first publications of the Danish thinker Kierkegaard, which until the 1920s were virtually unknown outside his own country, belong to the same period as the early writings of Karl Marx. Whereas the latter criticized the older philosophy, especially that of Hegel, from a materialistic standpoint, Kierkegaard – whilst, incidentally, making considerable use of Hegelian methods, as did Marx, notwithstanding all his criticisms – rejected systematic philosophy from the angle of the experiences of the self of a religious individual struggling with his conscience. Hegel's proposition: "Truth is the Whole" was for him an absurdity. There cannot be any such thing as a philosophical edifice which aims to present objectively the true principles of Being and the Whole by way of general and abstract concepts. Kierkegaard regarded objectivity, and thus almost the whole of older philosophy which aspired to objective knowledge, as a deceptive idol. "The desire for objectivity is falsehood," it alienates man from himself. "The only reality of which a living being does not merely "know," is his own reality, the fact that he exists, and this reality is his absolute concern." Truth cannot therefore be "known" objectively, it is subjective, and accessible only in an existential relationship of the individual to himself, to his reality and his potential for being. Especially in religious faith every man is "interested in an infinitely personal way in his relationship to this truth, in a passion directed towards his eternal salvation." In Kierkegaard's existential thinking an important part is played by "decisions," in which man plans his future and puts his past in a fresh light. Such decisions are "moments," a term which for Kierkegaard had a special meaning of its own, namely crossing points of the infinite (eternity) and the finite, the temporal. Man is finite, it is true, subject to time, but his freedom of choice and his "passion for the infinite" raise him in a certain manner above the temporal realm that is subject to necessity.

Since according to Kierkegaard there can be no general rules governing vital existential decisions, and since the particular can never be subsumed in the general, he could not put forward his philosophy in a dogmatic form. He had his writings published under various pseudonyms, in most cases in Latin, not in order actually to hide away as an author, as the "Socrates of Copenhagen" (as he has been called), but rather in order to keep differing standpoints, which are presented with literary artistry, open to mutual influence, as Socrates also did in his dialogues, and in order to encourage readers to form their own views.

POSITIVISM AND PRAGMATISM

August Comte

Positivism rejects any kind of metaphysics and sees the source of knowledge in what can be perceived by the senses, i.e. "positive" facts obtained by observation. As a young man, Auguste Comte, the founder of positivism as a philosophical movement, was for a time close to the social theoretician Saint-Simon. The latter with his followers, had drawn up a social utopia to be based on social equality during the period of restoration following the French Revolution, in which a scientifically based planned economy would

govern all areas of life and the economy. Comte did not by any means belong to this school of thought, but he too regarded empirical science as authoritative with regard to the methods by which it was possible to obtain knowledge in general, and as a basis for progressive social life. He was concerned not least with questions of social history and theory, and can be regarded as one of the founding fathers of sociology. Comte's goal was to build up sociology in the spirit of a positive science. For Comte human knowledge was not, as it was, for example, for transcendental philosophy or German idealism, to be explained in terms of universally valid principles, but had always to be seen in the context of history and society.

However Comte did attribute a certain necessity to the development of knowledge and of the mind, which he described in a model "law of the three stages." At the first, "theological" stage, all phenomena are explained in terms of divine (polytheistic or monotheistic) activity; the organization of society is warlike and theocratic. At the metaphysical stage, abstract principles are hypostasized, everything being determined, for example, by the conflict between Good and Evil; governmental power is held by educated political thinkers. At the positive-scientific stage empirical research and a theory of knowledge based on logic create optimal conditions of life; government is in

The positivism inaugurated by Comte was a rejection of metaphysics. In essence, his philosophy restricts itself to what is real, progressive and socially useful. In his *System of Positive Polity* Comte teaches that the human mind in its development passes through three successive stages (the "law of the three stages"). At the first, theological stage, man searches for the origin of being, for true knowledge, and finds them in a supernatural being (God). At the second, metaphysical stage divine power is replaced by abstract causes and ideas by which man allows himself to be governed. Only at the third, scientific and positive stage can the true laws governing reality be established by observation and experiment. Comte's watchword for positive science was: know in order to predict, predict in order to prevent. He is perhaps best known for his "Encyclopedic Law," which established Comte's notion of a hierarchy of the sciences. This allotted to "social physics" – which he was the first to call "sociology" – the task of investigating and organizing the complex workings of human society.

the hands of scientific and economic experts. For Comte the task of "positive" philosophy was to assess and categorize individual branches of knowledge in terms of their "positiveness," i.e. their certainty and freedom from metaphysical assumptions, thereby contributing to the theory of knowledge.

John Stuart Mill

Mill, like Comte, was concerned with working out a theory of science which would also be fruitful for politics and social science. He set out its basis in his *System of Deductive and Inductive Logic* (1843). Mill belonged to the tradition of British empiricism (especially Hume). For him there could be no such thing as a science that was not exclusively concerned with empirical facts. Along with statements concerning the observation of individual facts, he saw the transition from many congruent statements of this kind to general statements of fact, i.e. "induction," as the fundamental means of obtaining knowledge. Since like Hume he saw the basis of this kind of reasoning in associative regularities, that is to say in a function of the human psyche, the ultimate basis of all knowledge was psychological, even if this does not affect individual instances and does not mean, for example, that knowledge is in some way arbitrary. This kind of psychological conception of logic had many supporters in the 19th century. It was later attacked, especially by Edmund Husserl.

In his *System of Deductive and Inductive Logic* (1843) Mill begins by making a number of distinctions with regard to the function of terms which are still important today for linguistic analysis as the basis of logic and the theory of science. "General" terms are contrasted with "singular" terms, such as proper names, which can only refer to an individual object. "Concrete" terms, which can be directly related to objects, are distinguished from "abstract" terms such as "redness" or "liberty"; "denotation" of terms, i.e. what is described, is contrasted with "connotation," i.e. the manner in which it is described, or the term itself along with its overtones.

In subsequent chapters Mill adopts the view previously held by some of the empiricists of the Enlightenment, that the axioms of mathematics and formal logic are based on inductive generalizations derived from

empirical facts just as much as are all other branches of knowledge: they are always inductive. The notion of a general theory of knowledge, to be given specific form in the individual branches of knowledge, is at odds with other 19th-century ideas, according to which natural sciences and human sciences are two fundamentally different fields.

Importance is also attached to Mill's theses regarding "utilitarian" ethics (*Utilitarianism*, 1861), i.e. ethical thinking which sees moral criteria solely in the usefulness of actions (Latin *utilis*, useful). Here Mill modified the doctrine of Jeremy Bentham, whose intention it had been to apply, so to speak, the methods of physics to ethics. A positivistic tendency can be seen in this intention, and in the rejection of all "fictions" which cannot be derived from terms in the language of observation. Bentham gave his moral principle an anthropological foundation, arguing that nature had placed man under the governance of two sovereign rulers: pain and pleasure. Experience tells us that, as Hume had said earlier, actions are judged according to whether their ultimate effect – which may possibly be reached only by a very circuitous route – is to cause pain or pleasure. An action is "good" if it is conducive to the happiness of the people who are directly or indirectly involved. Bentham believed that moral norms had to be established and laws passed accordingly. He expressed the aim of utilitarianism as "the greatest happiness of the greatest number" of people. A "number of people" can of course be determined by counting, and Bentham believed that "happiness" could also be quantified. Mill added to this, among other things, a qualitative dimension of happiness, arguing that the source of happiness was not a matter of indifference. Intellectual pleasures, for example, perhaps that of looking back on the course of one's life, would, he thought in the long run bring greater happiness than pleasures of the senses, from which they had to be qualitatively distinguished.

Charles Sanders Peirce

In the very title of his paper "How to make our ideas clear" (1878), Peirce gave an approximate indication of the aims of his philosophical pursuits. We have always had many convictions that we cannot put into words but according to which we live our lives

Whenever habitual modes of behavior lead to failure, uncertainty is created, of which we try to rid ourselves by looking more closely at our assumptions and behavior, and by making changes as appropriate in order to restore the tranquillity of undisturbed behavior. That was how Peirce summed up, in simple terms that relate directly to life as it is lived, what we call the epistemological process. This has of course always been a topic for philosophy, which has to do, among other things, with the clarification of ideas. Peirce was principally concerned with problems of the theory of science and epistemology, but he always saw them in the context of practical living. One of the main areas of his work was semiotics (the theory of signs), since in epistemological processes we are always dealing with referential concepts and ideas, and are hence necessarily also concerned with linguistic signs. Peirce sees concepts as rules of behavior. Everything to which concepts refer has a "disposition" to enter into connections, to allow itself to be used, which gives rise to particular effects. Peirce then directly reduces all possible objects to these practical relations into which they can enter. In the paper mentioned above he formulates a "pragmatic maxim": "Consider what effects, which might conceivably have practical bearings, we conceive the object of our conception to have. Then, our conception of these effects is the whole of our conception of the object." Rules of behavior are concepts as the totality of these relations and effects which we produce, or which arise in connection with their use.

For example, we understand the concept of "hardness," if we know how particular things react to the effects of being struck, what is to be done and what consequences arise when we deal with hard things. Peirce assesses the meaning of propositions depending on whether or not they are verifiable in a particular way. This is only the case if the truth or falsity of propositions would make any difference to our potential perceptions or actions. There are no ultimate truths for Peirce, the meaning of concepts extends no further than an enumeration of contexts, which as a structure of relationships do not constitute an absolute. With this view, in which theories and concepts are assessed in terms of their practical significance, Peirce was the founder of Pragmatism, a philosophical movement

close to Positivism, which was particularly influential in English-speaking America.

John Dewey

Like Peirce, Dewey was of the opinion that knowledge and action, theory and practice cannot be separated from each other. Dewey rejected the interpretation of knowledge as a form of intuition, as it had frequently been seen in the philosophical tradition. This applied not only to a more or less mystical vision of ideas in the Platonic sense, but also in general to any analogy between seeing and knowing. Truth cannot be "seen" as an image of reality, it is not independent of context, of people and events. Truth is always a merely provisional response which extends our capacity for action when faced with problems that arise in particular situations. From the epistemological positions of Pragmatism, Dewey developed his so-called Instrumentalism. True statements are to be understood as suitable instruments for solving problems and are only true by virtue of this. But that does not in any way mean that Dewey accepted the voluntarist view that "what is useful to us is true." This view entails deciding the matter on the basis of subjective aims. But the network of functional relationships of the human organism, the environment, and interaction is a very dense one, and even if within this network truths are, to some extent, only tentative, not resting on any absolutely fixed point, they do have a certain objectivity.

A crowd of over a million people on the Coney Island bathing beach, Photograph, 1940

Even before the turn of the century, crowds of people and cavernous streets in the first rows of huge high-rise buildings were much sought after as photographic subjects intended to show the spectacular new appearance of modern America. As far as John Dewey, for example, is concerned, American pragmatism can surely not be thought of in complete isolation from the particular conditions, demands and social structures of this densely populated Western nation. Perhaps Dewey's philosophy even reflected the "unlimited opportunities" with which America is proverbially associated, when he used logical methods and rational thought as instruments for the solution of variable problems, rather than directing his attention to eternal truths.

The End of Philosophy?

The 20th Century

From the 19th to the 20th Century

20th-century philosophy is no longer confident of its right to exist. The catastrophes of our age have not only affected philosophers' own lives in many ways, but have also dealt a more lasting blow to their faith in the reality of reason, far more so than the experience of the estrangement between the old and the new in the age of revolutions was able to do. Philosophy has therefore, unlike classical idealism, lost confidence in its ability to heal that estrangement in the realm of thought. On the contrary, its most significant voices proclaim their own abdication, whether in favor of art, science or politics. More than in any previous age, the great philosophers now vociferously and unanimously sought salvation outside philosophy. Paradoxically this manifest self-negation goes hand in hand with an unprecedented determination to make philosophy into an academic subject with a "scientific" basis. Never before have there been more people in the universities and academies of the world for whom philosophy is their main occupation, never before have there been so many separate individual philosophical disciplines – disciplines which now need specialists to survey them in their entirety.

The first major blow to the its self-confidence to which 20th-century philosophy responded came above all from the work of three men: Karl Marx, Friedrich Nietzsche and Sigmund Freud. Marx had shown that the capitalist economic system is governed by laws of its own which cannot be controlled by reason and which create the potential for an imminent crisis. Nietzsche had unmasked the belief of the Enlightenment in human self-determination as nothing more than the product of the desire for power. Finally Freud proceeded to cast doubt on man's rational ability to control his own inner self, his emotions and instincts, by describing them as the forms taken by a ubiquitous sexual drive. All these ideas radically questioned the power of reason: in central areas of man's self-understanding it had turned out that it was not the self-assured subject but rather blind forces that were in control. The response of philosophy to this challenge varied: in some cases it led to the abdication of reason, in others to a radical restatement of the goals and beliefs of the Enlightenment, in order to face up to the powerful onslaught to which they had been subjected by those great enlighteners Marx, Freud, and Nietzsche. Even as regards the broad general public, by the late 19th century the belief that the world could be shaped by reason had begun to crumble as man was compelled to see himself, with fewer and fewer reservations, as part of the functional network of modern industrial societies. The First World War merely brought out into the open once and for all the fact that there was nothing left in the bourgeois notion of progress with which to oppose the destructive forces of the present.

THE 20TH CENTURY

The historian Eric Hobsbawm called the 20th century the **Age of Extremes.** Indeed, in no century have progress and regression, war and peace, enlightenment and barbarity co-existed so closely, both temporally and spatially, as in the 20th century.

The two major ideologies of the century, **fascism** and **communism,** brought men under the sway of the belief that they could control the course of history. The Second World War unleashed by Germany and the murder of European Jews constituted a break with civilization which gave the lie once and for all to the promise of political salvation for the Western world. The struggle between the opposing systems of capitalism and communism was eventually won by capitalism.

In the field of culture, an avant-garde art and literature began at an early stage to break the autonomous, enlightened bourgeois subject of the 19th century down into its component parts.

By the end of the 20th century, thanks to electricity, gramophone records, the telephone, television, PCs and the Internet, a **commercialized mass culture** had reached even the remotest corners of the earth. Since the student protests of the 1960s, conceptions of life geared to the existential experience of the self have to an increasing degree replaced the inflexible role models of modern industrial society. The **theory of relativity** and **quantum theory**

Thales of Miletus, Hans Arp, 1952, private collection

along with the discovery of **DNA** were the central scientific discoveries of the 20th century.

Philosophy faced up to the upheavals of the age. The certainties of the Enlightenment and Positivism were questioned. **The new topics** of **Life, Language and Society** moved into the center of **philosophical reflection.** Language became the principal topic of philosophy, because it seemed that the unity of experience within the multiplicity of possible perspectives could only be found, if at all, in linguistic communication. The guiding concept of "Life" took into account that, with the irreversible breakdown of traditional communities, a source of spontaneous vital energy had also been blocked off. Finally, society became a topic of philosophy because the multifaceted dependence of each individual on the world could no longer be credibly described in terms of theological concepts.

The spirit of the age was marked by the discontents of civilization and technology, along with mistrust of Enlightenment and rationalism. These were also the basic sources which nourished vitalism. The head-on confrontation with reason gave rise to that vitalist dualism which opposed the dynamic principle of life to the principle of rationality that had come to be felt as ossified.

Vitalism

The Frenchman Henri Bergson, probably the best-known vitalist philosopher, distinguished two fundamental principles of reality with two corresponding kinds of movement: Life, with its urgent rising movement, and dead matter with its falling movement. Matter is passive and can be known and manipulated with the aid of the scientific intellect. Life, in contrast, possesses an unruly energy which allows it to impose its will on matter: the *élan vital*. This *élan* is the dynamic force operating in all living things, creating life out of inanimate matter. Thus Bergson understood evolution not as the blind workings of random chance, but as a purposeful process in which life in the course of its development compels matter to yield higher and higher forms.

According to Bergson, society is also marked by the dualism of rigidity and dynamism. A fixed, dead morality provides rules for the masses, making it possible for them to function as cogs in the great mechanism of society. A fluid, living morality is reserved for the great individuals, heroes and saints, who are enabled by their intuitive insight into life as a whole to strike out on new paths. A similar distinction applies with regard to religion. The mind makes man's mortality endurable for him by inventing idols which promise him a deceptive security. True religiosity, in contrast, is mystical. It turns half-knowingly to the origin of the stream of life and detaches itself meditatively from the world of matter. Thus in the combination of elitist cultural critique and glorification of the irrational, a fundamental skepticism on the part of vitalism with regard to modern mass society found expression. Politically, it took the form of a profoundly anti-democratic way of thinking.

Phenomenology

A widespread discontent with the rationalism of the modern age also led to a fresh

start in Germany. At the beginning of the 20th century the younger generation was disillusioned with the sterility of academic philosophy, with its neo-Kantian orientation, which offered them an epistemology but not the concrete plenitude of life. It was Edmund Husserl's motto "To the things themselves!" which promised to restore life to philosophy. Unlike vitalism, phenomenology, as Husserl called his enterprise, was far removed from the cult of the irrational. On the contrary, having been trained as a mathematician and scientist, he always set store by the most stringent methodological controls in his thinking and meticulous, not to say laborious, care in presentation. Husserl's goal was to reconstruct philosophy as a strict science, starting with secure foundations. To this end he demanded that the natural stance towards the world be

The Philosopher, Ljubov Sergeyevna Popova, 1915, Russian State Museum, St. Petersburg

The 20th century is an era which was perceived as an age of enormous acceleration and the breakdown of a unified perspective from which to view the world. Both trends, which also affected philosophy, are succinctly expressed in Cubism. Perspective is broken down into innumerable individual perspectives, which exist side by side and no longer add up to the picture of a whole. At the same time it reveals an unprecedented dynamism of change, creating the impression that the perspectives are in constant flux. The response of philosophy to these tendencies was for the most part ambiguous. Either it welcomed, as did logical positivism for example, the dynamic progress of science and technology, while however rejecting the plurality of modes of knowledge. Or else it regarded progress as a disaster and accepted epistemological perspectivism, as did for example Heidegger.

abandoned and the existence of the outside world "bracketed." For the only thing that is certain is how things appear, not how they are in themselves. Phenomenology thus establishes its secure standpoint by strict methodological restriction to the direct evidence of what appears in consciousness, i.e. "phenomena."

Husserl's decisive insight was that consciousness is "intentionally" structured. Consciousness is not passive perception but a purposeful act. When somebody becomes conscious of something, he actively constitutes it as a particular thing. Kant had already urged this point against empiricism. Husserl then investigated, step by step, how an object is constituted in consciousness. In *Logical Investigations,* which is considered to be his main work, he began by turning his attention to the nature of logical and mathematical objects. Later, he also investigated our consciousness of time and, towards the end of his life, when he was ostracized because of his Jewishness, the constitution of the social world. It may be somewhat difficult today to understand the enthusiasm aroused by phenomenology at the time. But it must be remembered that – in principle at least – it made the entire plenitude of the world of experience accessible once more to a philosophy which had previously believed that it had to be modestly content with epistemology. However, it was above all Husserl's students and followers who fulfilled his promise of a return to things themselves and applied the phenomenological method to concrete contents of consciousness. Thus a rich phenomenological tradition came into being, especially in France, which continues to the present day. Whilst Husserl had already worked on the structure of the scope of human perception, the turn towards Existentialism which phenomenology took in France was expressed with particular clarity in the early major work by Maurice Merleau-Ponty *The Phenomenology of Perception* (1945). He began there by taking issue with psychological *Gestalt* theory in order to show that perception cannot be understood either in a sensual manner as mere processing of sensory data, nor in an idealist fashion as the outcome of constitutive processes in consciousness. On the contrary, perception is an active process in which the subject discovers his world for himself. As in an Impressionist painting, the structure of objects is not unambiguously fixed, but nor is it completely arbitrary. Thus in an Impressionist picture, for example by Monet, we see a cathedral because this is one of the possibilities that are culturally available to us of giving meaning to the confused mass of dots of which the picture consists. Perception thus transcends the dualism of mind and body, because perceptible objects can ultimately only be understood in relation to a subject which intervenes physically in the world.

The Persistence of Memory,
Painting by Salvador Dalí, 1931,
The Museum of Modern Art, New York

The dualism of space and time occupies a central position in Bergson's philosophy. Space is the medium of the natural sciences and technology: because all points in space are indistinguishable, any spatial event that has been scientifically described can in principle be replicated by technological means. This however presupposes that time is also conceived by science as "space-like." Science merely measures successive changes in the position of bodies in space. But the essence of time is to create new things continuously. No point in time is the same as any other. Dalí's picture is also based on insight into the true nature of time, which was described by Bergson as "duration." "Duration" catches up with the exact measuring instruments (clocks) which attempt to bring time under control. For its organic flow is not measurable, it can only be grasped by intuition.

Existentialist Philosophy

Phenomenology also gave rise to one of the most influential philosophical movements of the 20th century, a movement which many indeed see as *the* philosophy of the 20th century: Existentialism. The generation born around the turn of the century had been disillusioned by the First World War. They no longer cared anything for the bourgeois ideals of their fathers, nor had they any interest in the Church. In their eyes man, in his quest for the meaning of existence, had nothing but his own resources. The freedom to choose his own life and the danger of choosing wrongly: these matters are of central importance in the work of the Existentialist philosophers Martin Heidegger, Karl Jaspers and Jean-Paul Sartre.

Heidegger was undoubtedly one of the most important philosophers of the 20th century. His world-wide influence in that century can only be compared to that of Ludwig Wittgenstein, although his philosophy – like that of Wittgenstein – is couched in highly abstruse language and demands considerable prior knowledge of the subject. Heidegger's thinking also brought him for a time into the orbit of National Socialism, because he thought that Hitler's movement was a resolute attempt to rise above the degeneracy of the modern age. He rapidly realized his mistake and in 1934 resigned after one year as Rector of the University of Freiburg. Nevertheless, he never subsequently dissociated himself publicly from his earlier commitment to National Socialism. It was this silence that many of his enemies, and also former friends, were never able to forgive.

The subject of his major work *Being and Time,* which in 1927 made him, so to speak, famous overnight, is an analysis of human existence and its temporality. In it, following the phenomenological method of his teacher Husserl, he investigated the fundamental structures of human existence, the "existentials" *(Existenzialien).* These "existentials" describe, in the first instance, a relationship of man to space and time which is fundamentally different from the mode of existence of things. Being is always "being in the world," that is to say, it entails a relationship to a pre-existent environment with its own quite specific quality as regards existence. Hence the world is always "disclosed"

An Existentialist development of phenomenology in France originated with Emmanuel Levinas. He studied with Husserl and Heidegger, whose thinking was to have a lasting influence on his philosophy. But it was the particular combination of phenomenology and Jewish mysticism to which he turned with increased intensity after the experience of the Holocaust, which gives his thinking its special quality. Levinas's ethics are rooted in the gaze of the Other, which creates an infinite commitment for us. The Other, by means of his/her face, establishes obligations for us in such a way that feelings of guilt become a fundamental element in the human condition. For Levinas the experience of the Absolute is rooted in the knowledge that we have an unconditional desire to fulfill these obligations, but ultimately lack the ability to do so.

(erschlossen) in one way or another. However, existence cannot choose a predisclosed world for itself; it is "thrown" into the world. But existence that has been thrown into the world is not tied to any particular manner of being. It must first, at every moment and in every decision, make itself into what it wants to be. Heidegger gives the name of "concern" *(Sorge)* to this "existential," the fact that existence is "that Being which is concerned in its being with its being." In concern, the temporality of human existence, the knowledge of our own mortality, becomes visible. Existence is a "being unto death." Were it not for the certainty of death, were existence not "held out into Nothingness," there would not be the danger of wrongly choosing one's own authentic life. But as things are, only by being "resolute" can we escape inauthenticity, the helpless dependence on "Them." However, Heidegger leaves open the question of "resolute to what end?"

Analysis of existence is the subject of the first half of *Being and Time.* The second half was never published. However, the philosophy of the late Heidegger, following the so-called "change of direction" in the mid 1930s, can be understood as a further development of the approach in *Being and Time.* For the question to which *Being and Time* was intended to provide an answer and which Heidegger pursued throughout his life, was "What is Being?" According to Heidegger, traditional philosophy cannot answer this question because it

Existentialism goes back to Søren Kierkegaard, who used the word "existence" to denote man's relationship to himself. Despair when faced with the arbitrariness of hedonistic conceptions of life and anxiety in view of the absence of binding criteria for ethical behavior were given artistic expression by Edvard Munch. For Kierkegaard they could only be overcome by an awareness of divine grace. For mid 20th-century man this awareness was no longer available, and writers such as Sartre and Camus made the absence of divine assistance in the search for bearings in the world a major theme of their work. The atheistic rhetoric with which they presented their insights gave a new intellectual sense of direction to a whole generation of young people after the Second World War.

has "forgotten" Being. Western metaphysics in particular has failed to recognize Being by trying to describe Being *(das Sein)* or God as the highest and most perfect existing thing *(das Seiende)*. But Being is separated from "existing things" by an "ontological difference." It is not something that finds itself existing in the world, but it is that which causes the "things that exist" to have any existence. It is the active source of everything that is. Hence even the fact that Western philosophy has forgotten Being is something that has been brought about by Being itself. For Being itself, so to speak, punishes Western man, who has made himself master of the world, for his arrogance by withholding itself from him. The late Heidegger's philosophy can be understood as one long appeal for modesty, for precise attention to the quiet messages of Being, which, as he admits, is the vocation of the poet rather than the philosopher. Only when man has learned to be "calm," when he no longer tries, with the aid of technology, to bend nature to his will, only then will he be able to carry out his task as the "guardian of Being."

Unlike Heidegger, Karl Jaspers, who was initially a psychiatrist, took the unreliability of the world, which threatens the individual with failure, as the starting point of his thought. In the "extreme situations" *(Grenz-situationen)* of death and chance, guilt and struggle we see that we cannot rely completely on anything in the world. There is always an ultimate gulf remaining between subject and object, between us and that to which we relate. Jaspers calls on modern man to acknowledge this gulf and to take hold of his existence in a responsible manner. For it is all too easy to close one's eyes to the inescapability of failure and to console oneself with ideological or religious phantoms. Failure is then experienced merely as a blow dealt by Fate, not as a fundamental condition of human existence. For failure is the corollary of human freedom, which in extreme situations forces us ineluctably to choose between good and evil, between being ourselves and being alienated from ourselves. In this situation we are most likely to obtain a sense of the "encompassing" *(das Umgreifende)* which bridges the gulf between subject and object by encompassing both of them. The "encompassing" can, however, never be experienced directly. We only catch a gleam of it in "ciphers of transcendence," after which it immediately withdraws from us again. Thus it is above all in loving concern for others, in existential communication, that man can seize the opportunity to be himself. It was Jaspers's pessimistic, yet profoundly humane seriousness that enabled him to embody, as it were, the conscience of the nation in postwar Germany, a role which he used above all to keep awake an awareness of the guilt which the Germans had incurred during the era of National Socialism.

Jean-Paul Sartre occupied an even more prominent public position in French politics. Indeed he became to a virtually unique degree the epitome of the committed intellectual. Again and again Sartre became involved in public disputes – as, for example, in 1968, when he joined protesting students distributing leaflets. He also pursued a fruitful career as the author of novels, filmscripts and plays, for which he was awarded the Nobel Prize for Literature in 1964. However, he refused to accept it.

His relationship with Simone de Beauvoir, the founder of philosophical feminism, provided an often emulated model of an open relationship between a couple. Sartre was thus more than a philosopher, he was the inventor of existentialism as a world-view. Although he greatly admired Heidegger and saw himself as following in his footsteps, Heidegger entirely failed to understand him, for Sartre was not primarily interested in ontology but wished to create a philosophy of the subject for modern times. Human freedom played a key role in this. "Man is condemned to be free" is one of his most famous pronouncements. Nothing and nobody can take his decisions for him, he himself is solely responsible for his life. However, the idea that human life cannot be given any meaning from the outside is only part of Sartre's philosophy. For in his view the only legitimate response to this situation is "commitment." The content of this commitment remained vague to begin with, even though Sartre always sympathized with Marxism. In his stage plays he vividly illustrated the moral dilemma which arises from the necessity of being completely free and at the same time wholly committed. The characters in the novels and plays of Albert Camus find themselves in a similar situation. Camus describes this situation as absurd, because the world constantly resists man's unreasonable expectation that it should be rational. Thus there is nothing else for man to do but confront this world devoid of meaning with pride and to assert, with his head held high, the legitimate human demand for meaning, while aware that that demand cannot be met.

In his theoretical major work *Being and Nothingness* (1943) Sartre characterized human existence as "being for itself," as distinct from the "being in itself" of mere objects. Being for itself "is what it is not and not what it is." The second part of this paradoxical proposition conveys the idea that man is never completely defined by what he has – hitherto – been. Human existence constitutes a break in the seamlessness of Being, a Nothing *(néant)*, for man is the only existing entity which has no pre-given nature, no essence, but only existence. He himself can and must acquire his being, by repudiating his past and projecting himself into the future. This is the point of the first part of the paradoxical proposition. Thus man at every moment has to take the decision to choose his life anew – and he must also accept full responsibility for the consequences of that decision.

Being and Nothingness was a philosophical bestseller, not least because of its wealth of examples taken from everyday life and its vivid descriptions. For example, Sartre

illustrates the danger of denying the freedom of human existence to oneself, using the example of a waiter who conceives ("projects") himself as a waiter and only as a waiter, thereby failing to realize that he himself is to blame for uncritically adopting social role expectations. It was precisely at this point that Sartre began his large-scale second main work, the *Critique of Dialectical Reason* of 1960, in which he tried to integrate the social dimension of intersubjectivity into the subjective approach of *Being and Nothingness.*

Philosophical anthropology

Kant once remarked that the three fundamental questions of philosophy: "what can I know?," "what shall I do?" and "what may I hope for?" could basically be summarized in the single question: "what is man?" Philosophical anthropology tries to answer this question directly, by engaging in debate

Venetian Woman II, Bronze sculpture by Alberto Giacometti, private collection

Sartre saw Giacometti's sculptures as giving solid form to perceptual experiences which also figured in his philosophy. For example, a chapter in *Being and Nothingness* deals with "being looked at by somebody else." I am, Sartre imagines, alone in a park, projecting my feelings onto the surrounding landscape. Suddenly I become aware of a person watching me. At that moment I become an object defined by the other person. The experience of emptiness also gives expression to our location in the world, our necessary relatedness to others. For Sartre, Giacometti was a person who constantly carried his emptiness around with him. This emptiness is conveyed when contemplating his figures. They remain "absolutely detached" from the observer and appear as if at the horizon, drenched in backlight and hence divested of their volume.

Jean-Paul Sartre, 1905–1980
Photograph with Simone de Beauvoir, 1970

Jean-Paul Sartre was one of the most famous 20th-century intellectuals. He was the guiding intellectual force of philosophical existentialism, which is distinguished by its radical rejection of all meanings that are on offer. It calls on every individual to decide on a life and to take responsibility for that decision, without having any criteria for determining which decision is the right one and which is the wrong one. Man in the nature of his being is not fixed as something specific – as is a stone or a hammer – but has to give himself his own being by acting in the world.

with scientific research, especially in biology, and no longer indirectly, via epistemology, ethics or theology.

This approach was first prompted by a short work by Max Scheler, a Catholic who had been a pupil of Husserl, written in 1928 and bearing the title *Man's Place in Nature*. In it, Scheler asked himself what constituted man's special position in the universe. Unlike animals, Scheler argued, man possesses a special "openness to the world." His mind enables him to distance himself from his immediate environment and thereby to open himself to the world beyond the scope of his perceptions.

Helmuth Plessner's *Man and the Stages of the Organic* also appeared in 1928. In this work, Plessner defined Man's special position as an "eccentric positioning" of his organism that is peculiar to him. Animals are "centered" at the center of their environment, but the human organism, although, as *physis* *(Leib)*, it is the direct center of its environment, becomes, as body *(Körper)*, an object whose movements man can, as it were, control from the outside. The human organism is always both things at once: a medium of expression for direct "emotionality" and an instrument which can be used to a particular purpose. Plessner explains this dual nature of the organism by reference to the forms of human self-expression: whereas self-expression by means of gestures and language demands control of the body, making successful communication with others possible, a "mimic" expression such as, for example, blushing or turning pale, is involuntary – the organism expressing itself.

Finally, in laughter and weeping, the precarious balance between "being *physis*" and "having a body" breaks down, since here, according to Plessner, man is so overwhelmed by his physicality that he loses the ability to act as a whole.

In his book *Man, his Nature and Place in the World* (1940), considered to be the principal work of philosophical anthropology, Arnold Gehlen described man as a "deficient being" *(Mängelwesen)*, because, as regards acuity of the senses, physical strength, and instinct, deficient human equipment makes man far inferior to his natural enemies. His perceptions, motor functions and system of drives are highly unspecialized, but for that very reason they are also highly capable of development. Man perceives a much larger segment of reality, albeit less precisely, than animals do. His motor functions are not restricted to a fixed repertoire of sequences of movements, but have to be trained. His drives do not restrict him to particular patterns of behavior; he has instead to take decisions. These weaknesses, which are at the same time strengths, enable man to act, a concept which Gehlen, following Dewey, puts at the center of his analysis. At the same time they force him to act in such a way that he avoids the dangers of overstimulation, crude motor functions and diffuse drives, which he does by structuring his perceptions, shaping his needs and controlling his motor functions. According to Gehlen, avoiding such dangers is the function of institutions. Gehlen included language, among other things, among these institutions, but he was thinking in particular of those political,

social and cultural institutions which limit man's scope for action by means of received interpretations of the world and rules of behavior. The more these are exempt from criticism and revision, the better they fulfill their stabilizing function. It was above all this fundamental idea underlying his theory of institutions – along with his often acute sociological diagnosis of the age – which made Gehlen one of the most important intellectual spokesmen for conservatives in the postwar Federal Republic of Germany.

LANGUAGE

Hermeneutics

It was not until the 20th century that language as a medium of knowledge moved into the foreground of philosophical awareness. Certainly, linguistic philosophy had existed in earlier times, but language was usually thought of merely as a means of expressing ideas that had been conceived independently of language. This view of the matter began to change as it became more and more clearly apparent how difficult it was for a philosophy of consciousness to describe simply as a relationship between two things, viz. subject and object, the way the objects of experience are constituted. It became increasingly clear that a world which is shared with others, and is to that extent objective, can only be known in the form of different observers referring to the same reality through the medium of a shared language. The two great traditions of linguistic philosophy in the 20th century, which were for the most part hostile to each other and only towards the end of the century began to bridge the gap between them, took their bearings from two different kinds of science. While hermeneutics set about laying the basis of a theory of science for the human sciences, the ambition of analytic philosophy was to achieve the same ideal precision of statements as in the natural sciences.

Hermeneutics is the theory of understanding. It has its roots in the theological exegesis of sacred texts and took on philosophical form in the Romanticism of Friedrich Schleiermacher. Wilhelm Dilthey, in the spirit of vitalism, developed the idea that the scholar in the human sciences, whose business is to understand, unlike the natural scientist, whose business is to explain, must empathize with his object of investigation, that is to say the historical expressions of human life, in order to understand them by inwardly recreating them for himself.

However, it was Hans-Georg Gadamer, who in his work *Truth and Method,* published in 1960, brought the two strands together and elevated hermeneutics to the rank of a fundamental discipline for the human sciences. Gadamer shared his philosophical starting point with his teacher Heidegger. Man is "thrown" into a world of which he always has some prior understanding. Only by possessing a horizon of what has always been known can man appropriate the alien reality which he encounters everywhere. As he enters into communication with that alien reality, his own standpoint changes and his horizon is broadened. This process occurs in an exemplary form in the human sciences, especially in the interpretation of works of art, in which the power of language to reveal the world is to be found in concentrated form. For as he communes with the work of art, the interpreter's original horizon merges with that of the work. He thereby arrives, in the so-called hermeneutic circle, at a deeper understanding of what he began by presupposing. Since every age has its own questions, this process of appropriation is never-ending; we can only ever understand works of art – or our own existence – differently, never definitively.

Logical Positivism

Analytic philosophy is not content to accept the incomplete nature of understanding. It attempts to provide for philosophical knowledge the same exactness that distinguishes knowledge in the natural sciences. This way of thinking has set its stamp on academic philosophy, especially in the Anglo-Saxon countries, right down to the present day. It concentrates rigorously on the astute vindication and refutation of specific arguments and to a large extent eschews explicit attempts to form a world-view. The roots of analytic philosophy stretch back into the 19th century. The mathematician Gottlob Frege, in the course of his attempt to provide a foundation for arithmetic, had sketched out a form of logic with the help of which both the structure of any statements and their possible

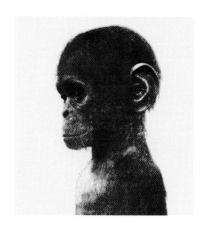

A young and an adult chimpanzee

Philosophical anthropology draws to a considerable extent on the findings of the empirical sciences, especially biology. Outstanding importance is attached to a discovery by the zoologist and philosopher Adolf Portmann, who proved that man, in comparison with his nearest relatives, is born too early, so to speak. Hairless, equipped with reduced instincts, and in many respects incomplete, Man, after being born, has to survive approximately a further year of a kind of pregnancy outside the maternal womb before his development is at the stage already reached by other animals at birth. Perception, motor functions and basic drives are, in comparison with animals, unspecialized; but this is compensated for by a high capacity for development, which animals do not have. This difference can be seen very clearly in the photographs, which show a newborn and an adult chimpanzee. The newborn chimpanzee shows a much greater similarity to man, so that it may be said that man remains, so to speak, newborn throughout his life.

Gottlob Frege, Photograph, c. 1920

The mathematician and philosopher Gottlob Frege is regarded as the father of analytic philosophy. In the course of his attempt to provide a foundation for arithmetic, he had sketched out a form of logic with the aid of which both the structure of any statements and their possible combinations could be formally described. Formal logic resembles a natural language such as English or German in having at its disposal a syntax, that is to say rules which lay down which sentences in the language are well formed and which are not. However, the propositions of formal logic tell us nothing about the real world, for whether they are true or not depends on the empirical truth or falsehood of the statements which they comprise. Thus the logical proposition "A AND B" is true if – and only if – statement "A" and statement "B" are both true, quite regardless of what "A" and "B" state about the world. Frege also owed decisive insights to semantics, that is to say the theory of the meaning of linguistic expressions. Thus, for example, the terms "morning star" and "evening star" both refer to the same object, i.e. Venus, but their sense is different, since it was an informational discovery to establish that morning star and evening star are identical.

combinations could be formally described. It was the English philosopher and mathematician Bertrand Russell in particular who then applied logical analysis to natural language. He became known to the broad general public by his courageous pacifist commitment, protesting against the First World War, and also against the Vietnam war.

The ideal of exactness which the emerging philosophy of linguistic analysis thus took over found expression in two quite different research programs, both of which were decisively shaped by Ludwig Wittgenstein, a pupil of Russell's: logical positivism, and "ordinary language philosophy." Logical positivism aimed to construct an exact scientific language free of the vagueness and contrariness of natural language. Its manifesto was Wittgenstein's early work of genius, the *Tractatus Logico-Philosophicus* of 1921, a continuously numbered sequence of apodictic assertions. At the heart of the *Tractatus* is the question of the relationship between language and reality. According to the famous first sentence of the *Tractatus* the world is "all that is the case," that is to say a composite fact. This fact can be unambiguously broken down into the simplest facts, which consist in their turn of simple things, viz. objects and qualities. A language which allows us to describe reality adequately must, according to Wittgenstein, be an exact "picture" of reality – it must show the same structure as reality. Since natural languages meet this requirement only very inadequately, Wittgenstein constructed in the *Tractatus* an ideal language in which simple names denote simple things and in which the syntactic structure of sentences copies the structure of the facts. What is epistemologically decisive here is that for Wittgenstein, objects and their qualities are given in reality independently of language and are merely "pictured" by language. Wittgenstein's deeper concern in the *Tractatus* was to demonstrate the difference between what can be said in language, viz. the way the world is, and what reveals itself in language. For the relationship of language to reality reveals itself in the sentences of a language. It follows from this, as Wittgenstein conceded, that the propositions of the *Tractatus,* like all philosophical attempts to say anything about the relationship of language to reality, are fundamentally

meaningless. Hence for Wittgenstein the task of philosophy cannot be to erect an edifice of theory. On the contrary he regarded philosophy as a therapeutic activity which was to cure us of the "bewitchment of our minds by our language." It is in particular those final meditative propositions of the *Tractatus,* with their almost mystical aura, in which Wittgenstein's passion for clarity takes on an existential concreteness.

From 1924 onwards a group of top-flight mathematicians, scientists, and philosophers had formed in Vienna around the physicist and philosopher Moritz Schlick, which soon became well known as the "Vienna Circle." Their aim was to lay the basis for a unified science, the statements of which, couched in the language of logic, were to be derivable solely from empirical observations. Any questions that could not be precisely answered in this way – including almost the whole of traditional philosophy – were rejected as "pseudo-problems" arising from the use of meaningless propositions. For the Vienna Circle, propositions were meaningful only if the conditions under which they were true could be stated. If these conditions are known, the meaning of the proposition is also known. Hence one has come to speak of the "verification principle" of meaning. It was Rudolf Carnap in particular who developed from this the "physicalist" program according to which all propositions of a theoretical scientific language had to be translatable into a language of observation.

Analytic Philosophy

After its members had fled from the National Socialists to the United States, the tradition of the Vienna Circle was continued there in altered form and reached new heights, particularly in the work of Willard van Orman Quine and Donald Davidson. Without aiming at a usage theory of meaning in the spirit of the later Wittgenstein, Quine, a pupil of Carnap, subjected the fundamental assumptions of logical positivism to a radical critique. At the center of his thought is the fundamental dependence of all linguistic meaning, and hence of all knowledge, on context. There cannot be any single correct description of the world, such as Positivism had aimed to provide, since it is perfectly possible for different systems of knowledge that canno be translated one into the other to coexist. Donald Davidson, in contrast, continued to explain the meaning of propositions with the aid of their conditions of truth. However, he no longer thought of these conditions as independent of understanding and interpretation in inter-personal communication. By extending the fundamental concept of interpretation to include the understanding of actions, he succeeded in combining theoretical and practical philosophy on a basis of linguistic analysis which by then was not far removed, as regards content, from the tradition of hermeneutics in continental Europe, but which rested on quite different methodological foundations.

In the preface to his *Tractatus* Wittgenstein had said that he had in essence provided final solutions to the problems of philosophy. It was, however, not least the problems faced by the Vienna Circle when working out the verification principle of meaning which impelled Wittgenstein to undertake a radical revision of his earlier position. The work which was to give a new direction to 20th-century philosophy, the *Philosophical Investigations* (1953), was not published until after his death. In it, Wittgenstein abandoned the view that reality is given, independently of language, and is merely "pictured" by it. On the contrary, the world only reveals itself when it is described in language. Hence there is no single correct description of the world; rather, which description is correct depends on which language is being used. For this reason Wittgenstein also relinquished any ambition to construct an ideal exact language which would have no need of the vagueness of everyday language. For everyday language is all right as it is. It is, rather, the aberrations of the philosophical (and scientific) use of language which creates problems. But these problems can be exposed as devoid of content by an exact analysis of everyday language. Thus what remains unaltered from his early philosophy is Wittgenstein's conception of philosophy as language therapy.

In the *Investigations* Wittgenstein starts from the view that speaking is an activity governed by rules, just as, for example, games are. Such a language game, as Wittgenstein called it, is embedded in complex practical contexts or forms of life, and its scientific description is merely one of many possible descriptions. The meaning of a word depends on the function which it fulfills within a language game, that is to say the meaning of a word is the way it is used. This unostentatious wording conceals a completely new theory of meaning. It is no longer the relationship to particular things in the world, be they objects or qualities, that gives a word its meaning, but purely and simply the social convention of correct

Ludwig Wittgenstein, 1889–1951, Photograph, c. 1930

In his early work, the *Tractatus Logico-Philosphicus* of 1921, Wittgenstein worked at laying the basis for an ideal scientific language, with the aid of which it was to be possible to "picture" reality exactly. In the 1930s Wittgenstein began to revise his ideas on the relationship of language and reality. The result was the *Philosophical Investigations*. There he repudiated the ambition of Positivism to provide a single correct scientific description of the world. He now regarded language as embedded in a form of life. Hence it is language, and with it the form of life, which pre-establishes the structure of the world, and no longer vice versa.

The house of Wittgenstein's sister in Vienna. Photograph by Margherita Spiluttini

After growing up in the high society of Imperial Vienna as one of the children in the highly musical family of a Jewish industrialist, Ludwig Wittgenstein studied engineering in Berlin and Manchester. During his studies he was intensely preoccupied with questions relating to the basis of mathematics. However, he became increasingly enthusiastic about philosophy and the theory of science, and on Frege's advice went to Cambridge to join Bertrand Russell, whose pupil and friend he became. He gave away his considerable fortune to a number of poets – including Rainer Maria Rilke and Georg Trakl – and, while on military service at the front, wrote the *Tractatus*, in which he thought that he had solved all the problems of philosophy. He then became a village schoolmaster in Austria and a gardener in a monastery. He returned to Vienna in 1926, built a house for his sister, and came into contact with the Vienna Circle, but remained quite aloof from its rationalism. In 1929 he went back to Cambridge, where he taught, with interruptions, until his death.

Scene from the film *Son of Franken-stein,* USA, 1939, directed by Rowland V. Lee; scene with Bela Lugosi, Boris Karloff, Basil Rathbone and Paul Muni

In analytic philosophy since the 1950s, the sub-discipline of the so-called philosophy of mind has emerged, which once again takes up, using different methodological approaches, the classical question of the mysterious relationship between body and soul. In the analytic philosophy of mind, a monistic position is usually adopted which allocates to the mind the role of an ostensibly independent sphere, which, however, in reality is merely a function of the brain. With the development of computers and information technology, representatives of the so-called cognitive sciences, which include the philosophy of mind, are at work on the development of artificial intelligence. But unlike the case of Dr. Frankenstein, it is not (yet) a matter of the creation of life but of the attempt to imitate, with the aid of computer programs, intellectual functions such as perception or learning.

usage. A word is used correctly if a generally accepted rule regarding its use is obeyed. But how is this done? When learning a language one learns how to use a word by way of examples, and one applies it in new cases without having any criteria to refer to which would guarantee that it is being correctly applied. Ultimately one must be content with the fact that the new case is sufficiently similar to the examples by means of which one has learned to apply the term in question. This entails on the one hand an unavoidable vagueness of terms. On the other hand Wittgenstein draws from it the anti-skeptical epistemological inference that the members of a linguistic community must agree not only as to definitions but also to a large extent as to judgments about the world.

"Ordinary language philosophy," also known as "Oxford Philosophy" from its intellectual center, took up Wittgenstein's suggestions und tried, in meticulous detailed studies, to solve philosophical problems by analyzing the use in ordinary everyday language of the concepts associated with them. John Austin's speech-act theory proved particularly fruitful. Starting from Wittgenstein's observation that people, when they speak, are also doing something, he showed how all speech-acts can be broken down into their locutionary content and their illocutionary role, that is to say what one is doing when one says something (for example promising, thanking etc.).

Theory of Science

After leaving Austria to escape from the National Socialists, Karl Popper, who had been a member of the Vienna Circle, was active in London in particular. But in his principal work on the theory of science, *The Logic of Scientific Discovery* (1934), he was not so much interested in the logical structure of an ideal scientific language as in the problem of how scientific knowledge can be obtained through observation at all. For science aspires to establish laws, that is to say general statements which apply to all cases to which the law in question is applicable. But how is it possible to deduce from a finite number of observations a general law that applies to an infinite number of cases? This is the so-called problem of induction. Popper's answer is: it is not possible at all. For no number of observations, however large, can guarantee that a contrary observation will not occur one day. The creative task of science is rather to put forward general hypotheses and test them experimentally, for hypotheses cannot be verified, but they can be falsified, i.e. disproved. By eliminating more and more theories, the "similarity to the truth" of the surviving theory is increased.

Quine has raised the objection to this view that empirically testable propositions drawn from observation cannot be derived from individual hypotheses, but only ever from complexes of hypotheses. In the case of an observation which is contrary to a hypothesis, it is, according to Quine, a matter for decision whether the hypothesis is dropped or whether one assumes that unknown disturbances are involved. This holistic conception of scientific knowledge has been emphatically supported by the American Thomas Kuhn with his research into the history of science in his book *The Structure of Scientific Revolutions* of 1962. For him, science is not a matter of the steady progress of knowledge through the accumulation of facts. This only applies to periods of normal science. One then speaks of the existence of a paradigm, which is characterized by generally accepted theoretical background assumptions and within which the valid theory is not questioned as a whole but is used to solve outstanding problems, so-called anomalies. If such anomalies prove intractable, a scientific revolution and a change of paradigm may occur. However, whether or not this happens depends on factors outside science, such as, for example, power structures. Since the old paradigm and the new are incommensurable, that is to say cannot be compared with each other, one cannot, in Kuhn's view, speak of scientific progress.

SOCIETY

Western Marxism

After the First World War, in Germany in particular, a way of thinking about modern society developed through discussion and conflict with the emerging science of sociology, which may be described as Western Marxism. This is, however, an inadequate description of this system of thought, which is nothing less than the attempt to provide a comprehensive interpretation of the situation of the modern subject as a whole, that is to say including its personal and cultural dimensions, in terms of social processes of modernization, and to communicate that interpretation through political practice. The theoretical reference point for this enterprise is above all the work of Karl Marx. Western Marxism, however, liberates Marxist thought from its fixation on the economic sphere. It thus differs from orthodox Marxism, which for a bare half century was the official doctrine of communist parties the world over and of the states which were under

their control. It differs both theoretically, by virtue of the major significance attached to the phenomena of the so-called superstructure, i.e. developments in social consciousness, and practically, by virtue of its far-reaching skepticism as regards the Soviet model of society.

Western Marxism was born in 1922, the year in which the Hungarian Georg Lukács wrote his *History and Class Consciousness*. He shared the view of Max Weber, one of the founding fathers of sociology, that a distinctive feature of modern society is the process of progressive rationalization, that is to say the expansion of areas of life in which people are no longer guided by communal values but only by self-interest. Lukács described this process as reification, that is to say, modern man increasingly sees both himself and other men as "things" with which he forms rational relationships. The origins of this process are to be found, according to Lukács, in the spread of wage labor, in which the worker regards his own labor as a thing that is split off from himself which he has to sell. As a result workers, unlike other social classes, have the opportunity of seeing through the fact that the capitalist economic system is the reason for this reification. Lukács's philosophy of history led him to hope that in the revolution the proletariat would put an end to both capitalism and reification.

Two thinkers who likewise had a decisive influence on the tradition of Western Marxism, but who were themselves influenced far less by Weber than by the intellectual heritage of Jewish mysticism, were Ernst Bloch and Walter Benjamin. Bloch, who was for a long time a close friend of Lukács, tried to combine the utopian aspect of Marxist thinking with the speculative philosophy of German idealism, in an "ontology of that-which-is-not-yet." For Bloch, what mattered was the waking dream that has not yet come true, the hope that has not yet been fulfilled, the possibilities of being. In his monumental work *The Principle of Hope* (1954–1959), he pursued, into the remotest areas of human life, the traces of that hope for the moment of fulfillment. In the work of Walter Benjamin, the place of Bloch's "hope" is taken by "redemptive criticism." He abandoned the

Karl Popper, 1902–1994,
Photograph by Ingrid von Kruse

Karl Popper was the founder of critical rationalism, a school of thought whose guiding principle was skepticism vis-à-vis any all-embracing interpretations of reality. Popper achieved early fame with his book *The Logic of Scientific Discovery* (1932), in which he was critical of the view that the development of science can be understood as a steady growth of knowledge. But it is not only the theory of science that owes important stimuli to Popper. In his work *The Open Society and its Enemies* (1945) he put forward the vision of an open, pluralistic society in opposition to the doctrines of Plato, Hegel and Marx on the philosophy of history. In his view these had potentially totalitarian implications because they singled out a particular form of society as the goal of history, which is incompatible with an open pluralistic society.

Swan in St. James's Park,
Photograph by Jon Player

Karl Popper used the example of swans to illustrate his famous thesis, according to which scientific statements cannot be proved but only disproved ("falsified"). Swans had been known in Europe since classical antiquity, and they were all white. The proposition "all swans are white" could therefore be regarded as well-attested. However, no number of observations of this fact, however large, could rule out the possibility of a contrary observation being made one day which would disprove the law that "all swans are white." But this is exactly what happened when, following the discovery of Australia, a variety of swan was found to exist, *cygnus atratus*, which is black. The hypothesis "all swans are white" was thereby definitively falsified, i.e. disproved. Popper drew from this the controversial conclusion that progress in science is only ever made when a hypothesis collapses, not when it is confirmed.

Theodor W. Adorno,
1903–1969, Detail of a
photograph, 1968

Theodor W. Adorno, the
philosopher and sociologist,
composer and musicologist was
decisively involved in the public
impact of Critical Theory. His
thinking focused primarily on the
notion of "non-identity," that which
cannot be "identified" under a
concept. He was critical of
Positivist epistemology, accusing
it of creating the impression of a
value-free science whereas in
reality it was dependent on the
compulsive exploitation of the
capitalist economy. He argued
that, avant-garde art and new
music enable us to see the non-
identical, but they cannot show
us a way out of the curse of
progress, since its unavoidable
corollary is the enslavement of
man's authentic drives.

Odysseus and the Sirens,
Painting by Francesco Primaticcio

In a central passage of their *Dialectic
of the Enlightenment* (1947), Adorno
and Horkheimer used the myth of
Odysseus to explain their conception of
the relationship between myth and
Enlightenment. They wanted to show
that the self-assertion of the rational
subject necessitates a steady advance in
the control over nature. The price for
this, however, is that human reason has
to suppress man's instinctual drives.
Having seen the sirens, who with their
beguiling song have until then lured
every seafarer onto their treacherous
rocks, Odysseus has himself lashed to
the mast by his comrades and orders
them to block their ears and row
through the straits. Thus Odysseus can
only assert himself by renouncing the
sirens' blandishments. He must forgo
the fulfillment of his desire in order to
survive as an autonomous subject,
while his comrades do not even enjoy
the dubious pleasure of temptation: they
– deputizing for the modern worker –
have to provide the material basis for
their master's self-preservation.

belief in an approach to utopia within the
world, replacing it with a paradoxical hope
of redemption for which justice is only to be
found in the commemoration of the name-
less victims of the catastrophes of history. He
gave expression to his sensitivity to the
plight and the revelations of the spirit of the
age as a literary critic, but also as a shrewd
observer of the culture of everyday life.

The attempt to combine the ideas of
Hegelian Marxism with empirical social
investigation was the distinctive feature of
the "critical theory" of the so-called Frankfurt
School. The *Institut für Sozialforschung*
(Institute for Social Research) had been
established in Frankfurt in 1924. From 1930
its director was the philosopher Max
Horkheimer, who, with his Institute, worked
on the project of an interdisciplinary social
theory which, drawing on the most recent
research in individual disciplines, was to
investigate the potential for emancipation of
modern societies. Along with economics, it
was psychoanalysis in particular, but also
jurisprudence and literary scholarship, which
were to help in discovering which tendencies in the way society was developing
supported the expectation – founded on
the philosophy of history – of the coming
revolution, and which were inimical to
it. Against the background of the waning
of revolutionary tendencies in Western

industrial societies, the Institute turned its
attention in particular to the mechanisms
which contributed to the pacification of
the potentially revolutionary working class.
Thus the increasing interpenetration of civil
society and capitalist economy, the structural
changes to the bourgeois nuclear family,
and the emergence of an industrially produced mass culture – these became the
Institute's central theoretical concerns.

The philosophy of Horkheimer and his close
friend and collaborator, the philosopher and
musicologist Theodor W. Adorno, revolved
from an early stage around the idea of a
"critique of instrumental reason." They saw
the process of rationalization in modern
society as the development of an instrumental rationality which uses technology to
bring under its sway not only external nature
but also the internal nature of man. The
treatment of people as unfit to take political
decisions, the loss of moral bearings even
in the process of socialization by the family,
and the dumbing-down of the mass media,
are so closely interconnected that it
becomes impossible for man to articulate
his real needs. But by these means people
are psychologically enabled to function as
part of the anonymous mechanism of the
capitalist economy. Critical theory took on
the task of using ideological critique to
unmask this false consciousness, which, in

terms of philosophy, it saw embodied in an exemplary form in the scientific self-image of logical positivism.

However, after the Institute had moved to New York to escape the National Socialists, Horkheimer and Adorno became more and more profoundly pessimistic. Faced with Stalinist barbarity on the one hand and American mass culture on the other, their diagnosis of the age grew into a concentrated vision of a wholly administered world which men, caught up in structures that render them totally blind, can no longer escape. The philosophical expression of this skepticism regarding belief in progress was *Dialectic of the Enlightenment* (1947), in which they saw the subjection of outer and inner nature as the corollary of all rationalization – not only that of instrumental capitalism. Only an "esthetic theory" – the title of Adorno's last work (*Ästhetische Theorie*) – can show how freedom can be glimpsed in great works of art as a means of coming into closer contact with nature.

Today, the tradition of the Frankfurt School is continued above all by the philosopher and sociologist Jürgen Habermas. After Horkheimer and Adorno had turned their attention, in their late works, to religious and esthetic experience, Habermas attempted to reestablish a connection with current theory in philosophy and the social sciences. His output, which extends into many fields, is dominated by the idea that the predominance of instrumental reason in the modern age is not a matter of fate but is merely a one-sided development of technological/ instrumental rationality at the expense of moral/practical and esthetic/expressive rationality. But all three forms of rationality are a part of reason, communicative reason, for according to Habermas reason is to be found wherever people communicate sincerely about something, not only where they rationally pursue their goals. Habermas specifies the spheres of action in which such a communicative approach predominates as the privacy of the family and public politics. In his principal work *The Theory of Communicative Action* (1981), he gave these spheres the joint name of *Lebenswelt* ("life-world"). In modern society this "life-world" confronts the spheres of action of the economy and the state apparatus, which are

held together not by communication but by control mechanisms in which language plays no part, i.e. money and power – Habermas calls this "the system." He then reformulated the diagnosis of the age provided by critical theory by explaining social problems in terms of the "colonization of the life-world" by the system, that is to say, the invasion of the private sphere and public life by money and power, the impact of which they may possibly be unable to absorb without harm. He thereby reconciled critical theory with the enlightened self-image of liberal democracies in the late 20th century.

Political Philosophy

This normative consent as regards the basic institutions of democratically constituted capitalism is also reflected in the rediscovery of political philosophy in the second half of the century. It was the particular achievement of Hannah Arendt, a pupil of Heidegger and Jaspers, to have established the preconditions of political life in all their radical quality. Her conception of politics was influenced by the direct democracy of the city-states of classical antiquity, in which free citizens met and conversed in the public space of the marketplace and the people's assembly. In her principal philosophical work, *The Human Condition* (1958), she therefore made a distinction between work and manufacture on the one hand, and action on the other. Whilst work serves to reproduce life (a private matter in

Student demonstration in Berlin,
Photograph, 13.Apr.1968

From the mid-1960s onwards, starting with Berkeley University in America, student movements had emerged in radical opposition to the established social order in all the industrialized countries of the West. In the USA their political commitment was directed against the Vietnam War; in France it was above all a protest against the rigid structures of the education system; in West Germany the young generation were asking questions about what their fathers had done during the Third Reich. All these movements had in common the use of Marxist rhetoric and the struggle for sexual emancipation. Thus in both the USA and Germany it fell to Herbert Marcuse, a member of the inner circle of the Frankfurt School who, unlike Adorno and Horkheimer, had remained in the USA after 1945, to play the part of an intellectual leading light of the student movement, for in his synthesis of Marxist social theory and psychoanalysis, sexual emancipation was the precondition of political revolution. Sartre also made himself the students' spokesman in Paris in May 1968, whereas for Horkheimer and Adorno in Germany the students' willingness to use violence recalled the era of dictatorship. Hence they saw only a confirmation of their pessimistic diagnosis of the age.

Panopticon, Jeremy Bentham

Michel Foucault developed a theory of power which makes it possible to interpret as the product of power structures even such forms of unfreedom as cannot be explained in terms of the control of one person over another. For Foucault, power is not tied to its exercise by particular persons. On the contrary, it is an anonymous phenomenon which insinuates itself into all social relations and sets its stamp on them. For Foucault as for Adorno reason always also entails subjection. In his work *Discipline and Punish* Foucault illustrates this with reference to the example of the Panopticon designed by Jeremy Bentham, a building in the middle of which there is a tower from which the cells, arranged in a circle, can along with their inmates be kept under complete surveillance, without the watcher in the tower being visible to the inmates. It is this piercing gaze of reason which in modern institutions – prisons, schools and factories, exercises physical discipline over the inmates.

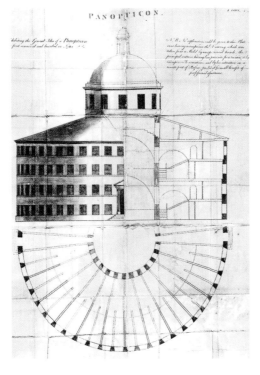

Piazza d'Italia, Charles Moore, 1978, New Orleans, Louisiana (USA)

In architecture from the 1970s onwards a conception of art had emerged which rejected the sober functionalism of the Bauhaus and its successors. So-called postmodern architecture makes uninhibited use of the formal inventory of architectural styles of the past in order to restore to the cities of the present that homeliness which it sees as having been banished by architectural modernism. In philosophy also there was much talk of postmodernism, whose chief exponent is considered to be Jean F. Lyotard. Philosophical postmodernism takes as its starting point the belief that the great promises of salvation for Western civilization have forfeited their credibility. The conclusions drawn from this conviction range from a pleasure-seeking attitude of "anything goes," to pessimistic cultural scenarios of the total domination of perception by the media, and the disappearance of the world.

the first instance), and manufacture serves to create products, action has no purpose in the narrower sense. However, it creates a social bond between people which enables them to tackle public issues jointly. According to Hannah Arendt, joint public speaking is the source of all political power. This is seen at its clearest during revolutions, which regularly find expression in grassroots democratic institutions. If in our time the public sphere is increasingly occupied by the work process (that is to say by economic necessity), the danger will increase that a totalitarian government may succeed in creating a particular social state of affairs entailing the destruction of political freedom. Of course, as a Jewess living in Germany, she had direct personal experience of this. John Rawls approaches the field of politics from a quite different angle. He is not interested in the conditions under which democratic politics can function, but rather the question of the justice of institutions and politics. His work *A Theory of Justice* (1971) brought to an end a period of decades of abstinence as regards questions of content in ethical philosophy. In order to guarantee the impartiality of his conception, Rawls presents a fictitious discussion between all members of society concerning a just or "fair" social order. The discussion takes place behind a "veil of ignorance," that is to say, none of the participants knows what abilities, social status or financial assets he actually possesses. In such a discussion, according to Rawls, there would be agreement on two basic principles for a just society. On the one hand, each person would have to have an equal right to the greatest possible number of basic liberties, on the other hand the so-called difference principle would ensure that social inequalities were arranged in such a way as to provide the best possible prospects for the least privileged.

Structuralism and Post-Structuralism

Structuralism, which had its intellectual home in the Paris of the 1950s and 1960s, is fundamentally opposed to "humanist" thinking, such as that of Sartre, for example, which allots a central position to the subject. On the contrary, the intention was to show, by means of an exact description of the structures underlying human thought and action, that it is anonymous processes which, in the modern age, create the illusion of an autonomous subject. Man is usually not able to see through the rules governing these processes, let alone change them. The modern subject's belief that he is his own master is thus exposed by structuralism as pure illusion, whether using the tools of ethnology (Claude Lévi-Strauss), psychoanalysis (Jacques Lacan), Marxism (Louis Althusser) or literary theory (Roland Barthes). The origins of structuralism go back to the linguistics of Ferdinand de Saussure. He conceived of language *(langue)* as a supra-individual system of signs with a structure independent of individual speech *(parole)*.

However, it was Claude Lévi-Strauss who applied the structuralist method, which he had encountered while in exile in New York, to the social sciences, by interpreting family relationships in primitive societies – which are the product of complicated rules governing marriage – as a structure analagous to language, in which, as it were, women were exchanged instead of words. The fascination of Lévi-Strauss's thinking becomes even clearer if one considers his romantic conviction that the supra-cultural structure of "savage thought" *(pensée sauvage)* conceals the knowledge of an original unity with the whole of nature, which modern man has irretrievably lost.

A distinction – not always an entirely clear one – can be made between structuralism and post-structuralism, along the lines that structuralism was concerned with uncovering a hidden deep structure, whereas post-structuralism aims to show that this deep structure does not exist. In this context the exposure of the fictionality of the subject becomes a liberating act. Michel Foucault, who transferred structuralist ethnology to the analysis of modern societies, occupies a key position here. Foucault sees the process of social rationalization as the subjection of the human body. In his early writings he tried to extract, so to speak archaeologically, the genesis of the modern subject from the "discourses of the human sciences" during the "classical era" between 1650 and 1800. With the aid of the distinction between madness and reason, health and sickness, the human sciences draw the boundaries of what may, and what may not, be considered as a rational subject, as a master of the anthropocentric world.

In the 1970s Foucault turned his attention to the phenomenon of power in order to determine more precisely how it is that discourses are able to discipline the human body. It comes about by discourses being linked to so-called practices. In the institutions, guided by science, of the lunatic asylum and the hospital, the prison and the barracks, the school and the factory, a more or less subtle network of power goes to work on the human body in order to shape a subject that is completely cut off from its own instinctual impulses. In Foucault's theory of power there is no

sovereign ruler exercising power over others. Power has become anonymous, so that even political commitment can no longer be directed towards changing government policy, but only against manifestations of oppression in particular situations.

Philosophical post-structuralism in its narrower sense was founded by Jacques Derrida with his project, which in many respects took up the ideas of the late Heidegger, of deconstructing Western "logocentrism." In a critique of Husserl's theory of signs Derrida tried to show that "sense" owes its existence to an immutable "différence," a difference between expression and meaning. This insight had always remained hidden, he argued, in the Western metaphysical tradition, because in its understanding of language it had always allowed itself to be guided by the spoken word *(parole).* But the transitoriness of speech makes it necessary to assume fixed meanings denoted by the spoken word. Derrida regarded this assumption as the heresy of Western logocentrism, to which he opposed the prime importance of writing. From Jewish mysticism he borrowed the idea that the world is revealed in a lost primal text, on which all existing writings are merely commentaries. The real meaning of the world remains hidden. It was to this conception of the world as an encrypted text that Derrida owed his enormous influence on literary scholarship, especially in America.

This Is Not a Pipe,
Painting by René Magritte, 1929,
County Museum of Art, Los Angeles

For Ferdinand de Saussure, the founder of the structuralist theory of signs, or semiology, a sign consists of two elements: the "signifier" and the "signified." The "signified" is not the object in the world to which one refers with the aid of the sign – that is the "referent" – but rather an abstraction, something like a concept. To this concept an arbitrary signifier is allotted by convention. It allows us to use the concept, which is abstract and hence cannot be perceived with the senses, in communication. This difference between signifier, signified and referent is expressed very clearly in Magritte's picture. The picture shows a pipe, but the caption reads: "This is not a pipe." As the representation of a pipe, the painted pipe is not a pipe, at most it refers to real pipes. But neither is the painted pipe a linguistic sign in Saussure's sense, because it has no signified. Unlike the word "pipe," it does not denote a concept. The picture thus has a referent, but no meaning. In this sense Magritte's pipe is not a pipe.

GLOSSARY

Terms in **bold** can be found under their own heading in the glossary

A priori, a posteriori (Latin, from [what came] before; from [what comes] after): With reference to an Aristotelian distinction (hysteron versus proteron), a pair of epistemological terms introduced by the **Scholastics**. A priori knowledge can be obtained through reason alone, independent of human experience. Kant summarizes under "a priori" the conditions that make knowledge possible in the first place, i.e. logically necessary and strictly general knowledge such as space and time, **analytical decisions**, **categories**, and concepts of reason. A posteriori knowledge, by contrast, comprises all the rest, e.g. sense-perceptions, with no claim to general validity.

Agnosticism: (Greek a-gnoéin = not to know): An **epistemological** concept coined by T. Huxley, meaning that only the outward appearance of what exists can be known, not its true being. Agnosticism disputes the possibility of solving the **metaphysical** problem of truth. The ancient Sophists and Skeptics were agnostics, as were later, among others, J. Locke, D. Hume, and H. Spencer. Nietzsche was critical of agnosticism on the grounds that the position of "not being able to know" the truth presupposed the knowledge of that very truth, which meant, he argued, that the frontier to the **Transcendental** had been crossed.

Agora: Name given in ancient Athens both to the assembly of citizens and to the place where they met (the market-place). Political discussion (agorein) was one of the most important civic duties in Athenian public life. Every male citizen was both entitled and indeed required to take part. The agora was thus an expression of the basic idea of the polis, namely that the state was founded on direct participation by its citizens in political life.

Academy (Greek akademeia): Originally the name of a temple area outside Athens named for the hero Akademos. It was here in 385 B.C. that Plato founded his philosophical school of the same name, which remained until 529 A.D., when it was closed by the Emperor Justinian. Even in Antiquity, the Platonic Academy was already the model for other schools **(Peripatos, Stoa)**, and it influenced the educational system of the Middle Ages. In 1440 Cosimo de' Medici founded an "Academia

Platonica" in Florence. Since then, academy has been a general term for a university, college or learned society.

Analytic and synthetic judgments: In the introduction to his *Critique of Pure Reason*, Kant distinguishes "judgments" (i.e. statements) according to the relationship between the subject and predicate (what is said about the subject). Analytical judgments are those in which the predicate is already contained in the definition of the subject, e.g. "All bodies possess extension" or "A bachelor is unmarried." Synthetic judgments by contrast give additional information about the subject in the form of knowledge gained from experience, e.g. "All bodies have weight," or "The Amazon is over 4000 miles long."

Archimedean firm place: An imaginary immovable fulcrum outside the confines of the Earth (or any system), and by extension, a foundation of knowledge beyond all possible doubt, from which all other knowledge can be supported or undermined. The term goes back to a saying by the Greek mathematician and engineer Archimedes (287–212 B.C.): "Give me a firm place on which to stand and I shall move the Earth."

Axiom (Greek axioma = demand, axioein = regard as true): General statement that cannot be proved itself but forms the basis for the proof of other statements. Euclid's geometry for example is founded on axioms, and there are axioms of logic (e.g. a statement cannot be true and false at the same time). In the natural sciences, an axiom is a statement confirmed by experience, but unprovable.

Being, to be (Greek on, ousia: Latin esse, ens): The meanings of these controversial basic concepts of philosophy can be divided into three: (1) existence, (2) identity, and (3) the logical relation between two terms, expressed by the copula "to be." Parmenides was one of the first to define being as permanence, non-transitoriness, as opposed to appearance, becoming and disappearing. By contrast, for Heraclitus there was no permanent being, all being was becoming. Aristotle thought of being as the existence of the existent thing.

Ontology usually understands being as the existence of things as such. Heidegger's existential ontology, on the other hand,

conceives Being itself not as something that is, but as a "process of de-concealment" (Entbergungsgeschehen) of what is.

Categories (Greek kategorein = to make a statement): Concepts of existence. A term introduced by Aristotle for the various kinds of statement which can be made about an object. Aristotle distinguished ten categories (substance, quantity, quality, relation, place, time, position, state, action, and affection), while Plato distinguished only four (identity, difference, persistence, and change). For Kant, the categories were both definitions of objects and **a priori** forms of knowledge, in other words mental concepts, which he derived from possible kinds of judgment. In this way, he arrived at twelve different categories, which he divided into four groups.

Categorical imperative: A general principle of behavior which Kant, in his *Critique of Practical Reason*, formulated as follows: "Always act in such a way that the maxims of your will could at all times constitute the principles of a general law."

Causality: The relation of cause and effect between two events taking place at different times. The principle of causality states that every event has a cause, and, conversely, that every cause has an effect.

Consciousness: Awareness of one's (spiritual or mental) existence. The term is understood in widely differing ways by philosophers, but is generally interpreted as the capacity to imagine objects. It comprises the total content of sensory perception, sensation, emotion, will and thought. The term in its modern sense is due to Descartes; in his **Methodical Doubt,** consciousness is the knowledge of the doubter that his doubt is beyond doubt. Descartes saw in this certainty of self the foundation of his concepts of existence and knowledge. With his concept of "transcendental consciousness," Kant introduced the connection between self-awareness and the unity of objects of experience: the subject is aware of his identity and of changing mental states, but is also aware of the unity of an object which can be seen in different ways. For Kant, "transcendental consciousness" is the basic condition of the possibility of knowledge. The **phenomenology** of Husserl defines consciousness as a consciousness that is always directed towards something and in this sense intentional. All reality is only such to the extent that it

relates to a perceptible, thinking, and remembering consciousness. For Husserl, the world is the correlate of acts of consciousness.

Copernican revolution: In the narrower sense, the revolution in cosmology resulting from the replacement by Copernicus of a **geocentric** universe by a heliocentric universe. By extension, any radical intellectual shift. Thus Kant regarded his theory that the "knower" imposed his mental structures on the objects of knowledge as a Copernican revolution in philosophy.

Cynics: A school of philosophy founded by Antisthenes (444–368 B.C.). The Cynics lived according to their ideal of an entirely untrammeled existence, despising all cultural values and notions of property. The modern use of the word goes back to their disregard for all social conventions and to their provocative pronouncements.

Deduction (Latin deducere = to lead down): Derivation of the particular from the general; obtaining a new statement from other statements by logical conclusions. See **Syllogism.** (see **Induction.**)

Deism (Latin deus = god): System of natural religion current in the **Enlightenment.** It recognized a God as creator and origin of the world, but not as a being which intervened in the affairs of the world, either through miracles or through revelation.

Dialectic (Greek dialégein = art of conversation): The **logic** of contradiction; method of philosophizing. As early as the Eleatics (Xenophanes, Parmenides, Zeno), also later in Socrates, dialectic was regarded as the art of investigating truth through dialogue. For Plato, dialectic is knowledge that arises from conflicting opinions. Kant described dialectic as the "logic of appearances," the art which invests falsehood with the appearance of truth. He used dialectic as a method of exposing sophistry. For Fichte (theory of science) and Hegel (science of logic), dialectic was that form of thought which includes contradiction (**negation**) of a thought or **idea** in itself. Their dialectical method shows how any concept (thesis) can turn into its opposite (antithesis), and how from the contradiction between these two a higher concept (synthesis) emerges, which is then subject to the same fate.

Empiricism (Greek empeiria = experience): The epistemological and philosophical standpoint which sees **experience** as the only source of knowledge. For the representatives of classical

Empiricism (Hobbes, Locke, Hume), there were no innate **ideas**; the whole content of consciousness was due to sensory experiences which could be collated into empirical knowledge by the principles of similarity and **causality**. Accordingly, permissible scientific methods for empiricists are observation and experiment. (See **Sensationalism**.)

Encyclopedia (Greek enkyklios = circular, paideia = teaching): The universal learning of the **Sophists**, comprising grammar, rhetoric, **dialectics**, arithmetic, music, geometry and astronomy. The modern encyclopedia aims at providing a written summary of current knowledge. In 1751, Diderot and d'Alembert, together with 142 authors ("encyclopedists") set about a systematic compilation of all human knowledge, a project concluded in 1772 with the *Encyclopédie ou dictionnaire raisonné des sciences, des arts et des métiers*.

Energeia (Greek activity, reality, realization): According to Aristotle, energeia is the principle that realizes potential. Taking the example of teacher and pupil, he explains the relationship between dynamis (movement, ability) and energeia. By imparting knowledge, a teacher can change the ability of a pupil, if the latter has the capacity to learn. As long as the pupil does not apply the knowledge he has acquired, he is only a potential "knower." Only when he implements this knowledge does this activity become energeia. It is defined as the realization of those aspects of dynamis, of the capacity to have an effect, of potentiality.

Enlightenment: A European intellectual movement of the 18th century, which sought to liberate itself from the ideas handed down by medieval and ecclesiastical authorities. While for Descartes it was still the radiant power of God that helped reason to discover truth, for the Enlightenment it was mankind itself whose own reason determined the rational and political order of the world. The leading philosophers of the Enlightenment were, in Great Britain and Ireland, Locke, Berkeley and Hume; in France, the **encyclopedists** Diderot, d'Alembert, Montesquieu, Rousseau; in Germany, Wolff, Lessing and Kant. Kant defined Enlightenment as "man's emergence from his self-imposed immaturity" and urged accordingly: "Sapere aude!" (Dare to use your brain). With their trust in **empiricism, reason** and the evolutionary progress of society, the Enlightenment however ran the risk of ushering in a new

immaturity, namely blind faith in the universal authority of science.

Entelechy (Greek entelecheia = having oneself as a goal): An expression which goes back to Aristotle, who stated that any existing thing contains the goal of its development already within it, as for example a seed has as its goal the fully-grown plant. The first entelechy of a viable organism is, for Aristotle, the soul. Leibniz described the **monads** as entelechies, as the purpose of their realization is contained within them.

Epicureanism: the teaching and way of life propounded by Epicurus (341–270 B.C.), in which happiness and a life of pleasure are seen as the greatest good. To attain to this good, Epicurus recommended a life of withdrawal and political abstinence.

Epistemology (Greek episteme = knowledge, understanding): The theory of knowledge. Epistemology is one of the basic philosophical disciplines; it is concerned with questions of the origins of the meanings, principles, methods and limitations of knowledge. Philosophical epistemology (in contrast to the philosophy of science) necessarily questions the validity of existing, scientific knowledge. Since, following the tradition of Descartes, a boundary exists between the understanding subject and the object to be understood, it is necessary to agree about understanding as a means. While Kant, in his epistemology, examines metaphysical knowledge, which is supposed to be independent of all **experience,** Fichte raises the question of whether science is possible at all. According to how these preconditions are interpreted, epistemology remains to this day divided between logical, psychological and transcendental-phenomenological schools.

Esthetics (Greek aisthetikós = relating to what is perceptible): Originally the theory of sensory perception; later, as one of the cardinal philosophical disciplines, narrowed down to the theory of art and beauty. Philosophical esthetics investigates the conditions under which judgments of taste arise, the effect of beauty on the beholder, and the relationship between art and reality. Esthetics has not been confined to any particular epoch in its pursuit of the connection between the sensuous and sense-formation: Plato and Plotinus understood beauty as the radiance of the Platonic **ideas** shining into the world; Aristotle saw order, regularity, and discrimination as the sources of beauty. With his *Aesthetica*

(1750) A. E. Baumgarten became the first to attempt to create a basic science of sensory experience. In his *Critique of Judgment,* Kant explained beauty as the symbolic visualization of the supra-sensory in the sensory; for Schelling, it was the finite representation of the infinite. Hegel and Schopenhauer understood art as truth made visible; according to Adorno, art aims for truth in the sense of a rescue of the Other, Non-identical.

Ethics (Greek éthos = custom): Moral philosophy. Ethics investigates the preconditions and the effects of human actions. In contrast to autonomous ethics, authority-based ethics denies that individuals have the capacity to formulate the maxims of their own behavior (an example would be the theological ethics represented by the Christian commandments). Normative ethics aims to formulate universally binding values and standards. **Utilitarianism** sees utility and the maximization of happiness as the only moral principles. The Stoics held that ethics was derived from a law of nature. Kant developed this idea in his **categorical imperative.** In place of the determination of man by nature, he proposed an autonomy of the will, which makes a law for itself. This enables the individual to justify the reasons for his actions. Practical ethics (P. Singer) develops options of action for problem situations, especially those arising from technological progress in medicine.

Existentialism: Philosophy of existence and being. Existentialism wishes to restore a connection between abstract thinking and the individual's concrete experience of the self and the world. This awareness of one's own self is created in extreme situations such as fear, guilt, and death. The main exponents of Existentialism are Kierkegaard, Jaspers and Heidegger **(ontology).** In France the term "existentialisme" denotes philosophical movements which, unlike essentialism, accept the primacy of existence over essence. In *Being and Nothingness* Sartre explained this primacy as signifying that man first exists, encounters himself, appears in the world, and then defines himself accordingly.

Experience (Greek: empeiria, Latin: experientia): Knowledge of the particular. Aristotle defined experience as the ability to recognize and judge things correctly. The precondition of every experience is memory. It takes many memories to create the faculty of forming general concepts on the basis of individual experiences. In

modern times (cf. **Empiricism**) experience has been regarded as the basis of scientific knowledge. Francis Bacon used the word "experientia" in the sense of exploration, meaning the process of learning, the method of obtaining general statements. The Empiricists (e.g. Locke) identified experience with perception. Locke distinguished external experience (sensation), the registration of the external world through the sense organs, from internal experience (reflection), the "inner life" of man accessible to mental capacity. Kant usually identified experience with empirical knowledge. For **Phenomenology** it is the relationship of experience to the practical life-world that is important, as it is the foundation for all scientific statements and for knowledge.

Frankfurt School: A school of thought concerned with the critique of society and science which takes its name from the Institute for Social Research founded in Frankfurt in 1923. Of its members, the authors Horkheimer and Adorno with their "critical theory" are associated with a program of analysis of social power structures. In *Dialectic of Enlightenment,* Horkheimer and Adorno exposed the veiled power-seeking of the Enlightenment and its shift into **myth,** while, however, also reflecting on their theory itself as part of the blindness of the Enlightenment. Marcuse and Habermas also belong to the tradition of the Frankfurt School.

Genealogy (Greek: genealogia): The study of origins and descent. In its narrower sense genealogy denotes the theory of human ancestry; in its broader sense it demonstrates the fundamental connections between ideas which are interrelated in their historical development, as did Nietzsche, for example, in his *Genealogy of Morals.*

Geocentric, heliocentric (Greek ge = earth, helios = sun): The view, current until the end of the Middle Ages, that the Earth was at the center of the universe, is termed geocentric. Copernicus ushered in the heliocentric view, whereby the Sun was at the center of the planetary system.

Hedonistic (Greek hedon = pleasure): The view of life which sees enjoyment and the pleasures of the senses as the aim and goal of human action (see **Epicureanism**).

Hellenism (Greek hellen = Greek): That period of classical Antiquity, between the 4th century B.C. and the rise of the Roman Empire, in which Greek civilization spread across the eastern Mediterranean with Arabic, Persian and Roman admixtures.

Hermeneutics (Greek hermeneuo = to interpret, techne = art, skill): the art of interpretation and understanding. Originally an auxiliary science of theology and jurisprudence, hermeneutics sought rules for the exegesis of canonical texts. Then Schleiermacher developed a comprehensive theory of understanding. The goal of his hermeneutic procedure was to understand an author better than he understood himself. The reader approaches this goal if he has full knowledge of the philological and biographical background of a text. The question of "correct" interpretation concerns all those human sciences that deal with works transmitted in language. The problem arises, inter alia, from the fact that understanding any individual part of the text presupposes an understanding of the text as a whole, which in its turn can only be acquired from the individual parts (the hermeneutic circle). It was Gadamer who, in his philosophical universal hermeneutics **(Truth and Method)** showed that there can be no understanding without prior knowledge. He described understanding as the merging of various horizons of meaning.

Humanism: A movement of the Italian Renaissance, marked by an interest in literary scholarship. Early leading exponents were Petrarch and Boccaccio. On a European level, it turned against the dogmatic bonds of **Scholasticism.** The Humanists sought to revive and preserve the linguistic culture of Graeco-Roman Antiquity, and, by means of comprehensive intellectual and artistic education, to open up for people a rich and dignified existence. Other leading humanists included Erasmus of Rotterdam, Michel de Montaigne and Ulrich von Hutten.

Idealism: In the broader philosophical sense, idealism describes any **epistemological** standpoint which sees things as complexes of ideas, or a philosophy which sees the world of human perception as a world of apparitions, behind which there is an unknowable "world-in-itself." Based on Plato's theory of ideas, in which **ideas** are seen as true reality, Idealism came to dominate the philosophy of the Middle Ages. Descartes was the first to raise the thinking receptive "I" to the supreme principle of philosophy. Berkeley formulates idealism thus: To be is to be perceived ("Esse est percipi"). By contrast,

Kant assumed the existence of a **thing-in-itself** which is not accessible to our perception; on the contrary, we could only ever see things as they appear, and not as they are. Fichte radicalized idealism with his theory of the absolute ego. Hegel's absolute idealism regards thought and ideas as the sole truth and reality.

Ideas (Greek idein = to see): In the special sense introduced by Plato, ideas are eternal, immutable archetypes of things, which can only be registered in the mind. Ideas stand for real existence; thus for Plato, true goodness is conveyed by the supreme idea of the good, which is what we strive for in our actions. Insofar as they are the images of ideas, things only have a share (methexis) in ideas. For Kant and the German **Idealists** ideas are concepts of reason, whose object cannot be encountered in **experience.** The term is also used by English-speaking philosophers in one of its everyday senses, namely as an image of a thing in the mind's eye, which can also be generated in the absence of the thing itself on the basis of **experience** and memory.

Illumination: As the light of knowledge, illumination is part of the tradition of Western light-imagery, in which the knowledge of truth is associated with bright clear light. St. Augustine's **epistemology** identifies the understanding of divine truth with illumination, the inflow of light.

Induction (Latin inducere = to lead into): In contrast to **deduction,** the scientific method which draws conclusions concerning general regularities from individual particular instances.

Leviathan: Originally, the sea-monster mentioned in the Book of Job. In his work of the same name (1651), Thomas Hobbes chose Leviathan as his symbol of a powerful state authority. He theorized that people transfer their individual rights to a regulatory body, i.e. the omnipotent state, which restrained power-seeking efforts on the part of individuals.

Linguistic philosophy: Linguistic philosophy investigates the nature, function and origins of natural languages. In doing so, it inquires after the contribution which language makes to the constitution of the reality of the world and of **consciousness.** For linguistic philosophy, speaking consists not only in expressing the content of thoughts and perceptions that are independent of language. On the contrary, such contents are always linguistically prefigured. In addition to

fundamental investigations by Humboldt and Herder, linguistic philosophy is the domain of **analytic philosophy** (Russell, Carnap, Wittgenstein, Quine).

Logic: The theory of thinking and reasoning. As the science of the conditions of the formal correctness and orderliness of thought, logic establishes rules for the drawing of conclusions from statements. Four basic logical systems have arisen in philosophy. (1) Formal logic as developed by Aristotle, elaborated by the Stoics, and further developed in the Middle Ages, focusing on the **syllogism,** based on four central principles: (I) the law of identity; (II) the law of contradiction; (III) the law of the excluded middle; (IV) the law of sufficient reason. (2) The transcendental logic of Kant, which aims to identify the concepts of objects as the condition of possible knowledge. (3) Hegel's dialectical logic, which developed the logic of the mind out of the dialectical evolution of human nature and history. (4) Mathematical logic, largely due to Leibniz, which seeks to represent conceptual relationships by unambiguous symbols on the pattern of mathematical symbols, and to operate with these algebraically.

Logos (Greek: word, language, reason): The faculty of reason as expressed in speech, the central value-concept in Greek philosophy. Logos is regarded on the one hand as the presentation of truth in an ordered form, and on the other (with Heraclitus and the Stoics) as the "mind" of the universe, uniting all **ideas** in itself. Finally, in Christianity, the Logos is seen as the Word and creative power of God.

Marxism: Socialist theory developed by Karl Marx (1818–1883) drawing on Hegelian **dialectics** and Feuerbach's **materialism.** Because of the economic contradictions between the ruling class (capitalists) and the increasingly pauperized class of workers (proletariat), Marxism prophesied overt class struggle, from which, with dialectical necessity, a classless society would emerge.

Materialism: The philosophical approach which regards **matter** (or material processes) as the fundamental cause of all existence and all the phenomena of **consciousness.** For materialists, matter is the only universal **substance.** All explanations can be referred to the scientific laws relating to matter. In classical Antiquity, the Atomists (Democritus, Epicurus, Leucippus) were the first materialists. Materialism was given new impetus in

the French **Enlightenment** by Diderot, Lamettrie and Holbach. Marx understood materialism differently. He saw existence and **consciousness** as standing in a dialectical relationship, whereby he regarded human consciousness primarily as a product of human material existence, i.e. the production process in which people found themselves at any particular time.

Matter: Via Latin materia (whence also material), used to translate the Greek word hylë, meaning the unformed original substance which Aristotle still strictly distinguished from the possibilities of the forms it could take on. Descartes regarded matter as extended **substance (res extensa)** as opposed to thinking substance **(res cogitans).** For epistemology, matter is that aspect of things which makes them spatially demarcated, perceptible bodies.

Metaphysics (Greek meta = behind, physis = nature): Umbrella term for a number of philosophical disciplines, including **ontology,** cosmology and philosophical theology. The word "Metaphysics" (from ta meta ta physika) was originally applied to 14 books of Aristotle's which were ordered after his *Physics*. This editorial arrangement accorded with Aristotle's progress towards knowledge, namely from what was sensorily perceptible to the supra-sensory: but as Aristotle defined metaphysics as the science of first causes, it does actually belong at the beginning of philosophy. It asks about existence over and above nature, about the existence of existing things. Via the genuinely metaphysical question concerning the reasons for existence, metaphysics moves on to, among other things, the question of God as the highest existing thing.

Methodical doubt: The systematic questioning of untested assumptions, in order to reach an ultimately valid core of truth not open to doubt. Descartes used methodical doubt to arrive at the certainty of his own existence (see **consciousness**).

Monads (Greek monas = unit): In philosophy, monad is the term used for the simple, the indivisible. For Plato, monads are the immutable **ideas.** Epicurus and Democritus understand them as atoms. Monads are at the center of Leibniz's philosophy. In his *Monadology* (1714), he understands them as immaterial centers of force turned in upon themselves, which go to make up the substance of the world.

Monism (Greek monos = alone): A philosophical system, which, unlike Pluralism, explains reality and the origin of the world by a single principle, a single original substance.

Myth: The term myth comprises the total tradition of a cultural community as contained in stories and tales of gods and heroes or (usually) anthropomorphized processes of nature. While **logos** has the function of representing reality as it is, myth makes no claim to literal truth. Plato saw in myth the unsecured, childlike knowledge of an earlier age, a kind of precursor of philosophy.

Negation (Latin: denial, opposition): The denial of a statement. In Hegel's **dialectics** the antithesis is the negation of the thesis. Synthesis emerges in its turn from the negation of the antithesis, hence also the "negation of negation."

Neoplatonism: A philosophical school of late Antiquity (3rd–5th century A.D.), founded by Plotinus. It renewed and developed Plato's teaching. For Neoplatonism, all "lower" levels of being emanate in a hierarchical sequence from the higher levels (hypostases) and ultimately from the One, without the latter losing any **substance.**

Nihilism (Latin nihil = nothing): the position of negation. Nihilism disputes the possibility and the usefulness of all knowledge and the validity of any truth or moral values. St. Augustine called people who believed in nothing "nihilisti." Later, heretics who either believed nothing or held false beliefs were known as "Nihilianista." Nietzsche understood nihilism as a state of meaninglessness, as the devaluation of the supreme values.

Nominalism (Latin nomen = name): Philosophical doctrine principally associated with **Scholasticism.** It holds that general terms (universals) are in truth only names given to things without any reality of their own. The Nominalists thus took one side in the medieval dispute over **universals.**

Nous (Greek, variously translated as "spirit" or "mind"): Anaxagoras (500–428 B.C.) represents nous as the guiding, ordering principle of the world. Plato understands by nous the "thinking soul"; Aristotle the human capacity for sensory perception, and the intellect.

Ontology (Greek on = being, logos = teaching): the theory of existence, or of general concepts of existence. Philosophical ontologies are part of **metaphysics;** starting with the **Presocratics**

and going on to Kant and Hegel, ontology poses the question about the place of the existing thing in the whole scheme of things. In Husserl's phenomenological ontology the **Being** of "what is" is understood for the first time as "that which shows itself." In Heidegger's analysis of existence, Being (Dasein) is distinguished from other things "that are" (das Seiende) by being that which is concerned in its Being with this very Being. Fundamental ontology is understood by Heidegger as a **hermeneutics** of existence which inquires into the meaning of Being.

Organon (Greek: instrument): Aristotle talks of the intellect as the organon of the soul; later Organon was the title given to his collected works on **logic.** Francis Bacon, in his Novum Organon (1620), developed an analytical, inductive method of scientific discovery, which derives its concepts and **axioms** from things themselves.

Pantheism (Greek pan = all, theos = god): The doctrine that God comprises everything. The word was coined by J. Toland (1705); it abolishes the distinction between God and creation, and sees God in all things.

Paradox (Greek para = against, doxa = opinion, expectation): In Antiquity, a paradox was a statement which conflicted with the general understanding of things and was thus (apparently) nonsensical. Thus Zeno's famous paradox of Achilles and the tortoise is based on the fact that an infinite series of movements never comes to an end. A paradox due to the **Stoics** is: "Only the wise man is rich"; it is resolved by defining "rich" not as "possessing much" but as "needing nothing". In **logic,** paradoxes are contradictory statements, which cannot be resolved. Thus "All Cretans are liars" when said by a Cretan, or Socrates' famous statement: "I know that I know nothing." The problem with such statements is one of self-reference.

Peripatetic: The school of philosophy founded by Aristotle, named after the promenade (Peripatos) in the Lyceum. The Peripatetic philosophers included Theophrastus, Eudemus and Aristoxenus.

Phenomenology: The theory of appearances. Phenomenology inquires after the contents of consciousness, i.e. it asks how the objects of knowledge present themselves. Hegel understood phenomenology as the theory which retraces the various stages of the manifestation

of the spirit on the way to pure knowledge: from sensory naiveté, morality, art, religion, science, philosophy to the absolute spirit. For Husserl, phenomenology was a methodological concept. Following his research motto: "To the things themselves!" his aim was to obtain philosophical knowledge through the analysis of intentional acts of consciousness, by looking at what is given to the reflective-contemplative gaze **(consciousness).**

Positivism: A scientific and philosophical position for which knowledge is based solely on concrete facts, sensory perception and experience and **metaphysics** is entirely rejected. Comte set out the principles of Positivism in Discours sur l'esprit positif (1844). According to this way of thinking only facts can be admitted as the objects of positive science. Positivism is not concerned with truth but with intersubjective certainty and with integrating knowledge that is obtained into theories that are secure. For Positivism being and consciousness are not identical, rather, human knowledge is relative and incomplete.

Postmodernism: This concept denotes recent theoretical positions in present-day philosophy. It was used by Jean F. Lyotard. Postmodernist philosophers reject the notion of an objective **epistemology** and regard human knowledge as historically conditioned and random. Examples of postmodernism include the work of Lyotard, Derrida and Foucault.

Potentia (Latin: ability): The **Scholastics** understood by potentia the essence of an existing thing. With reference to the Aristotelian distinction between dynamis and **energeia,** potentia was the immanent possibility within **substance** to achieve an existence appropriate to itself.

Pragmatism (Greek pragma = action): A philosophy developed essentially by Peirce, James and Dewey which tests and evaluates theories with regard to their practical relevance for human action. For Pragmatism the significance of a concept depends on the totality of possible behavior which could result from it under various circumstances. For Pragmatism, a thing is considered to be "true" if it is verifiable and practicable and is accepted by the research community.

Presocratics: Greek philosophers before Socrates, whose thought marked the transition from **myth** to **logos.** They include (1) the Ionian natural philosophers (e.g. Thales, Anaximander, Anaximenes), who inquired about the

primal substance that underlay all existent entities; (2) Heraclitus, who saw **being** as constant becoming; in contrast to him: (3) Parmenides and the Eleatic school whose **ontology** saw existent entities as characterized by immutability; (4) Pythagoras, who saw number as the supreme principle ; (5) the Atomists; (6) the elemental theories of Empedocles and Anaxagoras; (7) the **Sophists.**

Rationalism (Latin ratio = reason): Rationalism covers any philosophical position which derives knowledge primarily from rational thought. It thus contrasts with **Empiricism** and **Sensationalism,** because it seeks to establish a universal system of concepts, judgments and conclusions independently of all **experience** on the pattern of mathematics. Rationalist tendencies can already be discerned among the Eleatics and in Plato. Rationalism is the classic mode of thought of the **Enlightenment** (Descartes, Spinoza, Leibniz).

Realism (Latin res = thing): Realism, in philosophy, takes up Plato's theory of **ideas** and asserts that general terms **(universals)** precede things and are present outside **consciousness** as eternal **ideas** in God and inborn in the human mind. As one of the leading philosophical positions of **Scholasticism,** realism contrasts with **Nominalism.** In modern philosophy, realism asserts the scientific point of view that there is a reality independent of ourselves, which we can be aware of through sensory perception.

Representation (Latin representatio): The image of an object in consciousness, which can be produced even in the absence of the object and which is based on sensory **experience** and memory. Husserl distinguished the activity of representation from the images of representation, and distinguished these from the objects of representation to which representation refers.

Reality: Real existence independent of thought. In **metaphysics,** this is what objectively lies behind representation. For Kant, reality was one of the categories of qualities.

Res cogitans, res extensa (Latin: thinking substance, extended substance): The physical and the mental were for Descartes two different **substances** (res); he contrasted material, extended substance (res extensa) with an immaterial, non-extended substance (res cogitans) (dualism of substance). This leads on to the mind-body dualism, according to which the soul guides the body like a "ghost in the machine."

Rhetoric: The theory of the art of speaking. Gorgias, one of the **Sophists** defended rhetoric against Socrates as the art of debate, while Plato dismissed it as the unphilosophical art of flattery. Aristotle placed rhetoric as the theory of convincing argumentation alongside the exact sciences; Quintilian systematized rhetoric, seeing the education of the orator as a moral task. St. Augustine hoped to promote the interpretation and proclamation of scripture through rhetoric. In the Middle Ages, rhetoric was one of the seven liberal arts (alongside e.g. grammar and **logic**).

Scholasticism (Latin schola = school): The philosophy of the schools of the Middle Ages (9th–13th centuries). Scholasticism saw philosophy as the servant of theology; its task was to confirm Christian faith with the help of Aristotelian and Neoplatonic teachings. The Scholastic methods included reading and commenting on a text, and disputation, in which the correctness of proposed theses was tested by means of **syllogisms**. Truth according to the Scholastics (also known as "schoolmen") could only be found via church authorities.

Semiology (Greek sema = sign): Theory of signs. Semiology investigates linguistic systems/ processes of signs. Peirce, along with Saussure, formulated the three essential possibilities of reference for signs: 1. syntactical: the relationships of signs to one another; 2. semantic: the relationship between signifier and signified; and 3. hermeneutic/ pragmatic: the relationship between sign and interpreter.

Sensationalism: In the philosophical sense, Sensationalism regards all knowledge and thought as based on sensory data, or sensations. Locke's Sensationalist thesis was: "Nothing is in the understanding that was not first in the senses."

Sensibility: In the history of ideas, the capacity to respond to feelings, especially the feelings of others. It was the central idea of a chiefly literary movement of the late 18th century which sought to give sensory impressions particular importance through enhanced abandonment to feelings and emotions. **Esthetics** makes art the prime vehicle for sensibility. In his anthropology, Kant distinguishes sensibility ("Empfindsamkeit") from mere sentimentality ("Empfindelei"): the former is a strength, namely the

strength to allow a state of inclination or disinclination, or indeed to refrain from emotion.

Skepticism (Greek skepsis = test, examination): Philosophical skepticism casts total or partial doubt on the possibility of true knowledge. As well as the **Sophists** Protagoras and Gorgias, well-known Skeptics include above all Pyrrho of Elis. His ethical Skepticism refused all value-judgments, as he was of the opinion that in truth nothing could be just or unjust.

Sophists (Greek sophistai = teachers of wisdom): Originally, the term sophist was used to mean anyone striving for wisdom. In the 5th century B.C., the term was applied to a group of Greek philosophers (including Protagoras, Gorgias, Hippias), who as journeying teachers gave instruction in practical philosophy and **rhetoric**, as a rule for money.

Stoics: A school of philosophy founded in 300 B.C. by Zeno of Citium, and named after a colonnade (Greek: stoa) by the Athenian **agora** where it used to meet. The Stoics believed that the becoming and disappearing of the world was predestined in the plan of the divine **logos**. Their ideal was to live a rational life in accord with nature, free of passions and emotions.

Structuralism (Latin structura = constitution of a whole): Scientific method (in linguistics, literary scholarship, anthropology, psychoanalysis) which attempts to establish the function of elements in an encompassing whole from the total structure of the system. Structuralism analyzes the symbolic and linguistic orders which it sees as accommodating human existence.

Substance (Latin substantia, from substare = to stand firm): Descartes understood substance to be that which in its existence was dependent on nothing else. This criterion is fulfilled strictly speaking only by God, or, with qualifications, by the **res cogitans** and **res extensa**. Spinoza assumed God to be the only and all-inclusive substance. For Kant, substance was a concept permanently subsisting in the subject **a priori** (see **categories**) and necessary to assume the duration of a thing.

Syllogistics (Greek syllogizesthai = to put together, to form a conclusion): A system of rules for formal logical conclusions established by Aristotle and developed by the **Scholastics**. Syllogistics investigates what kinds of valid conclusion there are. A syllogism consists of at least two premises

and a conclusion. The distinction between quantity and quality gives rise to four possible kinds of premise: general affirmative (all x are y), general negative (no x is y), individual affirmative (some x are y) and individual negative (some x are not y).

Teleology (Greek telos = goal): The theory that all events, human actions, historical processes and natural phenomena have a purpose. While for Heraclitus the **logos** and for Plato the **ideas** represent the highest purpose or goal (telos), Aristotle and the **Scholastics** were of the opinion that things contained their purpose or goal within them.

Theodicy (Greek theós = God, dike = justice): Leibniz tried in his *Theodicy* (1710) to provide an answer to the question of how an omnipotent, loving creator God could allow evil and suffering in the world. The word now refers to any such attempt. It seemed to Leibniz that the imperfection of the world was a necessary evil. This was "the best of all possible worlds" in which evil was to be seen not as a shortcoming, but as a chance to achieve perfection.

Theory of Science: A branch of philosophy and **epistemology**, a meta-theory, since its subject is science itself and its methods. Its tasks include the development of a generally valid concept of science and the scrutiny of the methods which it uses as regards their soundness, reliabilty and consistency.

Thing-in-itself (German: Ding an sich): Something independent of our **consciousness**. A fundamental concept in **epistemology**. In pre-Kantian philosophy, it referred to something that was free of any sensory perception, accessible only to pure thought. In Kant's *Critique of Pure Reason*, the thing-in-itself remained in principle inaccessible to human knowledge; it could only be "thought." Thus the concept became, for Kant too, a methodological problem. The philosophical questions that arise as a result are: How can something which cannot be known be hypothetically thinkable? And how can the thing-in-itself possibly be accepted in any reasonable sense when it is inaccessible to every consciousness?

Transcendent, transcendental (Latin transcendere = to go beyond): In **epistemology**, something is transcendental if it is beyond the bounds of **consciousness** and **experience**. Kant uses the two words in distinct senses: for him, anything is transcendent which is

supra-sensory, i.e. beyond sensory experience and only knowable by means of reason, e.g. the concept of free will, of the existence of God and the immortality of the soul. "Transcendental" he uses to refer to pure **a priori** knowledge, the basic condition that we can rationally know and define things outside all sensory experience.

Universals, problem of: The problem of universals has been at the heart of a long-standing philosophical dispute, which can be discerned already in a disagreement between Plato and Aristotle as to whether general terms (universals) have any reality. The **Scholastics** were divided on the issue between the **Realists** and the **Nominalists**. The former, including William of Champeaux, asserted that universals not only existed, but preceded things (universalia ante res); the nominalists, including Roscelin of Compiegne, asserted that reality consisted only in individual things, whereby the general terms were merely names assigned later (universalia post res). A provisional synthesis was provided by Peter Abelard, who transferred the universals into the things themselves (universalia in rebus), according to which, corresponding to the term "human being" there is within (not outside) all human beings a universally human reality.

Utilitarianism (Lat. utilis = useful): The philosophy of usefulness. Utilitarianism regards an action as right if it produces just as great or a greater increase in utility and happiness for all concerned than any other action, and regards it as bad if it does not do so. Thus in 1789 Bentham demanded "the greatest happiness of the greatest number." Mill likewise saw the goal of human action as obtaining pleasure, but rated intellectual pleasures higher than the sensations of physical pleasure.

Will: The will is in general the ability to decide whether to act or not in particular cases. A complete act of will comprises: 1. the motive to act in one way or another; 2. one's own desire; and 3. the actual act of will. Kant defined the will as the **causality** of reason, as the ability to act in accordance with principles. He applied the term "free will" to desire that had been made free of subjective arbitrariness. Schopenhauer, an exponent of voluntarism, saw the will as the fundamental principle of being; the will stands as an independent driving force of **consciousness** above thought and feeling.

INDEX OF PERSONS

Terms in italics are explained in the Glossary

Abelard, Peter (1079 Le Pallet – 21 Apr. 1142 Chalon-sur-Saône): Theologian and philosopher, whose works in the field of epistemology and metaphysics make him one of the leading representatives of early *Scholasticism*. In the dispute regarding *universals*, he took a mediatory position between the *Nominalists* and *Realists*.

Adorno, Theodor W. (11 Sept. 1903 Frankfurt-am-Main – 6 Aug. 1969 Visp, Switzerland): Philosopher, sociologist, musicologist and composer. Co-founder of the *Frankfurt School* of critical theory, which sees modern mass-culture as a web of deception which blurs people's command over external nature and their own internal nature.

d'Alembert, Jean (16 Nov. 1717 Paris – 29 Oct. 1783 Paris): Mathematician, philosopher and writer, who together with Diderot published the *Encyclopédie*, the summary of knowledge within the French *Enlightenment*.

Anaxagoras (c. 500 B.C. Clazomenae – 428 B.C. Lampsacus): Ionian natural philosopher, who was the first to see *nous* as the principle of all things. For him, the elementary building blocks of the material universe were little particles put together by divine reason to form the world.

Anaximander (c. 610 B.C. Miletus – c. 546 B.C. Miletus): Ionian natural philosopher. He saw the basic principle of the world no longer as water, as his teacher Thales had done, but as the "unlimited" ("apeiron"), from which a vortex had created the Earth.

Anaximenes (c. 585 B.C. Miletus – c. 546 B.C. Miletus): Ionian natural philosopher. For him the basic principle of all things was air, which could appear in various forms, such as wind, clouds, water, earth or stone.

Arendt, Hannah (14 Oct. 1906 Hanover – 4 Dec. 1975 New York): German-American philosopher and political scientist, who regarded politics as a public space, without which co-operation between citizens would not be possible. She regarded this public space in the modern world as increasingly under threat from commercial interests.

Aristotle (384 B.C. Stagira – 322 B.C. Chalcis): Philosopher and universal scholar of classical Antiquity. His wide-ranging works, in which he created distinctions and coined terms which shape our thought even today, became the foundation of Western philosophy.

Augustine, Saint (13 Nov. 354 Tagaste, Numidia – 28 Aug. 430 Hippo Regius, Numidia): Bishop and Father of the Church, whose theological thought was characterized by the importance of the church community for man. As a philosopher of history, he abandoned the cyclical view current in Antiquity, adopting instead a linear approach involving six stages of salvation culminating in the Last Judgment.

Bacon, Francis (22 Jan. 1561 London – 9 Apr. 1626 Highgate): Statesman and founder of the modern notion of science, which, according to Bacon, should obtain its knowledge empirically, i.e. through observation, rather than deductively, i.e. by derivation from higher principles. This would make possible the subjection of nature and a peaceful society which could satisfy the needs of all.

Benjamin, Walter (15 July 1892 Berlin – 26 Sept. 1940 Port Bou, Spain): Marxist philosopher and cultural critic, who used thought patterns of Jewish mysticism to combine acute analysis of esthetic experience with a profound skepticism vis-à-vis progress. He took his own life while fleeing from the Nazis.

Bentham, Jeremy (15 Feb. 1748 London – 6 June 1832 London): Founder of *Utilitarianism*. The legislator should frame the laws in such a way that each citizen, by seeking his own happiness, i.e. pursuing pleasure and avoiding pain, would contribute to the sole object of legislation, namely "the greatest happiness of the greatest number."

Bergson, Henri (18 Oct. 1859 Paris – 4 Jan. 1941 Paris): Leading exponent in France of the philosophy of life; he rejected the principle of scientific reason, which he regarded as inflexible and life-denying, and in its place proposed the organic flow of time and the "élan vital" – the vital impulse.

Berkeley, George (12 Mar. 1685 Kilkenny, Ireland – 14 Jan. 1753 Oxford): Anglican bishop, and exponent of British *Empiricism*. He traced all *experience* back to sense impressions, radicalizing Empiricism into an *Idealism* which denied the existence of an outside world independent of the *consciousness*. For Berkeley nothing existed unless perceived.

Bloch, Ernst (8 July 1885 Ludwigshafen – 4 August 1977 Tübingen): Marxist philosopher, who placed the "hope principle" at the center of his thought. The category of the not-yet-existent described that utopian condition of the world in which all the potential present in people and things will be completely developed.

Bruno, Giordano (1584, Nola, Naples – 17 Feb. 1600 Rome): Natural philosopher who was burnt at the stake for asserting that the infinitude of the universe followed from the infinitude of God.

Camus, Albert (7 Nov. 1913 Mondovi, Algeria – 4 Jan. 1960, nr Villeblevin, France): French philosopher, novelist and playwright, who, as a representative of *Existentialism* stressed the absurdity of a human existence which consisted in man's continually trying anew to wrest some purpose from life while knowing that this attempt was doomed to a failure in a world devoid of purpose.

Carnap, Rudolf (18 May 1891 Wuppertal – 14 Sept. 1970 Santa Monica, Cal.): German-American linguistic philosopher and philosopher of science, who, as a leading exponent of logical *Positivism* tried to trace back the whole of *experience* to elementary observations from which a unitary body of science could be built up. He declared all other philosophical problems to be pseudo-problems.

Davidson, Donald (b. 6 Mar. 1917, Springfield, Ill.): Philosopher of linguistic analysis who gives a central importance for the explanation of linguistic meaning to the reciprocal interpretation of linguistic expressions by the speakers of a language.

Democritus (470 B.C. Abdera – c. 380 B.C.): Leading exponent of Atomism in ancient Greece. This philosophy assumes that everything that exists is composed of minuscule identical particles which are forever falling. By deviating from a straight line in their fall, they create turbulences which give rise to perceptible objects.

Derrida, Jacques (b. 15 July 1930 El Biar, Algeria): Leading exponent of philosophical Deconstructivism. For him, Western philosophy is characterized by "phonocentrism," a preference for the spoken word vis-à-vis the written. This finds its expression in "logocentrism," a fixation on reason, which Derrida regards as an error of thought to be "deconstructed" from within.

Descartes, René (31 Mar. 1596 La Haye-Descartes – 11 Feb. 1650 Stockholm): Founder of modern *Rationalism*. Methodical doubt in the existence of the external world led, for Descartes, to the certainty of his own existence: "I think, therefore I am." In addition, there are things with spatial extension, while God as the third *substance* guarantees the knowability of the external world.

Dewey, John (20 Oct. 1859 Burlington Vt. – 1 June 1952 New York): An exponent of American *Pragmatism*, he stressed the role of active intervention in reality when obtaining of knowledge. He also had great influence in the USA as a theoretician of democracy and as an educational reformer.

Dilthey, Wilhelm (19 Nov. 1833 Biebrich nr Wiesbaden – 1 Oct. 1911 Seis, Tyrol): Leading exponent in Germany of the philosophy of life. Dilthey was concerned above all with providing a foundation for the "understanding" humanities (the German term for which – "Geisteswissenschaften" – is due to him), which he saw as differing from the "explanatory" natural sciences in that the scholar of the humanities must place himself in his object of study, namely human expressions of life, in order to experience it once more.

Duns Scotus, John (c. 1265 Maxton, Scotland – 8 November 1308 Cologne): *Scholastic* philosopher who tried to draw together the Aristotelian and Augustinian traditions. He taught that the will was more important than the intellect, particularly in ethics.

Empedocles (c. 483 B.C. Acragas, Sicily – c. 430/20 B.C.): Wandering preacher and philosopher, who saw as the principle of all things the four elements which attract and repel each other through love and hate.

Epicurus (341 B.C. Samos – 270 B.C. Athens): The founder of the variety of *Hedonism* known as *Epicureanism*, he placed the avoidance of pain and the achievement of pleasure at the center of his teaching on correct living.

Feuerbach, Ludwig (28 July 1804 Landshut – 13 Sept. 1872 Nuremberg): Advocate of left-wing Hegelianism. In his examination of Hegel's philosophy of absolute spirit, Feuerbach understood the individual being as the only reality. In his critique of religion, he depicted God as the projection of human wishful thinking.

Fichte, Johann Gottlieb (19 May 1762 Rammenau – 29 Jan. 1814 Berlin): Founder of German *Idealism*. Taking Kant's philosophy as his starting point, he attempted to interpret the whole of reality as a construction of the *consciousness*, which refers itself to itself in such a way as to distinguish itself from itself by knowing itself. This distinction of knower and known he understood as an action in which the self-aware subject constituted itself.

Foucault, Michel (15 Oct. 1926 Poitiers – 25 June 1984 Paris): Leading exponent of philosophical *Structuralism*. Foucault understood the modern subject as the product of an anonymous process, by which the human sciences – which had developed since the 18th century – had turned the human mind and body into an object of observation shaped by the power of modern institutions such as the madhouse, the prison, the factory and the school.

Frege, Gottlob (8 Nov. 1848 Wismar – 26 July 1925 Bad Kleinen): Mathematician and logician who developed the formal *logic*, by means of which it can be determined how the truth of a compound statement depends on the truth of its parts. In addition he showed that terms can be represented as mathematical classes of objects.

Gadamer, Hans-Georg (b. 11 Feb. 1900 Marburg): Exponent of philosophical *Hermeneutics*. He has sought to show that the concept of understanding as current in the humanities is the central element in the basic constitution of human existence.

Gehlen, Arnold (29 Jan. 1904 Leipzig – 30 Jan. 1976 Hamburg): Leading exponent of philosophical anthropology. Gehlen characterized man as a deficient creature, who has to compensate his lack (compared with other animals) of physical strength, instinct and perception by developing his faculty for considered action.

Habermas, Jürgen (b. 18 June 1929 Düsseldorf): Philosopher and sociologist who continues the tradition of the *Frankfurt School*. In the process he seeks to combine the critical impulses of *Marxist* social theory with the self-image of democratic states governed by the rule of law, and to do this in such a way as to demonstrate the legitimate boundary between the system of state bureaucracy and business on the one hand and the living world of communication on the other.

Hegel, Georg Wilhelm Friedrich (27 Aug. 1770 Stuttgart – 14 Nov. 1831 Berlin): Leading exponent of German *Idealism*. In his system, Hegel represented the universe as the evolution of spirit. This evolution proceeded dialectically, in other words every manifestation of the spirit generated its own contradiction, the negation of the manifestation. The contradiction resolved itself in that the negation continued to be present in the new, higher manifestation and thus made it more concrete.

Heidegger, Martin (26 Sept. 1889 Messkirch – 26 May 1976 Freiburg): Leading German exponent of *Existentialism*. He characterized human existence as a design thrown into the world, something which found itself in an environment it had not sought, but which it must pass through into an uncertain future. In his later work, he made Western rationalism responsible for an absence of being.

Heraclitus (c. 550 B.C. Ephesus – c. 480 B.C. Ephesus): Ionian natural philosopher who saw fire as the principle of all things. He was opposed in particular to the Eleatic view that *being* was immobile, assuming that reality was in a state of constant flux.

Hobbes, Thomas (5 Apr. 1588 Bristol – 4 Dec. 1679 Chesterfield): Philosopher and constitutional theorist. On the basis of a materialist *epistemology* and anthropology, he made an implicit social contract the basis of the legitimacy of the modern state, whose function was to prevent the war of all against all.

Horkheimer, Max (14 Feb. 1895 Stuttgart – 7 July 1973 Nuremberg): Philosopher and sociologist, who as head of the Frankfurt Institute of Social Research combined a *Marxist*-inspired critical social theory with empirical social research.

Hume, David (7 May 1711 Edinburgh – 25 Aug. 1776): The advocate of an extreme epistemological *Empiricism*, he tried to reduce all knowledge to immediate sense-impressions and the ideas of them formed by the mind.

Husserl, Edmund (8 Apr. 1859 Prossnitz – 26 Apr. 1938 Freiburg): Founder of *Phenomenology*. He sought to re-found philosophy as an exact science of pure *consciousness*, emphasizing the intentionality or purposefulness thereof.

Jaspers, Karl (23 Feb. 1883 Oldenburg – 26 Feb. 1969 Basel): Psychiatrist and philosopher, exponent of *Existentialism*. For him, human existence can be experienced together with the "surrounding," especially in critical situations – failure, guilt, death. By contrast, human freedom is most perfectly realized in communication with others.

Kant, Immanuel (22 Apr. 1724 Königsberg [now Kaliningrad] – 12 Feb. 1804 Königsberg): Founder of modern critical philosophy and pioneer of German *Idealism*. He convinced himself of the limitations and possibilities of metaphysics and ethics by examining the conditions of the possibility of *experience* and action.

Kierkegaard, Søren (5 May 1813 Copenhagen – 11 Nov. 1855 Copenhagen): Philosopher and theologian, the founder of *Existentialism*. He radically acknowledged the despair and fear of man in the face of a God who his himself hidden.

Leibniz, Gottfried Wilhelm (1 July 1646 Leipzig – 14 Nov. 1716 Hanover): Philosopher and universal scholar, who hoped his *monad* theory would provide an ontological basis for modern science, and that his theory of pre-stabilized harmony would solve the body-soul problem.

Lévi-Strauss, Claude (b. 28 Nov. 1908 Brussels): Ethnologist who introduced linguistic structuralism into the social sciences by regarding the kinship structures of primitive societies as structures analogous to language.

Levinas, Emmanuel (30 Dec. 1905 Kaunas – 1995 Paris): *Phenomenologist* concerned primarily with the foundations of ethics. He saw the look of one's opposite number as something which imposes an infinite responsibility on us.

Locke, John (29 Aug. 1632 Wrington – 28 Oct. 1704 Oates): The founder of British *Empiricism*: nothing can be in the mind which did not enter it through the senses. As a political philosopher, he declared freedom, equality and the inviolability of the person to be the supreme desiderata, and based a liberal economic order on these principles.

Lucretius (c. 97 B.C. – 10 Oct. 55 B.C.): Poet and philosopher who presented the natural philosophy of *materialist Epicureanism* in a poem entitled "De rerum natura". According to this view, everything could be explained by natural laws in the interaction of atoms. This could also make possible a way of life free of fear of the gods or of fate.

Lukács, George (13 Apr. 1885 Budapest – 4 June 1971 Budapest): *Marxist* philosopher, who regarded the rationalization of modern society as a process of de-personalization in which social relationships between people were increasingly being seen in terms of relationships to things. This had its origins in the fact that labor in the capitalist economic system is treated as a commodity which the worker sells in return for wages and thus splits away from himself as a living being.

Machiavelli, Niccolò (3 May 1469 Florence – 22 June 1527 Florence): Founder of modern political philosophy. In his works he describes techniques of acquiring and retaining power; these, he said, were needed for the maintenance of public order, regardless of whether the government was legitimate or not.

Marcus Aurelius (26 Apr. 121 Rome – 17 Mar. 180 Vindobona [now Vienna]): Roman emperor and prominent *Stoic*. By being totally independent of external relationships, it was said, the Stoic would achieve a state of psychological equanimity.

Marcuse, Herbert (19 July 1898 Berlin – 29 July 1979 Starnberg): Social philosopher and member of the *Frankfurt School*. He investigated primarily the psychological effects of capitalism on human beings and founded his hopes of a revolution on the expectation of a revolt against the repression of natural urges by prevailing sexual morality.

Marx, Karl (5 May 1818 Trier – 14 March 1883 London): As a left-wing Hegelian, Marx understood world history as a process of progress which followed a *dialectic* logic. Albeit this consisted not in the self-realization of spirit, but the unfolding of productive forces. The modern age was witnessing the emergence of capitalism as a productive relationship, leading to crisis tendencies, which in turn would lead to the establishment of a new social order.

Merleau-Ponty, Maurice (14 Mar. 1908 Rochefort-sur-Mer – 3 May 1961 Paris): French *Phenomenologist* who derived from the way human beings fulfill themselves in life the notion that reason was rooted in the body. In particular in his phenomenology of perception he showed that perception is structure by man's possibility of practical intervention in the world.

Mill, John Stuart (20 May 1806 London – 8 May 1873 Avignon): Political economist. He defended and developed Bentham's *Utilitarianism* by making it more humane and less mechanistic. He sought to make the social sciences as exact as Newtonian physics by developing a general methodology for them.

Nicholas of Cusa (1401 Kues – 11 Aug. 1464 Todi): Mathematician, cardinal and philosopher. In his system he summarized the unity of the contrasts of God, angels, world and man, already formulating modern ideas of the relationship between God and man, for there was, he said, no clear knowledge of God, only learned ignorance.

Nietzsche, Friedrich (15 Oct. 1844 Röcken – 25 Aug. 1900 Weimar): Of the philosophical critics of the *Enlightenment*, Nietzsche had the greatest influence. He cast doubt on the notion of enlightenment by arguing that the motives to which the norms of enlightened *epistemology* and *ethics* are due are rooted in the resentment of those who are not sufficiently strong or courageous to accept the challenge of a free life.

Parmenides (c. 515 B.C. Elea – 445 B.C. Elea): Founder of the Eleatic theory of existence. He maintained that there is absolutely no change in reality; everything that we regard as change is mere illusion. Real existence, by contrast, is a sphere at rest in itself, which knows no change.

Peirce, Charles Sanders (10 Sept. 1839 Cambridge, Mass. – 19 Apr. 1914 Milford, Pa.): Physicist and philosopher. The founder of American *Pragmatism*, he sought to show that meaning can only be attributed to linguistic signs in the context of action. Peirce was the founder of the consensus theory of truth, according to which truth can be identified as a consensus, under ideal conditions, among all possible interlocutors.

Plato (428/27 B.C. Athens – 348/47 B.C. Athens): Founder of *Idealism* in philosophy. According to Plato, the world as we know it is a mere image of the *ideas*. Thus the idea of the horse is the pattern for all actual horses that exist in the world, while outshining them all in perfection. Merely by using the senses, however, it is not possible to see the ideas. For this purpose an intellectual vision is required, which emerges from a concrete vision as its idea.

Plotinus (c. 205–270 Mintumae): Leading exponent of *Neo-platonism*. Plotinus set up a hierarchy of existences, at whose pinnacle is God, as pure spirit or the Platonic idea of the good. The lower an object is in the hierarchy, the higher the proportion of *matter* in it. The hierarchy of existences is also linked to a value-judgment, according to which pure spirit is only good and pure matter only bad.

Popper, Karl (28 July 1902 Vienna – 17 Sept. 1994 London): Founder of critical *Rationalism*. In the theory of science, Popper showed that scientific progress is not to be understood as the collection of more and more confirmations of hypotheses, but rather as a falsification of

hypotheses. In political theory, he pleaded for an open society which did pursue any particular goal, but only the freedom of its citizens.

Pythagoras (c. 570 B.C. Samos – c. 480 B.C. Metapont): Mathematician and philosopher who assembled a secret society of adherents around himself, who, like him, saw the numbers as the principle of all things.

Quine, Willard van Orman (b. 25 June 1908 Akron, Ohio): Exponent of the philosophy of linguistic analysis who subjected the basic principles of logical *Positivism* to radical criticism by demonstrating the context-dependence of linguistic meanings and empirical knowledge.

Rawls, John (b. 21 Feb. 1921 Baltimore): Political theorist. He regards the same freedom for all as a basic principle against which all political institutions should be judged, and material inequality as permissible only if this inequality is judged to benefit all.

Roscelin of Compiègne (c. 1045 Compiègne – c. 1120 Saint-Martin-de-Tours): Philosopher and theologian who took the *Nominalist* position in the dispute regarding *universals*, namely that only individual things exist, and that the universals, i.e. general terms, are only sound and smoke.

Rousseau, Jean-Jacques (28 June 1712 Geneva – 2 July 1778 Ermenonville): Political and social philosopher, who made the legitimacy of governments dependent on a social contract designed to guarantee that in the process of the formation of political will, the particular interests of individuals merge into a general will.

Russell, Bertrand (18 May 1872 Trelleck – 2 Feb. 1970 Plas Penrhyn, Wales): Mathematician and philosopher, leading exponent of linguistic philosophy, by means of which he subjected statements in ordinary language to logical analysis. He was best known to the broader public as a pacifist and writer on philosophy.

Sartre, Jean-Paul (21 June 1905 Paris – 15 Apr. 1980 Paris): Leading exponent in France of *Existentialism*. He saw human freedom as characterized by its radical freedom. At every moment, a human being must decide for or against a particular course of action and take the responsibility for this decision.

Scheler, Max (22 Aug. 1874 Munich – 19 May 1928 Frankfurt-am-Main): *Phenomenological* philosopher and sociologist, who sought to replace the formalism of Kantian *ethics* with

a material value ethics. He founded philosophical anthropology by characterizing the place of man in the cosmos as a place between spirit and life.

Schelling, Friedrich Wilhelm (27 January 1775 Leonberg – 20 Aug. 1854 Bad Ragaz, Switzerland): Exponent of German *Idealism*, who parted company with Hegel after a common start. His system was based on the assumption of an absolute ego, which could not however be demonstrated by discourse, but could only be discerned through intellectual contemplation. If the original unity of the absolute ego had broken down, it was the duty of history and politics to restore it.

Schopenhauer, Arthur (22 Feb. 1788 Danzig [now Gdansk] – 21 Sept. 1860 Frankfurt-am-Main): Schopenhauer's thought is characterized by a basic attitude of extreme pessimism. Man recognized the world only through his own ideas, underlying which was the will, a force of nature which permeated everything.

Socrates (c. 470 B.C. Athens – 399 B.C. Athens): Founder of classical Greek philosophy. There are no writings by Socrates extant or recorded; his philosophy lives in dialogues handed down to us by, among others, his pupil Plato. Socrates was, like the *Sophists*, an enlightener, because he demanded reasoned explanations for things which had hitherto simply been accepted.

Spinoza, Baruch de (24 Nov. 1632 Amsterdam – 21 Feb. 1677 The Hague): Exponent of *Rationalist* philosophy. In Spinoza's system, there is only one *substance*, which is identical with God. Everything that exists, material objects and spiritual objects alike, consist of this substance.

Thales of Miletus (c. 625 B.C. Miletus – c. 547 B.C. Miletus): Thales was the founder of Ionian natural philosophy and is regarded in fact the founder of Western philosophy. In contrast to the previous mythic view of the world, Thales raised the question of the principle that underlies everything.

Thomas Aquinas, Saint (1225/26 Aquino – 7 Mar. 1274 Fossanova): *Scholastic* philosopher and Church teacher, who summarized the whole philosophical knowledge of his time in his "Summa theologiae", which combined the philosophy of Aristotle with Christian revelation in a view of the world which was thought out to the very last detail.

Voltaire (21 Nov. 1694 Paris – 30 May 1778 Paris): Philosopher of the French *Enlightenment*. He

did not create any philosophical work in the narrower sense, but his battle against conservatism and dogmatism led to his being considered one of the most important philosophers of the age.

William of Champeaux (c. 1070 Champeaux – 1121/22 Châlons-sur-Marne): Early *Scholastic* theologian, who took the extreme *Realist* position in the dispute over *universals*, asserting that only general concepts existed. This view implies that there are no individual things, and that therefore the only real aspect of a human being, for example, is his humanity, and not any of the things that make him a particular human being.

William of Ockham (c. 1285 Ockham – after 1347 Munich): Late *Scholastic* who took the radical *Nominalist* position in the dispute on *universals*, asserting that general terms are only signs, which exist in the soul but not in reality. He denied the possibility of using reason to discover divine truth.

Wittgenstein, Ludwig (26 Apr. 1889 Vienna – 29 Apr. 1951 Cambridge, England): Leading exponent of modern *linguistic philosophy*. He sought at first to develop an ideal language that would precisely reflect the structure of the world, but in his later work devoted himself to the philosophical investigation of ordinary language. He was concerned to eliminate philosophical problems by showing that they resulted from the misuse of language.

Xenophanes (c. 565 B.C. Colophon – c. 470 B.C. Elea): Founder of the Eleatic school of philosophy and critic of the mythological image of the gods current in ancient Greece. He said the popular view of the gods portrayed them as having weaknesses and faults; in other words it was an anthropomorphic view, which demeaned the gods. By contrast Xenophanes believed in a single God.

Zeno of Citium (c. 335 B.C. Citium, Cyprus – 263 B.C. Athens): Founder of *Stoicism*, which Zeno set against *Epicureanism*. Zeno taught that a good life had to be totally independent of all external influences. Emotions and the striving for external goods destabilized the tranquillity of the soul, and were thus to be avoided.

Zeno of Elea (c. 490 B.C. Elea – c. 430 B.C. Elea): Exponent of the Eleatic philosophy, who sought to use *paradoxes* (e.g. Achilles and the tortoise) to prove the unreality of all movement and thus defend the Eleatic view of the immutability of existence.

PICTURE CREDITS

The publisher would like to thank the institutions, archives and photographers for permission to reproduce illustrations, and for their kind assistance in the preparation of this book

© Archiv für Kunst und Geschichte, Berlin: 6, 7, 8 top and bottom, 12 top (Erich Lessing), 13 (Erich Lessing), 14 (Schütze/Rodemann), 15 bottom (Orsi Battaglini), 17 top (Erich Lessing) and bottom, 18 (Erich Lessing), 19 (Erich Lessing), 20, 21 (Cameraphoto), 22 top and bottom, 24, 25 bottom, 26 (Erich Lessing), 27 top (Erich Lessing) and bottom, 28 top and bottom, 29, 30, 31 top (Erich Lessing) and bottom, 32, 33, 34 bottom, 35, 36 bottom, 37, 38, 39 top and bottom, 40 top and bottom, 42, 43 bottom (Erich Lessing), 44, 46, 47, 49, 50, 52 top (Erich Lessing) and bottom, 53, 55, 56 (Michael Teller), 57 bottom, 58 bottom, 59, 60, 61, 62, 63 top and bottom, 64, 66 top and bottom, 67, 68, 70, 71 top and bottom, 72, 74, 76, 77, 78, 79 top and bottom, 80 top and bottom, 81, 82 top, 86 bottom, 87, 88 top and bottom, 89 top and bottom (Erich Lessing), 90, 91 top (Erich Lessing) and bottom, 92, 93, 94, 95 (Weegee), 96, 97 (Erich Lessing), 99, 100, 102 top and bottom, 104, 105 top, 106, 108 top, 108 bottom (Erich Lessing), 109

© Archivio Fotografico Electa, Milan: 101 bottom

© Bibliothèque nationale de France, Paris: 75

© Bildarchiv Steffens: Mainz: 16

© Bildarchiv Preußischer Kulturbesitz, Berlin 1999: 36 top, 51, 65, 107 top

© Bridgeman Art Library, London: 45 (Giraudon/BAL), 58 top, 73, 111

© Christoph Delius, Aachen: 34 top

© Descharnes & Descharnes, Paris: 98

© Fotomas Index, West Wickham: 110 top

© Graphische Sammlung Albertina, Vienna: 12 bottom

© Hulton Getty Picture Collection, London: 9, 84, 86 top, 107 bottom

© Kepler-Kommission der Bayrischen Akademie der Wissenschaften, München: 10

© Kunsthistorisches Museum, Vienna: 15 top

© Kunstmuseum St. Gallen: 83

© Digne M. Marcovicz, Berlin: 101 top

© Norman McGrath, New York: 110 bottom

© Niedersächsische Landesbibliothek, Hanover: 48 top and bottom

© Photothèque des Musées de la Ville de Paris: 69 (Berthier)

© Scala, Florence: 8 bottom, 11, 23, 25 top, 85

© Margherita Spiluttini, Vienna: 105 bottom